Myles

AN ELEMENTARY
HISTORICAL
NEW ENGLISH GRAMMAR

AN ELEMENTARY

HISTORICAL

NEW ENGLISH GRAMMAR

BY

JOSEPH WRIGHT

Ph.D., **D.C.L.**, LL.D., Litt.D.

Fellow of the British Academy; Professor of Comparative
Philology in the University of Oxford

AND

ELIZABETH MARY WRIGHT

HUMPHREY MILFORD
OXFORD UNIVERSITY PRESS

London   Edinburgh   Glasgow   Copenhagen
New York   Toronto   Melbourne   Cape Town
Bombay   Calcutta   Madras   Shanghai

1924

PRINTED IN ENGLAND
AT THE OXFORD UNIVERSITY PRESS
BY FREDERICK HALL

PREFACE

In writing this grammar we have followed as far as possible the same plan as that adopted in the elementary Old and Middle English grammars, as our object has been throughout to furnish students with a concise and historical account of the phonology and inflexions of the three main periods into which the English language is usually divided. This third volume, dealing with New English, should perhaps not be defined on its title-page as 'Elementary', but we have used the term designedly, in order to classify the book with the two preceding grammars dealing respectively with Old and Middle English. It will be found that this volume is much more comprehensive than either of the two. But these three volumes lay no claim whatever to being original and exhaustive treatises on the subject. In books of this kind, which are primarily intended for students rather than specialists, there is practically no scope for a display of either of these features.

In this volume, just as in the previous ones, we have designedly excluded word-formation, because it was considered that the subject could be dealt with more appropriately in our forthcoming *Historical English Grammar*, which will presumably be published by the end of next year.

Although the plan and scope of the present volume has precluded us from dealing extensively with the history of the orthography, it will nevertheless be found that the subject has been treated far more fully than is usual in English grammars. The ordinary general reader is apt to speak derisively of our English spelling, as of a thing born of

ignorance, grown up haphazard, and existing by pure con-
vention without any rhyme or reason for its being, or method
in its madness. We have endeavoured to show, as far as
was possible within circumscribed limits, that our English
orthography in itself contains much that is historically of
great interest to the student of language, and even to the
general reader, and that far from being devoid of law and
order, it is considerably more systematic than would appear
at first sight. Moreover, a comparison between the old
stereotyped symbols and the living sounds they now represent cannot fail to be of great use in enabling the student
to realize the actual natural growth and development of
a language through century after century.

As the modern dialects often throw very valuable light
upon many points connected with the historical development
of Standard English, we have not refrained from making
use of them for this purpose, wherever they help to elucidate
the course of development in the standard language.

Few students will begin the serious study of the Modern
period without a knowledge of Old and Middle English, and
for this reason many cross-references have been given to the
Elementary Middle English Grammar, where the links between
Modern and Old English will be found. In this manner
students will be enabled to gain, as it were, a full bird's-eye
view of the long line of development of the sounds or forms
in question.

A glance at the Index of nearly 4,000 words will show
that we have not shirked the drudgery of collecting large
numbers of examples to illustrate the sound-laws dealt with
in the phonology and accidence.

We gratefully acknowledge our indebtedness to many
other workers in the same field, such as Ekwall, Ellis, Franz,
Horn, Jespersen, Kaluza, Kluge, Luick, Morsbach, Skeat,
Sweet, Viëtor, Wyld, and Zachrisson ; and more especially
to the following works :—Horn's *Historische Neuenglische*

Grammatik, I. Teil: Lautlehre, Strassburg, 1908; Jespersen's *A Modern English Grammar on Historical Principles*, Part I: Sounds and Spellings, Heidelberg, 1909 ; Price's *A History of Ablaut in the Strong Verbs from Caxton to the End of the Elizabethan Period*, Bonn, 1910 ; Zachrisson's *Pronunciation of English Vowels 1400–1700*, Göteborg, 1913 ; and lastly to the *New English Dictionary*, which is a veritable mine of material for workers in the history and philology of the English Language.

In conclusion, we wish to express our sincere thanks to the Controller of the University Press for his great kindness in complying with our wishes in regard to special type, and to the Press reader for his valuable help with the reading of the proofs.

JOSEPH WRIGHT.

ELIZABETH MARY WRIGHT.

OXFORD,
    October, 1924.

CONTENTS

CHAPTER VII

CHAPTER VIII

ABBREVIATIONS, ETC.

AN.	= Anglo-Norman	Lat.	= Latin
C.Fr.	= Central French	ME.	= Middle English
dial.	= dialect	Mod.	= Modern
E.D.D.	= English Dialect Dictionary	NE.	= New English
ED. Gr.	= English Dialect Grammar	N. E. D.	= New English Dictionary
E.M.	= East Midland	NHG.	= New High German
EME. Gr.	= Elementary Middle English Grammar	OE.	= Old English
		O.Fr.	= Old French
EOE. Gr.	= Elementary Old English Grammar	OHG.	= Old High German
		ON.	= Old Norse
Fr.	= French	O.Nth.	= Old Northumbrian
Germ.	= German	S.	= Southern
Goth.	= Gothic	S.E.	= South Eastern
Gr. (Gk.)	= Greek	W.M.	= West Midland
Ken.	= Kentish	WS.	= West Saxon

ȝ initially	= **y** in **you**; medially between vowels = **g** often heard in German **sagen, siegen;** before consonants and finally = χ	þ	= **th** in **thin**
		ð	= **th** in **then**
		ž	= **s** in **measure**
		dž	= **j** in **just**
		š	= **sh** in **ship**
		tš	= **ch** in **chin**
ꞃ	= **n** in **finger, think**	χ	= **ch** in German **nacht, nicht**

For **ö, ō̈, ü, ṻ, ə, ə̄, ij, uw**, see §§ 57-8. The sign ˉ placed over vowels is used to mark long vowels. The sign ˛ placed under vowels is used to denote open vowels, as **ȩ̄, ǫ, ȩi, ǫi**. The sign . placed under vowels is used to denote close vowels, as **ẹ̄, ọ̄, ẹi, ẹu, ọu**. The asterisk * prefixed to a word denotes a theoretical form, as *ufen ' oven ',

INTRODUCTION

§ 1. What may reasonably be termed a standard literary language has existed in England since the early part of the fifteenth century, that is, some time before the end of the ME. period. This was chiefly brought about through the spread and influence of the London literary language and the gradual disappearance of the local dialect element from the literature of the period, but colloquial speech continued to be influenced by the dialects long after the dialect element had practically disappeared from literature.

§ 2. NE. embraces, that period of the English language which extends from about 1500 to the present day. The division of a language into fixed periods must of necessity be more or less arbitrary. What are given as the characteristics of one period have generally had their beginnings in the previous period, and it is impossible to say with perfect accuracy when one period begins and another ends. And just as it is impossible to fix the precise date at which one period of a language ends and another begins, so also it is not possible to do more than fix approximately the date at which any particular sound-change took place, because in most languages, and more especially in English, the changes in orthography have not kept pace with the changes in sound.

§ 3. The present standard language is regularly developed from the ME. East Midland group of dialects, especially the dialect of London and its environs. Although the present standard language is not quite free from dialect forms from other dialects, it is remarkable how few such forms have

crept into it, but in the course of dealing with the phonology
we shall see that in early NE. there were often two types of
pronunciation of the same word, and that later sometimes
the one type and sometimes the other has now become the
normal. From this statement it must not, however, be
assumed that there exists a uniform standard pronunciation
among the educated classes of all English-speaking people.
The English as spoken by the educated classes of Scotland,
Ireland, and the north of England is by no means uniform,
and it differs materially in pronunciation from what is
generally regarded as standard pronunciation. In treating
the history of the ME. sounds in NE. we shall, however,
confine ourselves almost exclusively to what is regarded as
standard English, and shall take as our basis: *An English
Pronouncing Dictionary on Strictly Phonetic Principles* by
D. Jones, London, 1917.

§ 4. Some scholars divide NE. into three periods :—The
first NE. period from 1500 to 1600, the second from 1600 to
1700, and the third from 1700 to the present day. Others
divide it into two periods :—Early NE. from 1500 to about
1650, and late NE. from about 1650 to the present day. In
this grammar we shall often simply use the terms early NE.
and earlier NE. By the former is meant from 1500 to about
1650, and by the latter from about 1650 to 1800. All such
subdivisions are rather arbitrary and can lead to no very
practical results. It is far more methodical to treat separately
the history of the individual ME. sounds in NE., stating
when possible the approximate dates at which any of the
sounds have undergone a change or changes.

§ 5. In the course of dealing with the phonology and
accidence the great characteristic differences between ME.
and NE. will become apparent, so that it is not necessary
at this stage to state them in detail, but it may, however, be
useful to state at the outset just a few of them :—

1. The great divergences between the sounds and the

letters or symbols used to express the sounds, which have arisen through sound-changes having taken place without the corresponding changes in the spelling.

2. The great influence which the liquids l and r have exercised upon a preceding vowel belonging to the same syllable.

3. The weakening of all ME. vowels and diphthongs to ə or i in initial, medial, and final unaccented syllables, and in ' careless' speech the eventual loss of the ə or i before liquids and nasals.

4. The loss of inflexional endings in nouns, adjectives, and verbs.

5. The great process of levelling and analogical formations which have taken place in the preterite and past participle of strong verbs.

6. The great number of ME. strong verbs which have become weak in NE.

§ 6. Before proceeding to the phonology it will be useful to state here what are the chief sources for ascertaining the approximate pronunciation of the speech-sounds of our ancestors. These are :—The statements of English grammarians, orthoepists, and phoneticians of the sixteenth, seventeenth, eighteenth, and nineteenth centuries, foreign writers of grammars for the learning of English, rhymes in early NE. poetry, and occasional phonetic or semi-phonetic spellings found in early writers. An extensive list of works dealing with the subject will be found on pp. vii–xiv of *Pronunciation of English Vowels 1400–1700* by R. E. Zachrisson, Göteborg, 1913 ; a list of English works on the subject will also be found on pp. 204–7 of *A History of English Sounds* by H. Sweet, Oxford, 1888. Valuable as these early authorities on pronunciation are the statements of even the best of them require to be carefully checked. In the earlier NE. period there was no such thing as a standard pronunciation in the precise sense that we now apply that term

to the pronunciation of educated and careful speakers of the
present day. There was, of course, a kind of standard pronunciation, but it was far from being sharply defined ; in
fact there was a considerable local colouring in the pronunciation of the educated classes, just as local colouring
exists to some extent in what is called the standard pronunciation of our own time. This is the main reason why
it is necessary to be careful not to accept the statements of
the early grammarians, orthoepists, and phoneticians without
being able to check them in various ways. These writers
belonged to various parts of the country—some of them
were not even Englishmen—and for that reason alone their
description of the pronunciation and their analysis of the
speech-sounds vary considerably, and it may also be added,
that in their description of sounds they were often greatly
influenced by the spelling. And furthermore the phonetic
knowledge of some of them was of a most rudimentary
nature, and their analysis of the speech-sounds was often
entirely wrong. Even the best authorities contradict each
other so much that it is sometimes almost impossible to
reconcile their statements. From what has just been stated
it must not, however, be inferred that these old authorities
are worthless. On the contrary, they furnish most valuable
materials for the investigator who knows how to make
proper use of them. It should also be remembered that the
scientific study of phonetics was practically unknown in
those days. The phoneticians of those days devoted their
attention almost exclusively to the acoustic side of phonetics,
and they knew little or nothing about the analytic and
synthetic side of the subject. And therefore, apart from
the local colouring in their statements, there is no wonder
that they often contradict each other, and that the modern
investigator often finds it difficult to interpret statements
about English pronunciation, which were written hundreds
of years ago. And although great progress has been made

during the last fifty years in the scientific and exact analysis
of speech-sounds, if any reader of this grammar will take
the trouble to write down on a separate slip of paper the
formation of each of the sounds found in standard English,
as given by our leading authorities on the subject, and then
compare the results, he will find abundant contradictory
statements in regard to some of the simple vowels and of
such common diphthongs as **ai, oi, au, ou.**

PHONOLOGY

CHAPTER I

ORTHOGRAPHY AND PRONUNCIATION

1. ORTHOGRAPHY

§ 7. To treat the history of NE. orthography in a comprehensive manner would require far more space than can be devoted to the subject in an elementary grammar. The following brief sketch is merely intended to draw the student's attention to the subject in a connected manner, and at the same time to account in some measure for the causes which have brought about the present great divergences between the sounds and the letters or symbols used to represent the sounds.

§ 8. In a fairly good system of orthography the same letter would always represent the same sound, and the same sound would always be represented by the same letter, but in NE. the same letter is often used to represent many different sounds, and the same sound is represented by many different letters; cp. for example the letter **a** in *man, any, wash, alive, village, father, all, take, care*; the letter **e** in *bed, English, butter, me, eh!, clerk, mercy, here*; the sound ī in *machine, me, feet, eat, ceiling, people, field, key, Beauchamp, Caius, quay*; the sound š in *she, schedule, sure, fuchsia, Asia, issue, mission, ocean, social, conscious, vitiate, nation*; and lastly the combination of vowels and consonants in *cough, rough, thought, through, though, plough.*

§ 9. In OE. and early ME. the orthography was to a great

extent phonetic, but during the ME. period it became less
phonetic, partly through the influence of the French system
of orthography upon it, such as the writing of u, ui for ü,
ou for ū, o for u, ie for ẹ̄, c for s, &c., and partly through
sound-changes which took place without the corresponding
changes in the spelling. Some attempt was made during
the ME. period to distinguish between long and short
vowels, but only Orm (*c.* 1200) made a systematic attempt
to indicate long vowels by writing double consonants after
short vowels. From the fourteenth century onwards long ẹ̄
and long ǭ were often indicated by writing them double in
closed syllables and when final, but single in open syllables,
as deed, but mẹ̄ten 'to meet'; cool, but sǭne 'soon'. The
reason why ā, ẹ̄, ǭ were not written double in open syllables
was doubtless due to the lengthening of early ME. a, e, o in
open syllables in the first half of the thirteenth century
(cp. *EME. Gr.* § 78). These new long vowels were always
followed by an e in the next syllable, and this e came to
be regarded as the sign of a long vowel in the preceding
syllable. And then later the e came to be used in a large
number of words to which it did not etymologically belong,
for the purpose of indicating a preceding long vowel. Long
and short ŭ came to be distinguished by writing the former
ou (ow) and the latter u (o). By some late ME. writers an
attempt was also made to distinguish between long and short
ĭ by writing the former y and the latter i.

§ 10. Early NE. orthography was based on that of late
ME., and it became to a great extent fixed at the time of the
invention of printing. The first English book was printed
by Caxton in 1473–4, and his system of orthography was
with slight variations a continuation of the ME. system.
In the sixteenth and seventeenth centuries many attempts
were made to put the orthography upon a more phonetic
basis, but they failed just as later attempts have hitherto
failed. Chiefly through the influence of the great printing-

houses a few improvements were gradually introduced and permanently fixed between 1500 and 1650, such as the omission of final -e in a great number of words, the writing of the digraph ea to represent what was at that time long open ẹ, and of the digraph oa to represent what was at that time long open ọ, the simplification of final double consonants after short vowels, the exclusive use of j, v as consonants and i, u as vowels, and the writing of -y for final -i (-ie). Apart from such minor changes the orthography has practically remained unchanged since the sixteenth century, although the sounds, especially the vowel-sounds, have undergone radical changes between that period and the present day. The result is that a great number of changes have taken place in the pronunciation without the corresponding changes in the spelling, and quite a number of changes have taken place in the spelling without the corresponding changes in the pronunciation. Consonants have changed comparatively little in the history of the English language, but vowels have continuously been on the change, and still are so. Therefore in a language like English the consonants chiefly form, as it were, the framework of the language, and the vowels are the clockwork or living organism. This is quite different from a language like French, where the consonants equally with the vowels have undergone great and radical changes in passing from popular Latin to the French of the present day.

§ 11. In the present language there has been hardly any fluctuation in the spelling of the same word since the seventeenth century, but we have great divergences between the sounds and the letters used to represent the same sounds in different words. In the following paragraphs we shall endeavour to give some indications of the manner in which these divergences have arisen.

NOTE.—Although the spelling of each individual word became fairly well fixed in the seventeenth century there is in the present language a considerable number of words which have double spellings, as *caldron, cauldron; carcase, carcass; faggot, fagot; fetish, fetich; gaol, jail; gibe, jibe; hithe, hythe; hooping-cough, whooping-cough; lacker, lacquer; licorice, liquorice; matins, mattins; rase, raze* v.; *sergeant, serjeant; shallot, shalot; selvage, selvedge; veranda, verandah; waggon, wagon*; &c. There is also fluctuation in the spelling of words like *connection (connexion), enquire (inquire)*, and verbs ending in *-ize (-ise)*. We sometimes have double spellings of the same original word with a differentiation in meaning, as *broach : brooch, clew : clue, course : coarse, draught : draft, flour : flower, metal : mettle, muscle : mussel*, &c. On the other hand in a large number of cases two or more different words have entirely fallen together in sound, but are kept apart in spelling, as *beer, bier; berth, birth; dear, deer; dew, due; die, dye; farther, father; hear, here; higher, hire; liar, lier, lyre; meat, meet, mete; miner, minor; pair, pare, pear; road, rode; succour, sucker; way, weigh, whey; right, rite, wright, write*; &c.

A. Vowels.

§ 12. The present language has the following simple letters: **a, e, i (y), o, u** which are used partly as simple vowels and partly as diphthongs; the following digraphs: **ai (ay), au (aw), ea, ee, ei (ey), eo, eu (ew), ia, ie, io, iu, oa, oe, oi (oy), oo, ou (ow), ui (uy)**; together with a few trigraphs like **eau, ieu (iew)**. In dealing with these simple letters and combinations of letters we shall generally take in order each simple letter followed by the combinations beginning with that letter.

a

§ 13. The pronunciation of what is written **a** in ME. has undergone a large number of changes in NE., although we still continue to write the changed sounds with **a**:—1. ME. short accented **a** normally became æ about the end of the sixteenth century, as *apple, bag, can, carry, flatter, glad, man, saddle, talent* (§§ 62–3). 2. Before voiceless spirants (**f, s, þ**)

and voiceless spirants followed by another consonant this æ
was lengthened to ǣ in the seventeenth century, and then
ǣ became ā in the eighteenth century (§ 93, 1), as *ask, bath,
brass, cast, chaff, clasp, craft, fasten, glass, path;* and similarly
with æ before final ·r and r + consonant (§ 108), as *bar, scar;
arm, card, garden, hard, large, mark, partner; far, mar, tar;
carve, darling, farthing, parson* (§ 110).   3. In a few words
we have the spelling of one form, but the pronunciation of
another, as *ate* (§ 365), *any, many* (§ 62, note), *Thames* (§ 64,
note).   4. ME. a preceded by w became o about the end of
the sixteenth century (§ 132), as *quality, squalid, swallow,
swan, was, wash, watch,* and we also have o in *yacht.*   In the
seventeenth century this o was lengthened to ǭ before final
·r and r + consonant (§ 111), as *dwarf, quarter, reward, war,
ward, warm, warp.*   5. ǭ from older au before final ·l(l) and
l + consonant (§ 102), as *all, ball, call, hall, wall; bald, chalk,
false, falter, paltry, talk, walk.*   6. ei from ME. ā (§ 69), as
*able, acre, age, ale, bake, grave, glaze, hate, lame, name, nation,
shame; angel, chamber, change, danger, strange* (§ 140); and
similarly with a, the first letter of the alphabet.   7. The ǣ
from older ā became ęǝ before r in early NE. (§ 119), as *bare,
care, dare, hare, rare, square.*   8. ǝ from ME. unaccented a,
as *about, ago* (§ 146); *infamous, relative* (§ 150); *distance,
elegant, fatal, general* (§ 156); *sofa, umbrella* (§ 167).   9. i
from ME. unaccented ā (§ 160), as *cottage, damage, image,
orange.*

§ 14. ai (ay) is generally written ay finally and before inflexional endings as well as medially before vowels, but ai
medially in other cases.   The digraph ai (ay) is used to
express quite a number of different sounds :—1. ei from
ME. ai (§ 82), as *abstain, aim, braid, brain, clay, daisy, day,
days, delay, frail, gray (grey), lain, lays, maiden, nail, raise,
say, straight, way.*   2. ęǝ from early NE. ei = ME. ai before
r (§ 128), as *air, chair, fair, lair, pair, stair; mayor, prayer.*
3. ai, as *aisle, aye* ' yes ', *Isaiah.*   4. ī, as *quay* (§ 83).   5. e

by shortening (§ 96), as *again, against, said, says, waistcoat.*
6. i in unaccented syllables, as *bargain, mountain* (§ 163);
Sunday, Monday, &c. (§ 170, 7).

§ 15. au (aw) is generally written aw finally and before
k, l, n, but au in other positions. The digraph au (aw) is
now used to express several different sounds:—1. ǭ from
early NE. au = ME. au, as *auger, aught, author, autumn,
awkward, awl, cause, claw, fraud, hawk, naught, pauper, sauce,
slaughter, sprawl, straw, taught, thaw* (§ 84); *brawn, daunt,
jaundice, spawn, saunter, tawny* (§ 85, 1). 2. The ǭ has been
shortened to o in the accented syllable of some words, as
cauliflower, laudanum, laurel, sausage (§ 84, 6), and is often
pronounced short in an unaccented syllable of others, as
austere, Australia, authority (§ 84, 6). 3. ā from early NE.
au (§ 84, 4), as *draught (draft), laugh, laughter.* 4. For the
au in *aunt; launch, laundry, staunch,* see § 85.

e

§ 16. The pronunciation of what is written e in ME. has
undergone a large number of changes in NE., although we
still continue to write the changed sounds with e:—1. ME.
short accented e has normally remained unchanged in NE.
(§ 64), as *bed, bend, bereft, bled, brethren, dwell, help, set, tell;
accept, address, correct, lesson, medicine.* 2. i from ME. e
before ŋ + consonant (§ 65, 3), as *England, English.* From
ME. e in unaccented syllables, as *behold, desire, eleven,
emerge, engage, prepare* (§ 146); *element, enemy, implement*
(§ 150); *basket, college, hundred, wicked* (§ 157, 3); *ended,
houses, melted* (§ 158); finally in learned words, as *acme,
anemone, apostrophe, catastrophe* (§ 170, 8). 3. ə in unaccented final syllables before l, n, r, as *chapel, model;
ardent, barren, happen, present, silence* (§ 157); *barber, father,
pattern, shepherd* (§ 165). 4. ā from ME. e before r + consonant (§ 110), as *Berkshire, clerk, Derby, Hertford.* 5. ī from
ME. ę̄ and ē̦, as *be, evening, evil,* and the pronouns *he, me, we,*

ye (§ 71); *concede, decent, equal, frequent, previous, tedious* (§ 71, 10); *besom, even, mete* (§ 72, 5); *complete, extreme* (§ 72, 6); e also = ī when used as a letter of the alphabet. 6. ə̄ = early NE. e, of whatever origin, before final -r and r + consonant (§ 112), as *certain, clergy, concern, deserve, err, herb, mercy, person, serpent, verdict.* 7. ęə from ME. ę̄ before r (§ 120), as *ere, there, where.* 8. iə from ME. ē̜ before r (§ 120), as *here, mere, severe, sincere.*

§ 17. After ME. final -e had ceased to be pronounced in all classes of words, it later also generally ceased to be written when the preceding stem-syllable contained a short vowel, as *bit* (ME. **bite**), *dog* (ME. **dogge**), *end* (ME. **ende**), and similarly *help, hip, sit, son,* &c. ; see *EME. Gr.* §§ 139–43, 153–4, but we still write e in *come, some,* and in words which underwent later shortening of the stem-vowel, as in *ate, done, gone, none, one,* &c. After long stem-vowels the final -e was generally retained in writing, and in late ME. and early NE. it came to be regarded as a sign for indicating that the preceding vowel was long, as *bare, make, name; mete; die, lie, tie; hope, nose,* &c., and the -e has been retained even after the diphthongization of the long vowel. And then -e came to be added analogically to all kinds of words with a long stem-vowel, which did not have it in early ME. (see § 9), as *foe, home, stone; life, wife, wine; duke,* &c., but the final -e is now not written, except after certain consonants and vocalic 1 (see below), when the old long vowels ę̄ (§ 72), ē̜ (§ 71), ǭ (§ 76), ǫ (§ 75), ū (§ 77) with their subsequent changes are written **ea, ee (ie), oa, oo, ou,** as *clean, leap, scat, teach; feed, green, keep, teeth; bier, field, thief, yield; boat, goat, loaf, road; bloom, cool, food; about, loud, owl, proud.* This adding of final -e was especially common in the latter part of the fifteenth century, the sixteenth century, and the early part of the seventeenth century, but it began to decrease during the seventeenth century, especially in the second half of the century, and by the end

of the century the orthography had become fairly well fixed
in its present form so far as final -e was concerned. Final
-e was, however, not only retained or added to indicate that
the preceding stem-vowel was long, it was also retained or
added for other purposes as well. It was retained or added
after u (= v), c = s, g (gg) = dž, th = ð to indicate that the
u was to be pronounced as v, the c as s, the g (gg) as dž, and
the th as ð, and the -e was retained after the u and g (gg)
had come to be written v, dg, as *give, have, love; believe,
sleeve, weave; advance, hence, whence; fleece, peace, piece;
mice, twice; age, bridge, edge, midge,* &c. ; *breathe, scythe,
seethe.* It was added after s = s or z to indicate that the
s was not an inflexional ending, as *cheese, else* (ME. **elles**),
false, geese, horse, house, pret. *rose, sense,* &c. The -e was retained in writing after l had become vocalic through the loss
of final -e in pronunciation, as in *able, fable, needle, single,
steeple, table,* and then after the analogy of such words many
words which in early ME. ended in -el came to be written
with -le, as *apple* (ME. **appel**), and similarly *cattle, fiddle,
riddle,* &c. And conversely after the e in the combinations
-er, -re had ceased to be pronounced and the r became
vocalic the words formerly ending in -re generally came to
be written with -er after the analogy of words which had -er
in ME., as *letter* (ME. **lettre**), and similarly *number, order,
powder,* &c. Final -e was also often added to monosyllables
ending in a vowel, sometimes with the object of distinguish-
ing pairs of words which would otherwise be spelled alike,
as *due, foe, shoe ; bee : be, doe : do, toe : to,* &c., cp. § 38.

For the loss or retention of e in final syllables ending in
a consonant, see § 158.

§ 18. In early ME. both ę̄ and ẹ̄ were expressed by e.
From the fourteenth until well on into the sixteenth
century both sounds were generally also expressed alike,
viz. either by ee in syllables which were closed in early
ME., and often finally, or by e followed by a single con-

sonant + e in syllables which were open in early ME., as
feet (OE. fēt), knee (OE. cnēo), and deed (OE. dēad 'dead'),
see (OE. sǣ 'sea'), but swete (OE. swēte 'sweet'), delen
(OE. dǣlan 'to divide'), lepen (OE. hlēapan 'to leap'), see
EME. Gr. §§ 52–3, 63–5.   Towards the end of the fifteenth
century and during the first half of the sixteenth century an
attempt began to be made to distinguish the two sounds in
writing.   The long close ē̜, which before this time had
become ī in sound, was expressed partly by ee, partly by
e followed by a single consonant + e, and partly by the
Central O.Fr. spelling ie which already in late ME. had
begun to be used to express long close ē̜ (*EME. Gr.* § 197, 2).
At first the ie was used in French words only, and then
later also in native words, especially before ld, f, and v.
And ē̜ came to be expressed by ea or by e before a single
consonant + e.   Caxton (d. about 1491) occasionally used ea,
but chiefly in French words only.   The ea was much more
common in Tyndale (d. 1536).   In early NE. there was
great fluctuation in the spelling of the same word, as **fele,
feile, feele, feel; feeld, feelde, feild, feilde, field; beme,
beem, beame, beam; pece, pees, peese, peas, pease,
peace.**   During the second half of the sixteenth and early
part of the seventeenth century the writing of ea became
fairly well fixed both in native and French words, although
a certain number of French words are now spelled with e, ei
which formerly had ea (§ 72, 6).   And at the same time the
spelling ee, ie (see above) became fairly well fixed for expressing the ī from older ē̜ in native and many French
words, but the writing of e + consonant + vowel remained
very common in French words of more than one syllable
(cp. § 70).

§ 19. The digraph **ea** is now used to express a large
number of different sounds which are chiefly due to the
various sound-changes undergone by ME. ē̜ during the NE.
period without the corresponding changes in the spelling :—

1. ī from ME. and early NE. ę̄ (§ 72), as *bean, beat, cheap,
clean, deal, eat, flea, heat, knead, leaf, meal, meat, speak, weave;
appeal, beast, conceal, defeat, disease, feature, peace, please,
reason, tea, treason, veal, zeal.*   2. **e,** the shortening of ę̄
before it became ī (§§ 64, 95), as *bread, breadth, cleanse,
feather, health, heather, heaven, leather, meadow, ready, stealth,
sweat, thread, tread, wealth, weapon; endeavour, jealous,
measure, peasant, pleasure, treasure.*   3. **i,** the shortening of
ī from older ę̄ (1 above), as in *guinea.*   4. **ā** from early ME.
e, later **a,** before r + consonant (§ 110), as *hearken, heart,
hearth.*   5. **ə̄** from early NE. e before r + consonant (§ 113),
as *dearth, Earl, early, earn, earth, heard, hearse, learn, pearl,
search, yearn.*   6. **ei** from older ę̄ (§ 72, note 1), as *break, great,
steak.*   7. **ęə** from older ę̄ before r (§ 122), as *bear* sb. and v.,
pear, swear, tear v., *wear.*   8. **iə** from ME. ę̄ or ę̄ before r
(§§ 120–2), as *dear, dreary, ear, hear, near, rear, shear, smear,
tear* sb., *weary, year; appear, arrears, clear.*   In French
words :—(a) in accented syllables, as *fealty, idea, ordeal, real,
theatre;* (b) in unaccented syllables, as *area, miscreant,
nausea.*   9. **i + æ** in Latin words, as *beatitude, meander,
reality.*   10. **i + ei** in Latin words, as *create, nauseate.*

§ 20. The digraph **ee** is chiefly used to express the sound
ī which arose from older ę̄ towards the end of the fifteenth
century (§ 71), as *beech, breed, cheese, creep, deed, deep, eel,
feed, feel, feet, flee, free, glee, green, greet, keep, knee, meet,
need, needle, reed, see, seek, sheep, sleep, sweep, sweet, weed,
week; agree, beef, degree, feeble, proceed.*   In a few words this
ī has been shortened to i (§ 97), as **bin** beside **bīn** 'been',
breeches, Greenwich : green, threepence; coffee.   And the ī has
become **iə** before r (§ 120), as *beer, career, cheer, deer, leer, steer.*

§ 21. **ei (ey)** is generally written **ey** finally and before
inflexional endings, but **ei** in other positions.   The digraph
ei (ey) is used to express quite a number of different
sounds :—1. **ei** from early ME. ei, later **ai** (§ 82), as *eight,
freight, grey (gray), neigh, neighbour, sleigh, they, weigh, whey;*

convey, deign, feint, inveigh, obey, prey, rein, survey. 2. **e** from
the shortening of **ei**, as *leisure*. 3. ęǝ from **ei** = ME. **ai**
before **r** (§ 128), as *heir, their.* 4. ī from ME. ę̄ (= AN. **ei**,
EME. Gr. § 205) in French words, which was generally
written **ea** in the sixteenth and seventeenth centuries
(§ 72, 7), as *conceit, conceive, deceive, perceive, receive, seize*; for
key, see § 83. 5. **i** from ME. **ai (ei)** in unaccented syllables
of French words, as *counterfeit, foreign, forfeit, surfeit,
sovereign* (§ 163); *abbey, alley, chimney, journey, medley, money,
parsley* (§ 170, 6); after the analogy of such words we now
write **·ey** for **·y** = ME. **·i** (§ 170, 1) in some native words, as
barley, honey. 6. **ai**: In a few words we have the spelling
of one form, but the pronunciation of another (§ 83), as *eider-
down, eye, height, sleight;* *either, neither.*

§ 22. Apart from learned foreign words like *georgics* with
ǭ, *geography, theology* with **iǫ**, and *peony* with **iǝ**, the
digraph **eo** is rare in accented, but common in unaccented
syllables:—1. ī from ME. ę̄ = the unrounding of AN. ȫ,
written **eo**, as in *people* (§ 71, 9); for *yeoman*, see § 75,
note 2. 2. **e**, the shortening of ME. ę̄ before it became ī, as
feoff, jeopardy, leopard (§ 71, 9). 3. **iǝ** beside **ǝ** in unaccented
syllables, as *courteous, duteous, hideous, piteous, plenteous,*
beside *bludgeon, courageous, gorgeous, luncheon, pigeon, surgeon*
(cp. § 17).

§ 23. The digraph **eu (ew)** is written **ew** finally, and
medially before vowels and inflexional endings, but generally
eu in other positions. Through the three early ME. sounds
ṻ (= AN. ü̈), **iu,** and **ęu (ęw)** all falling together in **iu**
during the ME. period, the **eu (ew)** came to be written in
words to which it did not originally belong, see § 86; and then
later the **iu**-sound underwent further changes in pronunciation without the corresponding changes in spelling. The
iu became **jū** in the sixteenth century, and then the **jū**
became ū after **ch** (= tš), **j** (= dž), **y, l,** and **r** about the end
of the seventeenth or beginning of the eighteenth century;

and similarly the ME. diphthong ęu (ęw) became **iu** in the
seventeenth century, and then **jū** in the eighteenth century
with the further change of **jū** to **ū** after **l** and **r** (§ 87).
1. **jū** from **iu** (= AN. **ü**, § 79), as *pew, stew*. 2. **jū** from **iu**
(= early ME. ęu (ęw), § 86, 1), as *knew, new*. 3. **jū** from
iu (= early ME. **iu** (**iw**), § 86, 3), as *spew, steward*. 4. **jū**
from **iu** (= ME. ęu (ęw), § 87), as *dew, ewe, few, hew, newt;
deuce, feud, neuter, pewter*. 5. **jū** from **iu** in unaccented
syllables (§ 172), as *curfew, nephew, sinew*. 6. **ū** from **jū**
(§ 86), as *chew ; Jew, jewel; yew ; blew, brew, clew (clue), crew,
grew, threw; lewd, shrew, strew*. On the pronunciation of
sew, see § 86 note, and of *shew*, see § 87 note.

i (y)

§ 24. OE. **ў** was unrounded to **ĭ** during the OE. period
(*EME. Gr.* §§ 49, 57), although the old spelling with **y** was
generally retained, so that in early ME. **y** was often used to
express both old long and short **ĭ**. This writing of **y** for **ĭ**
became very common during the ME. period, but attempts
were made by some late ME. writers to distinguish between
long and short **ĭ** by writing the former **y** and the latter **i**.
In the early NE. period there was still great fluctuation in
the spelling, but in the early part of the seventeenth century
the present usage became fairly well established, viz. to write
i initially and medially, and **y** finally, as *beautiful : beauty,
cities : city, holier : holy, tried : try*, but **y** is always written
before a following **i** in order to avoid the writing of double **i**,
as in *crying : cry, dying : die* ; it is also generally retained in
diphthongs like **ay, ey, oy, uy** before inflexional endings, as
plays, played : play, obeys, obeyed : obey, boys : boy, buys : buy,
but in *lay, pay, say* we have **i** in the pret. and pp. *laid, paid,
said*, and **y** in the present *lays, pays, says* ; it is also often
retained before such endings as are more or less felt as
independent words, as *juryman, ladyship, shyness, twentyfold*.

For the writing of **-ey** for final **-y** after l and n, as in *alley,
journey, money, valley,* see § 170, 6.

§ 25. Already in late ME. the diphthongs **ai, ei, oi** were
often written **ay, ey, oy** finally, and this became the
established rule in early NE.

§ 26. **y** = Greek **υ** is generally retained in Greek loan-
words, as *crypt, hymn, lyre, myrrh, myth, nymph, psychology,
system, tyrant,* but occasionally we have **i** beside **y**, as in
pigmy beside *pygmy.* A few words are now spelled with **y**
through a false assumption that they are of Greek origin, as
scythe (OE. **sīþe, sigþe**), *sylvan* beside *silvan* (Lat. **silvānus**),
style (Lat. **stilus**), *tyro* beside *tiro* (Lat. **tīro**), *wych-hazel* beside
wich-hazel (OE. **wice-**), *rhyme* (OE. **rīm**) through a false
association with *rhythm* (Gr. ῥυθμός).

§ 27. In early NE. **i** was often written for j-consonant
(= **dž**) and **j** for i-vowel, especially initially ; for the origin
of this twofold function, see *N.E.D.* sub **i, j.** By about the
middle of the seventeenth century the present differentiation
in the usage of the two letters had become fully established.

§ 28. **i** is now used to express various different sounds
chiefly through sound-changes which have taken place
between the ME. period and the present time without the
corresponding changes in the spelling:—1. ME. short **i** has
normally remained unchanged in NE., as *bid, children, drink,
fifth, fish, kitchen, live, midge, nimble, ring, sit, twig; admit,
city, dinner, finish, miracle, spirit, timid* (§ 65) ; in unaccented
syllables, as *diminish, divide, improve* (§ 146); *animal, feminine,
radical* (§ 151); *evil, famine, malice, novice, punish, profit* (§ 159).
2. **ə̄** from older **i** before final -**r** and **r** + consonant (§ 141), as
birch, bird, birth, circle, fir, firm, mirth, Sir, stir, third, thirst.
3. **i** = **ī** in late French loan-words (§ 73, 8), as *antique,
clique, fatigue, machine, oblique, police, routine, unique.* 4. **ai**
from ME. **ī** (§ 73), as *arise, bind, bride, fight, find, high, life,
mice, mile, mind, nine, ride, smite, thigh, wife; bribe, invite,
malign* ; **i** = **ai** when used as a letter of the alphabet. 5. **aiə**

from ME. ī before **r** (§ 123), as *fire, hire, iron, wire; admire, desire, squire.*

§ **29.** In unaccented combinations like **ia, ie, io, iu** the **i** generally became **j** (= **y**) after consonants together with the weakening of the **a, e, o, u** to **ə** in the late sixteenth or early seventeenth century, and then the combinations **sj** (**tj** = **sy**) and **zj** became **š, ž** with loss of the written **i** in pronunciation (cp. §§ 150–1), as *Canadian, filial, guardian, immediate, miniature, valiant; clothier, courtier, frontier, obedience, salient; behaviour, companion, copious, million, onion, opinion, previous; genius, medium, odium; Asia, partial, special; ancient, conscience, glazier, patience; action, admission, anxious, cushion, fashion, nation, pension.*

§ **30.** The digraph **ia** is now used to express:—1. **aiə** from ME. ī + ă in accented syllables (cp. § 73), as *iambic, giant, phial*; for *briar, friar,* see § 121. 2. **i + ei** from ME. ĭ + ā (cp. § 69), as *mediate* v., *obviate,* &c.

§ **31.** The digraph **ie** is now used to express several different sounds which have mainly arisen through sound-changes having taken place without the corresponding changes in the spelling:—1. ī from ME. ẹ̄ (§ 71) = Central O.Fr. **ie**, AN. ẹ̄ (*EME. Gr.* § 197, 2). Central O.Fr. **ie** began in late ME. to be written for the sound ẹ̄ in loan-words (§ 70), and in the early NE. period it had become very common in such words; from the loan-words it gradually spread to native words, and by about the middle of the sixteenth century it had also become fully established in some native words, especially before **ld, f,** and **v.** Examples of loan-words are :—*achieve, brief, chief, grief, grieve, liege, niece, piece, reprieve, siege*; and of native words :—*belief, believe, field, fiend, lief, priest, shield, thief, thieve, wield, yield.* 2. **e,** the shortening of the ME. ẹ̄ before it became ī (§§ **64, 97**), as *friend, friendly.* 3. **i,** the shortening of ī from older ẹ̄ (§ **97**), as *kerchief, mischief, sieve.* 4. **iə** from the ME. ẹ̄-sound before **r** (§ **120**), as *bier, fierce, pier, pierce, tier.* 5. **ai** from ME. ī

(§ 73), as *die, died, flies* v., *hie, lie, pie* (cp. § 17).   6. **aiǝ** from ME. ī + vowel, as *diet, hierarchy, piety, science* ; for *fiery,* see § 123.

§ 32. The trigraph **ieu (iew)** only occurs in a few words, and represents **jū** from early NE. **iu** (§ 86, 2), as *adieu, lieu, view.*

§ 33. The digraph **io** is used to express **aiǝ** from ME. ī + vowel in accented syllables (cp. § 73), as *lion, pious, prior,* but *priority* (= **prai-ǫriti**).

o

§ 34. The pronunciation of what is written **o** in ME. has undergone a large number of changes in NE., although we still continue to write the changed sounds with **o** :—1. ME. short accented **o** has normally remained in NE. (§ 66), as *absolve, body, college, copper, dog, fodder, follow, historic, holiday, holly, long, plot, profit, smock, song, wrong.*   2. **a** from older **u** (§ 67) : through the influence of the AN. system of orthography **u** was often written **o** in ME., especially before and after **m, n, w,** and **u = v** (*EME. Gr.* § 9), whence NE. spellings like *come, company, dove, dozen, govern, honey, love, money, onion, shove, some, son, won.*   ME. **u** from older **o** before ŋ (§ 139), as *among, monger, mongrel.*   Early shortening of **ū** from ME. **ǭ** before **u** became **a** in the late sixteenth or early seventeenth century (§§ 67, 99), as *brother, done, glove, Monday, month, mother, none, other.*   3. **u = ME. u** (§ 133), as *wolf, woman.*   4. **ǝ** from older **o** in unaccented syllables, as *compare, obey, official, polite, society, voracious* (§ 146) ; *apologize, chocolate, information, innocence, reasonable* (§ 150) ; *beacon, bishop, bottom, bullock, carol, doctor, effort, iron, provost, vendor.*   5. **ǭ** from the lengthening of **o** before final -**r** and **r** + consonant (§ 115), and before the voiceless spirants **f, s, þ** (§ 93, 2) in the seventeenth century, as *abhor, born, corn, for, horn, horse, morning, mortal, nor, organ, sworn, torn, worn ; accord, cord, force, ford, forth, pork, sort* (cp. § 116);

cloth, croft, loss, moss, soft.   6. ū from ME. ǭ (§ 75), as *do, lose, move, prove, to*; ME. ǭ (older ǭ) preceded by **w** (§ 75, 3), as *two, who, whose, whom, womb.*   7. ə from ME. **u** in the combination **wur** + consonant (§ 117, 3, 4), as *word, work, world, worm, worse, worship, worth.*   8. **ou** from late ME. ǫu (older **o**) before final ·l(l) and l + consonant (§ 103), as *bolster, bolt, gold, molten, roll, soldier, toll*; from late ME. ǫu (older ǭ) before ld (§ 106), as *bold, cold, fold, hold, old, sold, told*; from ME ǭ (§ 76), as *alone, broken, cove, drove, explode, frozen, go, grope, home, no, notice, only, pole, post, robe, rope, token, woven*; **o** = **ou** when used as a letter of the alphabet.   On the final **o** (= **ou**) in words like *grotto, hero, potato*, see § **168.**   9. ǭ (ǫə) from ME. ǭ before **r** (§ 125), as *adore, bore, core, lore, more, score, snore, sore, tore.*

§ 35. OE. had no long open ǭ, and long close ǭ was expressed by **o** in this period of the language.   Long open ǭ arose in early ME. from various sources, see § 125.   Both ǭ and ǭ were expressed by **o** in early ME.   From the fourteenth until well on into the sixteenth century both sounds were also generally expressed alike, viz. either by **oo** in syllables which were closed in early ME. and often finally, or by **o** followed by a single consonant + **e** in syllables which were open in early ME., as **goos** (OE. gōs ' goose '), **doo** also **do** (OE. dōn ' to do '), and **boot** (OE. bāt ' boat '), **too** (OE. tā ' toe '), but **loken** (OE. lōcian ' to look '), and **gropen** (OE. grāpian ' to grope ').   During the first half of the sixteenth century an attempt began to be made to distinguish the two sounds in writing.   The long close ǭ, which by this time had become ū in sound (§ 124), was expressed by **oo** and the long open ǭ was expressed by **oa** before a final consonant or by **o** before a following consonant + **e**, and **oe** finally.   This distinction in the writing of the two sounds became fairly well fixed during the seventeenth century, but in early NE. there was a great deal of fluctuation in the writing of both sounds, as **food, fode, fud(e), foode, foade,** beside **road, rod, rode,**

roode, road(e) 'rode'; it is remarkable that the spelling with **oa** has not become fixed in the preterite of any of the strong verbs belonging to class I (§ 336). The writing of **oa** to express the old ǭ sound was based on the analogy of writing **ea** to express the old ę̄ sound. Caxton (d. about 1491) occasionally used **ea** for ę̄, but never **oa** for ǭ. Tyndale (d. 1536) used both **oa** and **ea**.

§ 36. The digraph **oa** is chiefly used to express the sound **ou** which arose from older ǭ through the intermediate stage ọ̄ in the seventeenth century (§ 76), as *boast, boat, coach, coal, coast, coat, encroach, float, foal, foam, goad, goat, groan, loaf, moan, oak, oath, road, roast, soap, toast, throat*. It is also used to express ǭ (ǭə) from ME. ǭ before final -r and r + consonant (§ 125, 1), as *boar, board, hoar, hoard, hoarse, oar, roar, soar* v. ; and ə in the unaccented second element of compounds, as *cupboard, waistcoat* (§ 173).

§ 37. The digraph **oo** is normally used to express the ū which arose from ME. ǭ towards the end of the fifteenth century (§ 75), but through sound-changes which have taken place during the NE. period without the corresponding changes in the spelling, it is now used to express various other sounds. Furthermore medial antevocalic ọu (ọw) became ū during the ME. period, although the ·ou·, ·ow· were retained in writing through the influence of the Anglo-Norman system of orthography (*EME. Gr.* § 114, 2), and then in late ME. and early NE., especially in the sixteenth century, the ū from older ǭ was often written **ou** in many words which now have **oo** again, as **broum, loum, touth** beside *broom, loom, tooth*, but the spelling **ou** has survived in *ousel, ouzel* (OE. ōsle) beside the obsolete form *oozle*:—1. ū from ME. ǭ (§ 75), as *brood, broom, choose, cool, doom, food, fool, goose, groom, loop, loose, mood, moon, noon, ooze, proof, rood, roof, roost, root, shoot, soon*; ME. ū before labials, or when preceded by **w** (§ 134), as *coomb, coop, droop, room, stoop, troop, swoon, woo*. 2. **a,** the shortening of ū from ME.

ǭ before u became a (§ 99), as. *blood, flood.* 3. u, the shortening of ū from ME. ǭ after u had become a (§ 99), as *book, brook, cook, crook, foot, good, hood, look, nook, rook, soot, stood, took; wood* (cp. *EME. Gr.* § 84, 2). 4. uə (ǫə) beside ǭ (ǫə) from ME. ǭ before r (§ 124), as *boor, moor, poor; door, floor.*

§ 38. Apart from words like *poem* (Lat. **poēma** from Gk. πόημα), *poesy, poet, poetry* with ou·i, and *poetical* with ou·e, the e in the digraph oe generally has no etymological value. In late ME. and early NE. final ·e was often added to monosyllables ending in a long vowel to indicate that the vowel was long, as *doe, foe, roe, sloe, toe, woe* beside *wo,* all with o = ou from ME. ǭ (§§ 17, 76), and similarly in *mistletoe;* shoe with o = ū from ME. ǭ (§ 75). In *does* the e is an inflexional ending, and the o = a is an early shortening of ū from older ǭ before u became a (§ 99). The two ME. sounds ǫu (ǫw) and ǭ fell together in the seventeenth century, although they are still generally kept apart in spelling (see §§ 76, 89), but a few words now have the spelling oe for older ow after the analogy of such words as *foe, toe,* as *hoe, roe* 'of a fish', *throe* beside older *how(e), row(e), throw(e),* and similarly in *felloe* beside older *fellow, felly,* see § 171.

§ 39. oi (oy) is generally written oy finally and befoıe inflexional endings as well as medially before vowels, but oi in other positions. The oi (oy) in most of the words containing this digraph was pronounced ai (= ME. ui) from the late sixteenth century down to the early part of the eighteenth century, and then the ai came to be pronounced oi through the influence of the spelling, see § 88. Examples with ME. oi (oy) are:— *boy, choice, coy, employ, foible, joy, loyal, moist, noise, voice;* and of those with earlier NE. ai:— *anoint, boil* v., *coil, join, loin, oil, ointment, point, poison, soil, spoil, toil,* &c. In unaccented syllables the oi has regularly become ə in sound, as *porpoise, tortoise.* In words like *egoism, heroic, heroine* the o (= ou) and i belong to separate syllables.

§ 40. ou (ow) is generally written ow finally and before final l, n as well as medially before vowels, but ou in other positions. This digraph was used to express two different sounds in ME., viz. long ū and the diphthong ǫu (ǫw), see *EME. Gr.* §§ 56, 113–14. Through the influence of the Anglo-Norman system of orthography ou (ow) was often written for ū from the second half of the thirteenth century, and became general in the fourteenth century. This spelling has also been preserved in NE., although the old ū has become the diphthong au. Owing to various sound-changes which have taken place during the NE. period without the corresponding changes in the spelling, the ou (ow) is now used to express a large number of different sounds:—1. au from ME. ū (§ 77), as *about, allow, bough, bound, bounty, brown, cloud, couch, cow, crowd, doubt, doughty, down, found, fowl, gown, ground, house, loud, mouse, owl, plough, pouch, pound, powder, sound, town, thou.* 2. a, the shortening of ME. ū before it underwent diphthongization (§ 67, 4), as *country, couple, courage, cousin, double, flourish, nourish, southern, touch, trouble ; chough, enough, rough, tough.* 3. auə from ME. ū before r (§ 126), as *flour, hour, our, sour ;* for the written e in *bower, flower, power, shower, tower,* see § 126. 4. ǭ from ME. ǫu before ght (§ 90), as *bought, brought, fought* pp., *ought, nought, sought, thought, wrought ;* ME. ǫu before r + consonant (§ 131), as *fourteen, fourth ;* ME. ū before r + consonant (§ 127), as *court, courtier, discourse, mourn, source.* 5. o, the shortening of older ǭ from ǫu (§ 90), as *cough, trough,* see however § 93. 6. The old ū-sound has remained in *you, youth* (§ 77, note 1), *wound* sb. (§ 134, 1), and in late French loan-words, as *group, rouge, route, soup* (§ 77, 5). 7. ə̄ from older ū before r + consonant in French words, as *adjourn, journal, journey, scourge, sojourn.* 8. ə in unaccented syllables (§ 161), as *curious, famous, pious ; armour, favour, flavour.*   9. **ou** from ME. **ǫu** (§ 89), as *blow, dough, grow, know* (shortened to **o** in *knowledge*), *low, own, slow, snow, soul, though* ; late ME. **ǫu** from older **o** before final **-l**(l) and **l** + consonant (§ 103), as *bowl, mould, smoulder* ; from ME. **u** before **l** + **d** or **t** (§ 104), as *coulter, poultice, poultry, shoulder* ; finally in unaccented syllables (§ 171), as *arrow, barrow, fallow, follow, hollow, meadow, shadow, window.*

u

§ 41. In late ME. and early NE. **v** was often written for **u**, especially initially, and also medially in the neighbourhood of nasals, as **vse, mvse, tvne** ; and **u** for **v** medially between vowels, as **euer, giuen.** By about the middle of the seventeenth century the present usage of writing **v** for the consonant and **u** for the vowel had become fully established for all positions.

§ 42. The combination **kw** was written **qu** in O.Fr., and in French loan-words this spelling has been retained down to the present day, as *conquest, equal, quality, quest* (see § 179), but during the ME. period **qu** was substituted for **kw** (= OE. **cw**) in native words also, as **quellen** (OE. **cwellan**), **quęne** (OE. **cwēn** 'queen'), **quik** (OE. **cwic**). We have also retained or restored the spelling **qu** in words where it is now pronounced **k** (cp. *EME. Gr.* § 254), as *liquor* (ME. **likour**), *quoit*, and in late French loan-words, as *bouquet, etiquette.* And in like manner **gu** is written for **gw** in French loan-words, as *anguish, distinguish, languish, language* (§ 179) ; and **su** for **sw** in some French words, as *assuage, persuade, suave, suite.* In the O.Fr. system of orthography **gu** was written for the explosive **g** before **e, i,** and sometimes also before **a,** in order to indicate that the **g** was an explosive and not **dž,** and this spelling has been preserved in French loan-words down to the present day, as *beguile, disguise, guarantee, guard, guerdon, guide ; dialogue, intrigue,*

plague, rogue, vague. After the analogy of such words the
gu was introduced into a few native and ON. words so early
as the sixteenth century, as *guess, guest, guild, guilt, tongue*
(§ 267).

§ 43. Already in late ME. the diphthongs **au, eu, ou**
were often written **aw, ew, ow** finally, and this became the
established rule in early NE.

§ 44. The pronunciation of what is written **u** in ME. has
undergone a large number of changes in NE., although we
still continue to write the changed sounds with **u** :—1. ME.
short accented **u** normally became **a** in the late sixteenth or
early seventeenth century (§ 67), as *adult, begun, blush, butter,
crutch, cut, dust, fund, furrow, gum, hundred, hurry, judge,
luck, much, number, nut, public, rudder, run, shut, sum, sun,
thunder, trust, uncle.* 2. **u** = ME. **u** preceded by a labial and
followed by l(l), and also simply after a labial in a number of
words (§ 133), as *bull, bullet, full, pull, pulpit ; bush, butcher,
pudding, push, put,* &c. 3. **ū** from older **jū** after **j** (= **dž**), **l**,
and **r** (§§ 80, 86), as *allude, brute, conclude, delude, flute, frugal,
June, lute, plume, prune, rude, rule, salute, truce, truth.* 4. **ə**
in unaccented syllables, as *submit, succced, suppose, upon*
(§ 146) ; *guttural, Saturday* (§ 150) ; *augur, awful, cherub,
column, focus* (§ 156) ; *censure, creature, fortune, measure,
nature, treasure, venture, verdure* (§ 162). 5. **ə̄** from ME. **u**
before final **·r(r)** and **r** + consonant (§ 117), as *burr, cur, curse,
curtain, demur, furnish, nurse, spur, spurn, turf, turn* ; from
late ME. **·ir·** (§ 114, 2), as *burn, burst* ; from early ME. **·ir·**
(= OE. **·yr·**), later **·ur·** (§ 114, 3), as *burden, church, hurdle,
murder.* 6. **i** from ME. **iu** in unaccented syllables (§ 162), as
lettuce, minute sb. ; in *bury* with **e** (§ 64) and *busy* with **i**
(§ 65, 2) we have the spelling of one form and the pronunciation of another. 7. **jū** from ME. **iu** (§ 79), as *abuse,
accuse, curious, duke, duty, fume, huge, human, minute* adj.,
use ; **u** = **jū** as a letter of the alphabet. 8. **jŭ** from ME. **iu** in
unaccented syllables (§ 162), as *deluge, regular, volume.* 9. **juə**,

jǫə beside jǫə, jǭ from older jū (= ME. iu) before r (§ 129), as *cure, endure, mature, pure, secure.*

§ 45. Apart from a few dissyllabic loan-words like *cruel, cruet, duel, duet, fuel, gruel, suet,* the e in the digraph ue is partly a remnant of ME. final -e (§ 17), and partly a final -e which was added in late ME. or early NE., as *ague, blue, continue, cue, due, flue, glue, hue, rescue, rue, sue, value*; and we also have an unpronounced e in *gruesome, Tuesday* (§ 86, 3).

§ 46. AN. ū was often written ui, and although the sound iu was substituted for the ū in ME. loan-words the spelling with ui was retained, and has remained down to the present day (§ 78). ME. iu became jū in the sixteenth century, as *nuisance, pursuit, suit*; and then the jū became ū after j (= dž), l, and r about the end of the seventeenth century, as *bruise, bruit, cruise, fruit, juice, recruit, sluice.* In unaccented syllables early NE. had the spelling ·i·, ·e· beside ·ui·, and we now have the spelling of the latter, but the pronunciation of the former, as in *biscuit, circuit, conduit* (cp. § 162). In the native word *build,* pret. and pp. *built,* the spelling builden, buylden occurs so early as the fifteenth century, see *N. E. D.* s. v. In *buy* the spelling buye occurs so early as the thirteenth century, cp. *EME. Gr.* § 122, 3. In words like *genuine, suicide ; druid, fluid, ruin* the ui was dissyllabic in ME. (= iu-i), and has remained so in NE., viz. jū-i, ū-i.

B. Consonants

§ 47. In all periods of the language the consonants have undergone fewer changes than the vowels. The existing divergences between consonant-sounds and the letters used to express them are due to various causes, the more important of which will be dealt with in the following paragraphs, and the remainder in the phonology proper.

§ 48. Chiefly through sound-changes, which have taken place during the NE. period, consonants have often disappeared in pronunciation, but have been preserved in

writing:—1. Initial **g** and **k** ceased to be pronounced before
n in the seventeenth century, as *gnash, gnat, gnaw* (§ 268);
knave, knee, knight, know (§ 262). For **gh** in words like *high,
night; bought,* see § 50. 3. Final **·b** disappeared after **m** in
early NE., as *climb, comb, crumb, dumb, lamb, succumb, thumb*
(§ 214). 4. The **g** in the final combination **gn** was never
pronounced in English, as *assign, reign,* &c. (§ 269). 5. Final
·n was never pronounced after **m**, as *autumn, condemn, damn,
hymn, solemn,* but *autumnal, condemnation, damnation, hymnal,
solemnity* (§ 200). 6. **r** ceased to be pronounced in the
eighteenth century medially before consonants, and finally in
pausa, although it is always retained in writing, as *arm, bird,
court, hard; better, order, star* (§ 191). 7. After **ā, ǭ** (§ 102),
o = ou (§ 103, 3), 1 ceased to be pronounced in early NE.
before **f, v, m,** and **k,** as *calf, half; calve, halve; balm, calm;
chalk, talk, walk; holm, folk, yolk.* 8. **t** disappeared in pronunciation in early NE. between **s, f,** and a following **l, m,
n** (§ 227), as *bristle, bustle, castle, chasten, chestnut, Christmas,
fasten, gristle, hustle, jostle, listen, mistletoe, moisten, often,
soften.* 9. Initial **w** ceased to be pronounced before **r** in the
seventeenth century, as *wrack, wretch, write, wrong* (§ 180).
w also regularly disappeared in late ME. or early NE.
between a consonant and a back vowel, but we still write it
in some words, as *sword, two; who, whose, whom* with **wh** from
older **hw** (§ 181). And we still continue to write the **w** in
the second element of compound proper names like *Greenwich, Warwick,* &c., although it ceased to be pronounced in
early NE. (§ 182). 10. Loss of voiceless sounds through
assimilation of consonants, as *blackguard* (§ 264), *cupboard,
raspberry* (§ 207). 11. The **p** was never pronounced in
English in learned words like *pneumatic, psalm, pseudonym,
ptarmigan, Ptolemy.*

§ 49. In early NE. the **·ed** in the preterite and past
participle of weak verbs regularly became **t** after voiceless
consonants except **t,** but we still continue to write **·ed** in

many verbs, and -ed beside -t in others, as *asked, fixed, hoped,
kissed, laughed, rushed ; blessed, dressed, stepped,* beside *blest,
drest, stept,* see §§ 231, 390.

§ 50. The spelling with gh to express the guttural
explosive g was very common in early NE., especially in
Caxton's works. It was introduced by Caxton from the
Netherlands, where it was used to express the voiced spirant
ʒ. In the present language it has only been preserved in
aghast, ghastly, gherkin, and *ghost* (§ 267). We still continue
to write the old palatal gh, although it ceased to be pronounced in late ME. or early NE., as in *eight, fight, high;
night, right, thigh* (§ 271) ; and we also continue to write the
old guttural gh, although it has partly become silent, and
partly become f in pronunciation, as in *bought, daughter,
slaughter, sought, thought ; cough, enough, laugh, rough, tough,
trough* (§ 272).

§ 51. The ME. spirant ʒ continued to be written and
printed much later in Scotland than in England. It came
to be written y initially and gh in other positions at an
early period in England. And as ordinary printing-houses
did not have the letter ʒ they substituted for it medially
the letter z, whence such spellings as *capercailzie, Dalziel,
Mackenzie, Menzies,* which are pronounced with y in Scotland,
but often with z in England.

§ 52. For the writing of c, ck, ch, q, qu (-que) for the
k-sound, see § 261; c, sc, sch, ss for the s-sound, as in
*advice, certain, deceive, defence, mercy, recent, since, twice ;
descend, scene, science ; schism ; lesson, vessel,* see §§ 241, 243, 5 ;
s, sc, ss for the z-sound, as *besom, discern, possess,* see § 250 ;
c, ch, s, sc, sch, ss, t for the š-sound, as *ocean, social,
special ; champagne, chivalry, douche, machine ; nauseous,
pension, sugar ; conscience ; schedule ; issue, passion ; condition,
nation, patient,* see §§ 185, 246, 259 ; g, s for the ž-sound, as
prestige (§ 278) ; *casual, division, vision,* see § 258 ; ch, t, tch
for the affricata tš, as *achieve, chair ; creature, nature ; flitch,*

witch, see §§ 184, 274; ch, d, dg, g, gg, j for the affricata dž, as *Greenwich, spinach; soldier, verdure; badge, cadge; age, courage, gem, pigeon; suggest; judge, juice*, see §§ 185, 276, 278–9.

§ 53. OE. and ME. regularly had a large number of words containing double consonants preceded by a short vowel, as OE. **biddan, cyssan, fyllan, sittan, swimman** = ME. **bidden, kissen, fillen, sitten, swimmen**, and these double consonants have regularly been preserved in NE. in the medial position, as *bidding, sitting, swimming* beside *bid, sit, swim*. After the analogy of such words it became fairly common in late ME. to double medial consonants (except th, u = v) after short stem-vowels in order to indicate that the preceding vowel was short, as *alley, ballad* beside earlier **aley, balade**, and similarly *babble, banner, barrel, belly, bottle, cannon, cattle, emmet, gobbet, little, merry, penny, saddle, sorry, tallow*, &c. ; with ck, as *cricket, fickle, pocket, wicked*; and in the preterite and past participle of a large number of weak verbs, as *barred, crammed, dragged, hopped, robbed, tanned*, &c.

§ 54. After the loss of ME. final unaccented -e in writing (§ 17) all double consonants except ·ck, ·ff, ·ll, and ·ss became simplified, as *rib* (ME. **ribbe**), *bad* (ME. **badde**), pret. *bled, fed, met* (ME. **bledde, fedde, mette**), *bag* (ME. **bagge**), *swim* (ME. **swimme(n)**), *sun* (ME. **sunne**), *lip* (ME. **lippe**), *bar* (ME. **barre**), *sit* (ME. **sitte(n)**), and similarly with a very large number of other words, as *bed, bid, club, cup, dog, frog, hen, moth, stag, star, war, web*, but we still have the solitary form *ebb, wrath*. We now write ·ck, ·ff, ·ll, and ·ss irrespectively as to whether these consonants were double in ME. or not. We now write ck finally after vowels which were short in ME., but not after those which became short in NE., as *back* (ME. **bak**), *black* (ME. **blak**), and similarly *quick, sick, stick, suck, thick*, &c., but *book, crook, took*, &c. (§ 99). We now also write ff, as in *chaff* (ME. **chaf**), *cuff, off, stiff,*

but f in the unaccented particles *if, of.* We now write ll
after short vowels, and also after a long vowel which has
nothing to indicate that the vowel is long, but l after long
vowels which are indicated as such by the digraphs **ea, ee,
oa,** as *bill* (ME. **bil**), *fill* (ME. **fillen**), and similarly *bull, full,
sell, shall, tell,* &c. ; *all, fall, tall ; deal, heel, foal. Ass* (ME.
asse), *dross* (ME. **dros**), and similarly *cutlass, cypress, kiss,
miss,* &c. ; all words formerly ending in **-les, -nes,** as in
useless, goodness ; and in words with NE. lengthening of the
stem-vowel, as *brass, grass* (§ 93, 1).

§ 55. About the time of the revival of learning in the
sixteenth century there was a perfect mania among scholars
both in England and France for restoring what was called
etymological spelling. The result was that letters were
often introduced into words to which they did not originally
belong, or letters were restored which had previously
regularly disappeared, or a letter was substituted for one
which at the time had an entirely different pronunciation.
Although most of these strange spellings never became fully
established, we still have many remnants of them in the
language of the present day. A few examples are:—1. In
some words a **b** or a **p** was restored which was never pronounced in English, as *debt* : Lat. **dēbita** (ME. **dette**), *doubt* :
Lat. **dubitāre** (ME. **douten**), *subtle* : Lat. acc. **subtīlem** (ME.
sutill, sotill), *receipt* : Lat. **receptum** (ME. **recẹt, receit**).
2. In *indict* : Lat. **-dictāre** (ME. **indīte,** also spelled **indight**
in the sixteenth century !), and *victuals* (O.Fr. **vitailles**) the
c was never pronounced in English, but it is now pronounced
in *verdict* : **vēre dictum** (ME. and early NE. **verdit**). ME.
perfit, parfit (O.Fr. **parfit, parfeit**) has been completely
ousted by *perfect.* 3. Initial **ad-** was introduced or restored
in many words which at an earlier period had **a-,** as *admiral*
(ME. and O.Fr. **amiral**), and similarly *adjourn, administer,
advance, advantage, adventure, advice,* &c. 4. Early NE.
bankroute became *bankrupt* through the second element

being supposed to be from Lat. **ruptus**. 5. An l was restored
in a number of words, as *assault* (O.Fr. and ME. **assaut**),
and similarly, *altar, balm, default, falcon, fault, realm* (ME.
rẹme, older **rẹume, reaume**), *salmon, vault,* &c.; and in
moult (ME. **mouten, mūten**, Lat. **mūtare**) it had no etymological justification.   6. ME. and early NE. **īland** was
changed into *island* through being associated with *isle*, with
which it is not etymologically connected; *scissors* (ME.
sisoures, O.Fr. **cisoires**) was thought to be the same word
as Lat. **scissor : scindere** 'to cut', whence the spelling with
sc-.   7. Lat. **-ti-** regularly became **-ci-** (= **-si-**) in O.Fr., and
in French words introduced into English the **-si-** regularly
became **-š-** (§ **246**), and then the **-t-** was introduced again,
whence the great divergence between the spelling and pronunciation in words ending in *-tion, -tial, -tious, -tience, -tient,*
as in *nation* (ME. **nācioun**), *patient* (ME. **pācient**), and
similarly *ambitious, condition, essential, partial, patience,* &c.

2. PRONUNCIATION

A. Vowels.

§ **56**. In order not to have a too complicated system of
transcription of the simple vowel-sounds, and of the first
and second elements of diphthongs, we shall sometimes
include under one symbol two sounds which have a slight
phonetic difference, as for example there is a slight difference
between i in accented and unaccented syllables; between a
and the first element of **ai, au**; between o and the first
element of **oi, ou**; &c.; and what we here transcribe as ī, ū
are in reality diphthongs which from a strictly phonetic
point of view would be written **ij, uw**. The present standard
spoken language is generally regarded as having the following
simple vowel-sounds, diphthongs, and triphthongs:—

Short Vowels a, æ, e, i, o, u, ə

Long   „   ā,   ī, ǭ, ū, ə̄

Diphthongs **ai, ei, oi ; au, ou ; eə, iə, ọə, uə**
Triphthongs **aiə, auə**

§ 57. In this paragraph we shall state the various ways in which each of the above sounds is written :—

a, usually written **u, o, oo, ou,** as in *blush, sun, up ; come, mother, son ; blood, flood ; couple, rough, tough.*

æ, usually written **a,** as in *apple, hat, man* ; rarely **ai,** as in *plaid, plait.*

e, usually written **e, ea,** as in *bed, let, tell ; heaven, peasant, tread* ; rarely **a, ai (ay), ei, eo, ie,** as in *any, many ; again, said, says ; heifer, leisure ; jeopardy, leopard ; friend.*

i, usually written **i, y,** as in *bid, drink, sit ; city, hymn* ; rarely **e, u, ea, ee, ei (ey), ie, ui,** as in *England ; busy, lettuce, minute* sb. ; *guinea ; breeches ; forfeit, valley ; kerchief, sieve ; build, biscuit* ; often **a, ai (ay), e** in unaccented syllables, as in *damage, orange ; bargain, mountain, Sunday ; acme, basket, enough.*

o, usually written **o, a,** as in *fodder, long, not ; swan, was* ; rarely **au, ou,** as in *laurel, sausage ; cough, trough.*

u, usually written **u, o, oo,** as in *full, put ; wolf, woman ; book, good, wood* ; rarely **ou,** as in *should, would.*

ə, as a simple sound occurs only in unaccented syllables, and is variously written **a, e, o, u, eo, oa, oi, ou,** as in *about, infamous ; barber, chapel, happen ; bullock, innocence, polite ; awful, submit, venture ; gorgeous, luncheon ; cupboard ; porpoise, tortoise ; famous, favour.*

ā, written **a, e, ea, au,** as in *ask, craft, hard ; clerk, Derby ; heart, hearth ; aunt, draught, laugh.*

ī, written **e, i, ea, ee, ei (ey), ie,** as in *besom, evil, me ; clique, machine ; cheap, meat, reason ; cheese, feeble, seek ; conceit, key, seize ; achieve, priest, shield* ; rarely **ay, eo,** as in *quay ; people.*

ọ, written **o, a, au (aw), oa, ou,** as in *born, cloth, nor ; all, dwarf, walk, water ; aught, draw, taught ; broad, oar ; bought, fourth, thought.*

D

ū, generally written **oo**, but often also **o, u, ou, ui**, as in *brood, fool, room ; do, lose, move ; blue, brute, truce ; group, route, wound* sb. ; *bruise, fruit* ; rarely **ew, oe**, as in *chew, jewel ; shoe.* jū is variously written **u, eu (ew), ieu (iew), you, ue, ui**, as in *abuse, duke, volume ; dew, few, neuter, pew ; adieu, view ; you, youth ; hue ; nuisance, pursuit.*

ə, written **e, i, o, u, ea, ou** before final **-r(r)** and **r** + consonant, as in *err, herb ; birch, bird, fir ; word, work ; churn, cur, furnish ; earn, pearl ; journal, scourge.*

ai, usually written **i, y**, as in *bite, fight, write ; cry, defy* ; rarely **ai, aye, ei, eye, ie (ye), uy**, as in *aisle ; aye* 'yes' ; *height ; eye ; die, dye, pie ; buy.*

ei, usually written **a, ai (ay)**, as in *bake, name, take ; aim, nail, say* ; rarely **ea, ei (ey)**, as in *break, great, steak ; eight, they, weigh.*

oi, written **oi (oy)**, as in *boy, choice, toy.*

au, written **ou (ow)**, as in *about, bound, brown, clown, cow.*

ou, usually written **o, oa, oe** (finally), **ou (ow)**, as in *gold, hero, toll ; coal, foal, goat ; foe, toe, throe ; arrow, blow, bowl, dough, mould, soul.*

ęə, written **a, e, ai (ay), ea, ei** before **r**, as in *bare, snare ; ere, there, where ; air, pair, prayer ; bear, pear, swear ; heir, their.*

iə, written **e, ea, ee, eo, ie**, as in *here, sincere ; dear, idea, shear ; beer, leer, steer ; hideous, peony, piteous ; bier, pierce.*

ǫə beside ǭ, written **o, oa** before **r** and **r** + consonant, as in *adore, tore ; boar, hoard.*

uə beside ǭ, written **oo, ou, u** before **r**, as in *boor, door, poor ; tour, your ; sure.*

aiə, written **i, ia, ie, io**, as in *fire, wire ; briar, friar, giant, phial ; diet, fiery, quiet, science ; lion, prior.*

auə, written **ou, owe**, as in *bower, flour, our, power.*

§ 58. Philologists generally regard vowels from the acoustic point of view, whereas phoneticians generally regard them

Narrow (Tense)

	high-front	high-back	high-flat
high	ī: *be*		
mid	ME. ē: *fēt*	a: *sun, son*	
low	ME. ē̜: Fr. *père*		ə̄: *bird*

Narrow-Round

	high-front	high-back	high-flat
high	ü: Fr. **lune**	ū: *food*	
mid	ö: Germ. **schon**	ọ̄: Fr. **beau**	
low		ǭ: *all*	

Wide (Slack)

	high-front	high-back	high-flat
high	i: *big*		
mid	e: *red*	ā: *hard*	ə: *abide*
low	æ: *cat*		

Wide-Round

	high-front	high-back	high-flat
high	ü: Germ. **Hütte**	u: *put*	
mid	ö: Germ. **Götter**	o: Germ. **Gott**	
low		o: *cot*	

from the organic point of view. It is therefore not usual
in philological books to use the terms narrow (tense), wide
(slack), but to speak of close and open vowels. It is, however, important to remember that the terms close and open
do not always mean the same thing as narrow and wide.
We speak of a close or open e according as it lies nearer to
i or a. Thus the e in NE. *get* is an open vowel and at the
same time a mid-front-wide vowel, and the e in German
beten is a close vowel and at the same time a mid-front-
narrow vowel. The first element of the diphthong in NE.
air (ęə) is a low-front-narrow vowel, but it is an open vowel ;
and similarly the ǫ in NE. *all* is a low-back-narrow vowel,
but it too is an open vowel. In like manner we speak of
a close or open o according as it lies nearer to u or a ; and
of an open i or u according as it lies nearer to e or o.
When close and open vowels are distinguished in writing,
it is usual to place the sign . under the vowel to indicate the
former, and ˛ to indicate the latter, as ẹ, ọ; ę, ǫ. In the
table on p. 35 the NE. simple vowel-sounds, and a few
others which will be required in the phonology proper, are
classified from the organic point of view.

B. Consonants.

§ **59.** The divergences between the sounds and the symbols
or letters used to express the sounds is not so great in consonants as in vowels. In describing consonants philologists
generally use the terms explosive and spirant. For explosive
phoneticians often use plosive, stop, shut or momentary
sound ; and for spirant they often use fricative, continuant,
or open-consonant. The following table contains the NE.
consonant-sounds :—

		Labial	Inter-dental	Dental	Guttu-ral	Pala-tal
Explosives	voiceless	p		t	k	
	voiced	b		d	g	
Spirants	voiceless	f	þ	s ; š		
	voiced	v	ð	z ; ž		
Nasals		m		n	ŋ	
Liquids				l ; r		
Semi-vowels		w				j
Aspirate	h					

Of the above b, d, f, g, l, m, n, p, t, v, w are clearly
expressed by their symbols ; k, s, z, š, ž have been dealt
with in the orthography and need no further comment (§ 52) ;
for h, see §§ 281–3 ; and for j, which is always written y
initially, see §§ 151, 184–5. The following require a few
words of explanation :—, r, þ,   ð.

ŋ is written n before k and c = k, as in *ink, uncle* ; ng
when the g belongs to the same syllable, as in *sing, singer,*
but n when the g belongs to the following syllable, as in
finger.

r is pronounced initially and medially before vowels, and
also finally when the next word in the same sentence begins
with a vowel, but it is not pronounced medially before consonants, and finally in pausa, and when the next word in
the sentence begins with a consonant (§§ 190–1).

Both þ and ð are always written th, as in *thin, method,*
oath ; then, mother, smooth.

CHAPTER II

THE NE. DEVELOPMENT OF THE ME. VOWEL-SYSTEM OF ACCENTED SYLLABLES

§ 60. Standard ME. had the following simple vowels and diphthongs (cp. *EME. Gr.* §§ 22–3, 105, 3) :—

Short Vowels a, e, i, o, u

Long   ,,   ā, ẹ̄, ę̄, ī, ọ̄, ǭ, ū, [ü]

Diphthongs ai (ei), ǫi, ui, au, ęu, iu (ęu), ǫu

In this chapter we shall trace the NE. development of the above simple vowels and diphthongs of accented syllables, and in doing so we shall first deal with the independent and then with the dependent changes which they have undergone in NE. By independent changes we mean those which have taken place independently of neighbouring sounds, and by dependent changes those which have depended upon or are due to the influence of neighbouring sounds.

1. INDEPENDENT CHANGES

A. The Short Vowels.

§ 61. ME. a, u have become æ (§ 13, 1), a (§ 44, 1), but the vowels e, i, o have undergone no independent changes.

a

§ 62. ME. a, of whatever origin (*EME. Gr.* §§ 41–3, 59), became æ about the end of the sixteenth century, but in the northern and nearly all of the Midland dialects it has remained down to the present day, as *apple, arrow, bag, barrow, black, cap, cat, dash, fallow, fathom, flag, flat, flax, gallows, gap, gather, glad, had, latter, marrow, narrow, sack, saddle, sallow, sat, scab, scatter, scratch, shadow, shallow, sparrow, tallow, that, wax, wrap.* Early shortenings, as *an, ant, bad, bladder, chapman, clad, fat, hallow, ladder, lather, tadpole; savage,* cp. *EME. Gr.* §§ 90–1, 213, ɪ.

French words:—1. In syllables accented in both languages, as *ample, attack, carry, cash, catch, distract, fact, flatter, marry, plan,* &c. 2. In syllables accented in English, but unaccented in French, as *animal, anguish, ballad, banish, battle, baron, barren, cabbage, carrot, chapel, grammar, imagine, jacket, language, manage, matter, national, palace, satisfy, talent, valid, valley, valour,* &c.

Note.—NE. *any* (ME. **ani, eni**, OE. **ǣnig**, see *EME. Gr.* § 91, 2) is the ME. form **ani** in spelling, but the form **eni** in pronunciation ; and similarly *many* (ME. **mani** 'many', ME. **menige**, OE. **menigu** 'multitude', cp. NE. *a great many*) beside *manifold*.

§ 63. ME. **a** (**o**) before nasals :—Before nasals earlier ME. had **o** beside **a**. In the late fourteenth and early fifteenth century the forms with **o** were gradually ousted by those with **a** before **m, n** not followed by a different consonant, **mb, nd,** and **nk,** and then the **a** regularly became **æ** at the same time as old **a** became **æ** (§ 62), but the forms with **o** became generalized before **ng,** cp. *EME. Gr.* §§ 72–4. Examples are :—*began, can, cram, ham, hammer, man, pan, ran, than; candle, drank, hand, lamb, land, sand, sank, stand, thank,* but we still have *bond* beside *band* with differentiated meaning ; *long, song, strong, thong, throng, tongs, wrong* (§ 66, 2). Preterites like *sang, sprang* were formed after the analogy of those like *drank, ran, sank,* &c. Forms like *fang, gang, hang* have crept into the standard language from the dialect area north of where the standard language arose.

e

§ 64. ME. **e,** of whatever origin, = NE. **e,** as *bed, beg, bell, bend, better, bless, cherry, delve, drench, dwell, edge, egg, end, fell* v., *fetch, fresh, guest, hell, help, hemp, hen, kettle, leg, length, melt, men, neck, nest, net, penny, self, sell, send, set, settle, seven, spell, step, stretch, tell, then, twelve, web, wedge, went,*

when, yellow. Kentish forms with e from OE. y (*EME. Gr.*
§ 49, 2), as *bury* with Ken. pronunciation and southern
spelling, *ember days, fledge, hemlock, knell, left* adj., *merry,
shed* sb. Early shortenings of ME. ę̄ and ē̜ (*EME. Gr.*
§§ 91–2), as *bereft, cleanly, cleanse, empty, errand, ever, every,
feather, flesh, health, heather, heaven, heavy, herring, leather,
lend, less, meadow, never, ready, steady, stealth, wealth, weapon,
weather,* preterites and past participles like *dealt, leant, led,
left, lent, meant, read; brethren, depth, devil* beside dĭvl in
many dialects, *fellow, friend, shepherd, stepfather, ten, theft,*
preterites and past participles like *bled, bred, crept, fed, held,
kept, knelt, met, slept, sped, swept, wept,* pret. *fell.*

French words:—1. In syllables accented in both languages,
as *accept, address, arrest, attempt, condemn, correct, debt, defend,
dense, event, expect, expel, gender, gentle, letter, meddle, neglect,
November, possess, press, prevent, protect, regret, revenge, request,
select, text, tremble.* 2. In syllables accented in English, but
unaccented in French, as *cherish, destiny, domestic, essay,
lecture, lesson, perish, precious, preface, present, remedy, second,
sentence, several, tepid, very.*

Note.—In *Thames* (OE. Temes, Lat. Tamisia) NE. has preserved the OE. e in pronunciation, but the Lat. a in spelling.
NE. *thrash* (O.Nth. þærsca, þearsca) and *thresh* (WS. þerscan),
with metathesis of the r, began to be differentiated in meaning in
the seventeenth century, viz. ' to thrash a person ', but ' to thresh
corn ', both forms being pronounced þræṣ̌.

i

§ 65. ME. i, of whatever origin, = NE. i. Examples are :—
1. ME. i = OE. and ON. i (*EME. Gr.* §§ 45, 164), as *bid,
bit, bitter, children, chin, crib, drink, fish, gift, his, lid, lip, live,
middle, nimble, quick, rib, ring, ship, sinew, sink, sit, skill, smith,
spin, stick, swim, thick, twig, widow, will, win, window, winter,
wit,* and in the past participle of strong verbs belonging to
class I (§ 336), as *bitten, driven, ridden, risen, written.*

2. ME. i = OE. y (*EME. Gr.* § 49), as *bristle, built, cripple, did, din, dizzy, drip, fill, giddy, guilt, hip, inch, kiln, kindle, king, kiss, kitchen, methinks, midge, sin, sip, sister* (ON. **syster**), *thin, vixen*; *busy* with southern spelling (§ 44, 6).

3. ME. i from older e (*EME. Gr.* § 132) before **nk, ng,** and palatal **ng** (= **ndž**), as *blink, cringe, fling, fringe, hinge, ink, linger, link, mingle, singe, sprinkle, string, swinge, think, wing*. *England* and *English* have the old spelling, but in ME. and early NE. they were often written **Ingland, Inglish**. The NE. standard pronunciation of *engine* (spelt **ingin(e), engin(e)** in the fifteenth century) has been influenced by the spelling. The regular form with i has been preserved in the dialects.

4. ME. shortening of ī before consonant combinations (*EME. Gr.* §§ 86, 93), as *christen, Christmas, ditch, fifth, fifty, stirrup, thrift, vineyard, width, wisdom, women* (early ME. **wimmen,** *EME. Gr.* § 124). Forms like *fivepence, grindstone* beside older **grindstone, fippence** are new formations from *five, grind*.

5. ME. shortening of ī = OE. ȳ (*EME. Gr.* §§ 57, 93), as *filth, fist, grisly*, pret. and pp. *hid, kith, thimble, wish*.

6. French words, as *admit, brick, city, consider, consist, deliver, dinner, dish, enlist, equip, familiar, fiction, figure, finish, issue, liquid, pity, prince, prison, rich, signal, simple, submit, ticket, timid, visit*, &c.

NOTE. — Before **r(r)** + vowel the standard language formerly had ə beside **i,** and most of the modern dialects still have ə in this combination, as *miracle, squirrel, stirrup; spirit* (AN. and ME. **spirit**) beside ME. and earlier NE. **sperit** (O.Fr. **esperit**).

o

§ 66. ME. **o,** of whatever origin, = NE. **o.** It is probable, however, that ME. **o** was mid-back-wide like the **o** in NHG. **Gott,** whereas in NE. it is low-back-wide (§ 58). Examples are :—

1. ME. **o** = OE. and ON. **o** (*EME. Gr.* §§ 47, 164), as *aloft, body, borrow, bottom, cock, copper, crop, dock, dog, drop, fog, follow, fox, frog, from, God, hog, hollow, holly, hop, knock, knot, lock, lot, morrow, odd, on, ox, poppy, pot, rotten, smock, sorrow, top, trodden.*

2. ME. **o** = OE. **a** (**o**) before **ng** (§ 63), as *belong, long, song, strong, thong, throng, tongs, wrong.* This **o** became **u** in the west Midland dialects of the ME. period (*EME. Gr.* § 133), and a few words from these dialects have crept into the NE. standard language with regular change of **u** to **a** (§ 67), as *among, monger, mongrel,* see § 139.

3. OE. and early ME. shortening of **ọ̄** (*EME. Gr.* § 94), as *blossom, fodder, foster, gosling, soft, shod*; and early ME. shortening of **ǭ**, as *holiday* beside the NE. new formation *holy day* with differentiated meaning, *sorry; hot* may be a back formation from the comparative *hotter* where **ǭ** was regularly shortened to **o** (*EME. Gr.* § 359).

4. French words: — 1. In syllables accented in both languages, as *absolve, adopt, coffin, lodge, offer, plot, ponder, prompt.* 2. In syllables accented in English, but unaccented in French, as *abolish, college, common, conquer, conscience, contrary, cotton, doctor, folly, forest, historic, pocket, popular, porridge, problem, profit.*

NOTE.—In some of the dialects, especially the south Midland, southern, and south-western, NE. **o** had a tendency to become **æ** through the intermediate stage **a**, and the earlier standard language had many words containing this **æ**, which now have **o** again, as *plot* beside obs. *plat* (2 Kings ix. 26 in the authorized version of the Bible). We still have *strap* beside *strop.* But in *nap* (**noppe** of a clothe, *Promp. Parv.* about 1440), *scrag, sprat, stab* beside obs. *scrog, sprot, stob* only the forms with **æ** have survived, see § 137.

u

§ 67. ME. **u,** of whatever origin, became **a** in the late sixteenth or early seventeenth century, but in the dialects of

the north of England and in many of the Midland dialects
it has remained down to the present day (*ED. Gr.* § 98).
Examples are : —

1. ME. u = OE. and ON. u (*EME. Gr.* §§ 48, 164), as
*begun, buck, butter, cup, cut, drunk, furrow, hundred, hunger,
hunt, hurry, luck, lull, mud, nut, rub, run, scrub, scull, shudder,
summer, sun, sung, sunk, thunder.*   Through the influence of
the Anglo-Norman system of orthography u was often
written o in ME., especially before and after m, n, w, and
u = v (*EME. Gr.* § 9), whence NE. spellings like *come,
honey, love, monk, some, son, tongue, won, wonder,* &c.   The
stem-vowel is also written o in *borough, thorough* ; ou in
young ; and o in many French words, as *colour, company,
cover, dozen, front, govern, money, sponge, stomach,* &c.

2. ME. u = OE. y (*EME. Gr.* §§ 125–6), as *blush, clutch,
crutch, cudgel, much, rush, shut, shuttle, such, thrush ; worry*
(*EME. Gr.* § 123).

3. French words : — 1. In syllables accented in both
languages, as *crust, drug, front, fund, grudge, number, plunge,
pulse, pump, sponge, stuff, sum, supple, ton, trunk, uncle.*
2. In syllables accented in English, but unaccented in
French, as *abundance, bucket, button, comfort, company,
custard, custom, gutter, money, mutton, onion, subject, sudden,
supper, tunnel,* see 1 above.

4. ME. shortening of ū, of whatever origin, as *but, crumb,
dove, duck* v., *dumb, dust, husband, plum, rust, shove, southern,
suck, sup, thumb, trust, udder, us* (cp. *EME. Gr.* § 95) ; *chough,
enough, rough, tough* ; French words, as *country, couple,
cousin, double, flourish, nourish, touch, trouble* (*EME. Gr.*
§ 201).

Forms like *outer* and *outermost* beside *utter* and *utmost* are
late new formations.

5. Late ME. u = O.Fr. (AN.) ü (*EME. Gr.* § 184, 4) :—
1. In syllables accented in both languages, as *adult, bust,
humble, judge, just, result.*   2. In syllables accented in

English, but unaccented in French, as *culture, duchess, justice, public, punish, study,* &c.

NOTE.—1. NE. *oven* points to an OE. form *ufen (cp. *EOE. Gr.* §§ 23, 66) beside ofen, ofn which has not survived in NE. *shovel* (OE. scofl) has been influenced by the verb *shove* (OE. scūfan), see 4 above.

2. Through the influence of the spelling the o in a number of French words is now pronounced o or o beside a, but formerly only a from older u, as *bombard, bombast, combat, frontier, sojourn, sovereign* ; and through the same cause the o in *cony* (*coney*), formerly written *cunny*, and *wont* (late ME. wunt) is now pronounced ou.

3. *thorough* and *through* are originally the same word (OE. þurh = ME. þurh, þoruh, þorouȝ) which in NE. has been differentiated in form and meaning. The ū in the preposition þrū 'through' with metathesis of the r is a NE. lengthening.

B. THE LONG VOWELS.

§ 68. All the ME. long vowels have become diphthongs in NE.: ā, ī, ọ̄, ū have become ei, ai, ou, au, and ē̜ (ẹ̄), ọ̄ have become ij, uw (§ 56); for AN. ü, see § 78. Before tracing the history of the separate ME. long vowels ā, ẹ̄, ē̜, ī, ọ̄, ọ̄, ū in NE. it may be useful to state in a connected manner the independent changes which these vowels underwent partly in late ME. and partly in early NE.:—The vowels ī, ū were diphthongized, and then ẹ̄, ọ̄ became ī, ū, and ē̜, ọ̄ became ẹ̄, ọ̄ ; ā was fronted to ǣ, and then later raised to ẹ̄. Their further history will be treated under the separate vowels.

ā

§ 69. ME. ā (*EME. Gr.* §§ 79, 195) has become ei through the intermediate stages ǣ, ẹ̄. The ā was fronted to ǣ in the fifteenth century, ǣ was then raised to ẹ̄ in the sixteenth century, and then the ẹ̄ was diphthongized to ei in the

seventeenth century, and thus fell together with the **ei** from
ME. **ai (ei)**, see § 82.   Examples are :—*acre, ale, ape, awake,
bake, bathe, behave, cake, cradle, dale, game, gape, gate, glaze,
grave, graze, hate, lame, lady, late, make, name, race, raven,
sake, take, tale, tame, wade, wave.*

French words :—1. In syllables accented in both languages,
as *able, blame, brave, case, chaste, debate, engage, escape, fable,
fade, fate, grace, grape, page, persuade, place, table, taste.*
2. In syllables accented in English, but unaccented in
French, as *bacon, basin, capable, famous, fatal, favour, flavour,
matron, nation, native, nature, occasion, paper, pastry, patient.*
The **a** in *female* (Fr. **femelle**) is due to the influence of *male.*

Note.—1. *have, hast, has (hath)* beside *behave* are the unaccented forms which have become generalized (cp. *EME. Gr.*
§ 79, note 2).
2. Through ME. ā and **ai (ei)** falling together in the seventeenth
century a few words are now spelled with **ai** which formerly had
a, as *gait* (rare until the seventeenth century) beside *gate; mail*
(ME. **māle**, O.Fr. **male**) ; *waist* (ME. **wāst**) was rare until it was
adopted by Johnson in his Dictionary (1755).
3. The long ā has remained in late borrowings from foreign
languages, as *drama, lava, promenade, tomato. vase,* formerly
pronounced **veiz (veis)** and also **vǭz,** is now treated as if it were
a late French loanword.

ę̄ and ę̄

§ 70.   Before tracing the history of ME. long close ę̄ and
long open ę̄ in NE. it is desirable to state how these sounds
were expressed in early and late ME., and how the subsequent
sounds are expressed in NE.   In early ME. both ę̄ and ę̄
were expressed by **e.**   From the fourteenth until well on
into the sixteenth century both sounds were generally also
expressed alike, viz. either by **ee** in syllables which were
closed in early ME., and often finally, or by **e** followed by
a single consonant + e in syllables which were open in

early ME., as feet (OE. fēt), knee (OE. cnēo), and deed (OE. dēad ' dead '), see (OE. sǣ ' sea '), but swete (OE. swēte ' sweet '), and delen (OE. dǣlan ' to divide '), lepen (OE. hlēapan ' to leap '), see *EME. Gr.* §§ 52-3, 63-5. Towards the end of the fifteenth century and during the first half of the sixteenth century an attempt began to be made to distinguish the two sounds in writing. The long close ẹ̄, which before this time had become ī in sound, was expressed partly by ee, partly by e followed by a single consonant + e, and partly by the Central O.Fr. spelling ie which already in late ME. had begun to be used to express long close ẹ̄ (*EME. Gr.* § 197, 2). At first the ie was used in French words only, and then later also in native words, especially before ld, f, and v. And ę̄ came to be expressed by ea or by e before a single consonant + e. Caxton (d. about 1491) occasionally used ea, but chiefly in French words only. The ea was much more common in Tyndale (d. 1536). During the second half of the sixteenth and early part of the seventeenth century this writing of ea became fairly well fixed both in native and French words, although a certain number of French words are now spelled with e, ei which formerly had ea (§ 72, 6). And at the same time the spelling ee, ie (see above) became fairly well fixed for expressing the ī from older ẹ̄ in native words and many French words, but the writing of e + consonant + vowel remained very common in French words of more than one syllable (cp. § 71, 10). The system was, however, by no means consistently carried through. There is quite a number of words spelled with ea in present-day English, which must have had long close ẹ̄ in standard ME., as *cleave* (ME. clẹ̄ven, OE. clēofan), *read, seal* ' animal ' which were often spelled reede, seele in the fifteenth and sixteenth centuries, &c., but some such words with ea may have crept into the standard language from dialects which regularly had ę̄ in ME., cp. *EME. Gr.* § 52, 1.

ē̦

§ 71. ME. ē̦, of whatever origin, became ī towards the end
of the fifteenth century. This change of ē̦ to ī must have
taken place after ME. ī (§ 73) had begun to be diphthongized
in the latter half of the fifteenth century, otherwise the two
sounds would have fallen together. In southern standard
English the ī from older ē̦ was diphthongized to **ij** some time
before the end of the eighteenth century. Examples are :—

1. ME. ē̦ = OE. lengthened ē (*EME. Gr.* § 53), as *he, me,
thee, we, ye.*

2. ME. ē̦ = OE. i-umlaut of ō (*EME. Gr.* § 53), as *beech,
beseech, bleed, deem, feed, feel, feet, geese, green, greet, keen,
keep, meet, queen, seek, seem, speed, sweet, teeth, weep.*

3. ME. ē̦ = OE. ēo (*EME. Gr.* § 65), as *be, bee, cleave,
creep, deep, fiend, flee, fleece, free, freeze, knee, lief, meek* (ON.
mjūkr), *priest, reed, seal* 'animal', *see, seethe, thief, three,
tree, weed, wheel.*

4. ME. ē̦ = the OE. lengthening of **e** before **ld** (*EME. Gr.*
§ 71), as *field, shield, wield, yield.*

5. ME. ē̦ = WS. īe, non-WS. ē̦ (*EME. Gr.* § 66), as
believe, cheese, need, sheet, sleet, sleeve, steel, steeple.

6. ME. ē̦ = WS. ǣ, Anglian and Kentish ē, Germanic ǣ
(*EME. Gr.* § 52), as *deed, eel, evening, greedy, leech, needle,
seed, sleep, speech, street, weeds* 'garments'.

7. ME. ē̦ = WS. ēa, non-WS. ē (*EME. Gr.* § 64), as
cheek, sheep; leek (*EME. Gr.* § 35).

8. ME. ē̦ = early ME. i in open syllables (*EME. Gr.* § 85),
as *beetle, evil, glede* 'kite', *week, weevil.*

9. ME. ē̦ = the unrounding of AN. ȫ (*EME. Gr.* § 198),
as *beef, people, reprieve* ; and *jeopardy, leopard* with shortening
of the ē̦ before it became ī.

10. ME. ē̦ in French words :—1. In syllables accented in
both languages, as *achieve, agree, brief, chief, concede, degree,
feeble, grief, grieve, niece, piece, proceed, relief, siege.* 2. In

syllables accented in English, but unaccented in French, as *convenient, decent, equal, frequent, genius, legal, obedient, previous, recent, secret, tedious.* In late French loan-words like *esteem* (Fr. **estimer**), *redeem* (Fr. **redimer**) ee was used for ī after ME. ę̄ (written ee) had become ī in English words.

NOTE.—*chuse* (OE. cēosan) is a southern and west Midland dialect form which crept into standard ME. in the fourteenth century (cp. *EME. Gr.* § 65). It is still in general use in many of the modern dialects, pronounced **tšiuz**, and was far more common than *choose* (§ 75, 2) in the standard language from the sixteenth century until well on into the nineteenth century, when it gradually became obsolete, see 3 above.

ę̄

§ 72. ME. ę̄, of whatever origin, became ē̜ towards the end of the fifteenth century, that is, soon after old ē̜ had become ī (§ 71). It then became ī in the latter part of the seventeenth century, and thus fell together with the ī from old ē̜, although the ē̜-sound was often used in rimes until a later date. It, like the ī from old ē̜, was diphthongized to ij in the southern standard language some time before the end of the eighteenth century. Examples are :—

1. ME. ę̄ = OE. ǣ, the i-umlaut of ā (*EME. Gr.* § 52, 2), as *bleach, clean, deal, each, heal, heat, heath, lead* v., *lean* adj., *least, leave, mean, reach, sea, seat, teach, tease, wheat.*

2. ME. ę̄ = WS. and Germanic ǣ (*EME. Gr.* § 52, 1), as *bleat, breathe, meal-time, read.*

3. ME. ę̄ = OE. ēa (*EME. Gr.* § 63), as *beacon, beam, bean, beat, cheap, dream, east, flea, heap, leaf, leap, seam, sheaf, steam, stream.*

4. ME. ę̄ = ON. ei before k (*EME. Gr.* § 168, note), as *bleak, weak. steak* (ON. **steik**, early ME. **steike** beside later **stę̄ke**) has the pronunciation of the former ME. form and the spelling of the latter.

5. ME. ę̄ = OE. e in open syllables (*EME. Gr.* § 80), as

bequeath, besom, breach, eat, even, heave, knead, meal ' flour ',
meat, mete, reap, speak, weave, wreak.

6. French words : — 1. In˚ syllables accented in both
languages, as *appeal, beast, cease, cheat, conceal, defeat, eager,
eagle, ease, feast, feat, grease, increase, neat, peace, plead, please,
preach, treat, veal, zeal.* Words like *conceive, deceive, receive,
seize* were generally spelled with **ea** in the sixteenth and
seventeenth centuries (cp. § 21), and similarly with words
like *complete, extreme,* &c.   2. In syllables accented in
English, but unaccented in French, as *demeanour, reason,
season, treason.* See *EME. Gr.* §§ 196, 205, 217.

Note.—1. The regular pronunciation of *break* and *great* would
be **brīk** and **grīt** just as in many of the modern dialects, and also
very often in the standard language of the eighteenth century.
The present forms (**breik, greit**) crept into the standard language
from those dialects in which ME. **ę̄** was regularly diphthongized to
ei (cp. *ED. Gr.* §§ 61, 181). Perhaps *steak* may also be due to the
same cause, but see 4 above.

2. NE. *slay* (OE. **slēan**) for *slea is a new formation from the
past participle, and similarly *flay* from the now obsolete pp. **flain.*
The pronunciation of *yea* (ME. **ʒę̄**) is due to the influence of *nay.*

ī

§ 73. ME. **ī,** of whatever origin, has been diphthongized
to **ai** in standard NE., and has also become a diphthong in
all the modern dialects, but often, however, with a different
vowel (**o, e**) in the first element of the diphthong. It became
ij in the latter half of the fifteenth century, and then **ei** by
about 1500 or soon after. The **ei** then became **ai** in the
seventeenth century. It should be noted that the **ī** must
have begun to be diphthongized before ME. **ę̄** became **ī** (§ 71),
otherwise the two sounds would have fallen together, and
then have had the same further development in common.
Examples are :—

1. ME. **ī** = OE. **ī** (*EME. Gr.* § 54), as *abide, alive, arise,
bite, chide, drive, five, glide, ice, idle, life, like, mile, mine, pipe,*

*ride, shine, side, slide, smite, swine, thine, thrive, tide, time,
while, white, wide, wife, wine, wise, write.*

2. ME. ī = OE. and ON. ȳ (*EME. Gr.* § 57), as *bride, dive,
hide* sb. and v., *kine, lice, mice, sky, why.*

3. Early ME. ĭȝ = OE. ĭ + palatal g (*EME. Gr.* § 122), as
*bridle, Friday, hie, lie down, nine, scythe, sigh, stile, sty, thrice,
twice.*

4. Early ME. ĭȝ = OE. ў + palatal g (*EME. Gr.* § 122), as
buy, dry, lie sb., *rye.*

5. Early ME. ę̄ȝ = late OE. ē + palatal g or h (*EME. Gr.*
§ 107, 5, 6), as *fly* sb. and v., *high, island, lie* v., *nigh, sly* (ON.
slœ̄gr), *thigh, tie* v. The difference in spelling in *die* and
dye is quite modern ; both words were spelled *die* or *dye* in
the eighteenth century. *eye* has the old Midland spelling
with the regular southern pronunciation.

6. ME. ī = OE. i, y before **ld, mb, nd** (*EME. Gr.* §§ 71–3),
as *child, mild, wild ; climb ; bind, blind, find, kind, mind,
wind* v. *build, gild* have ĭ from the pret. and pp. *built, gilt*
beside the new formation *gilded.* *wind* sb. is a back-formation
from forms like *windy, windmill.*

7. Late ME. ī + **ght** = late OE. i (y), of whatever origin,
+ **ht** (*EME. Gr.* § 46), as *bright, fight, flight* (OE. **flyht**),
fright (OE. **fyrhto, fryhto**), *knight, light* sb. and adj., *might,
night, plight, right, sight.* *weight* for *wight* (OE. **wiht**) is
a new formation from the verb.

8. French words : — 1. In syllables accented in both
languages, as *advise, apply, arrive, beguile, bible, bribe, crime,
cry, decline, deny, entice, fine, guide, invite, July, miser, polite,
price, provide, rice, sign, spy, strive, tiger, type, vine* (*EME. Gr.*
§ 199). 2. In syllables accented in English, but unaccented
in French, as *climate, client, denial, liable, libel, licence, lion,
piety, pious, private, quiet, silent, society, tyrant, violent* (*EME.
Gr.* § 218). 3. In English secondary accented syllables, as
exile, multiply, realize, signify, suicide. 4. In syllables unaccented in both languages, as *idea, fidelity, vivacity.*

The ī has remained in late French loan-words, as *antique, critique, fatigue, invalid, machine, marine, police, ravine, routine, unique*. In the seventeenth and eighteenth centuries, and well on into the last century, *oblige* was treated as being a late French loan-word, and was accordingly pronounced with ī, as it still is in many of the modern dialects (cp. *ED. Gr.* § 223).

Note.—In late ME. the ī was also often diphthongized in secondary accented syllables which now have -y (= ĭ) and -ly only. In the sixteenth and seventeenth centuries these endings often rimed with the diphthong in accented syllables, and such rimes were sometimes preserved traditionally by poets of the eighteenth and nineteenth centuries, as *adversity : tie, charity : tie, happily : high*. The ending -lai is still common in some dialects, especially in the pronunciation of adverbs like *accordingly, surely*.

ǭ and ǫ

§ 74. Before tracing the history of ME. long close ǭ and long open ǫ in NE. it is desirable to state in a connected manner how these two sounds were expressed in early and late ME., and how the subsequent sounds are expressed in NE. OE. had no long open ǫ, and long close ǭ was expressed by o in this period of the language. Long open ǫ arose in ME. chiefly from : (1) the rounding of OE. ā in early ME. ; (2) the rounding of early ME. ā before ld, mb; (3) the lengthening of OE. o in open syllables; (4) the lengthening of o in AN. words, see *EME. Gr.* §§ 51, 71–2, 81, 200. Both ǭ and ǫ were expressed by o in early ME. From the fourteenth until well on into the sixteenth century both sounds were also generally expressed alike, viz. either by oo in syllables which were closed in early ME., and often finally, or by o followed by a single consonant + e in syllables which were open in early ME., as goos (OE. gōs 'goose'), doo also do (OE. dōn) and boot (OE. bāt 'boat'), too (OE. tā 'toe'), but loken (OE. lōcian

E 2

'to look'), and **gropen** (OE. **grāpian** 'to grope'), see *EME.
Gr.* §§ 51, 55. During the first half of the sixteenth
century an attempt began to be made to distinguish the
two sounds in writing. The long close ǭ which before this
time had become ū in sound (§ 75) was expressed by **oo,** and
the long open ǭ was expressed by **oa** before a final consonant
or by **o** before a following consonant + **e,** and **oe** finally.
This distinction in the writing of the two sounds became
fairly well fixed during the seventeenth century. The
writing of **oa** to express the old ǭ-sound was based on the
analogy of writing **ea** to express the old ę̄-sound. Caxton
(d. about 1491) occasionally used **ea** for ę̄, but never **oa**
for ǭ. Tyndale (d. 1536) used both **oa** and **ea.**

ǭ

§ 75. ME. ǭ, of whatever origin, became ū towards the
end of the fifteenth century. This change of ǭ to ū must
have taken place after ME. ū had begun to be diphthongized
in the latter half of the fifteenth century, otherwise the two
sounds would have fallen together. In southern standard
English the ū from older ǭ was diphthongized to **uw** some
time before the end of the eighteenth century. Examples
are :—

1. ME. ǭ = OE. and ON. ō (*EME. Gr.* § 55), as *behoof,
bloom, boon, booth, brood, broom, cool, do, doom, food, gloom,
goose, hoof, hoop, loom, mood, moon, noon, roof, root, shoe,
smooth, soon, spoon, stool, too, tool, tooth.*

2. ME. ǭ from OE. eó, older éo (*EME. Gr.* § 65, note), as
choose, lose, shoot.

3. ME. ǭ from older ǭ = OE. ā preceded by **w** (*EME. Gr.*
§ 128), as *swoop* v., *two, who, whose, whom, womb* (*EME. Gr.*
§ 72).

4. French words, as *boot, fool, move, proof, prove* (*EME. Gr.*
§ 198).

Note.—1. In late ME. and early NE., especially in the six-teenth century, the ū from older ǭ (see above) was often written ou in words which now have oo again, as broum, loum, touth, &c. beside *broom, loom, tooth,* &c., but the spelling with ou has survived in *ousel, ouzel* (OE. ōsle) beside the obsolete form *oozel.*

2. The pronunciation of *don't, behove* (ME. bihǭven, OE. be-hōfian) beside *behoof,* and *yeoman* (ME. ȝǭman) has been influenced by the spelling.

ǭ

§ 76. ME. ǭ, of whatever origin, has become ou through the intermediate stage ọ̄. The ǭ became ọ̄ in the early part of the sixteenth century, that is, soon after old ọ̄ had become ū (§ 75). Then the ọ̄ was diphthongized to ou in the seven-teenth century, and thus fell together with old ǫu (§ 89). Examples are:—

1. ME. ǭ = OE. ā (*EME. Gr.* § 51), as *alone, arose, atone, boat, bone, both, clothe, clover, doe, drove, foam, foe, go, goat, ghost, groan, grope, holy, home, load, loaf, moan, no, oak, oath, oats, only, road, roam, rode, roe, rope, so, soap, stone, stroke, those, toad, toe, token, whole, woe, wrote,* and similarly ME. ǭ before mb (*EME. Gr.* § 72), as *comb.*

2. ME. ǭ = OE. o in open syllables (*EME. Gr.* § 81), as *broken, chosen, cloven, coal, cove, doze, float, foal, frozen, hole, hope, nose, open, over, spoken, stolen, throat, woven, yoke.*

3. French words:— 1. In syllables accented in both languages (*EME. Gr.* § 200), as *boast, coach, coast, coat, cloak, host, noble, note, poach, pole, post, propose, roast, robe, rogue, rose, suppose, toast, tone, vote; broach* beside *brooch* with differentia-tion in spelling and meaning. 2. In syllables accented in English, but unaccented in French, as *devotion, local, moment, notable, notice, notion, odious, poem, sofa, total.*

Note.—1. *one* is a dialect form which crept into the stan-dard language before the end of the fifteenth century, although it was rarely written *won(e), woone,* see *N.E.D.* s. v. As the old spelling with initial o has generally been retained all along, it is only possible to state hypothetically the course of the development of the present pronunciation from ME. ǭn, viz. that ǭn became **wan** (§ 67) through the intermediate stages **wǭn** (cp. *EME. Gr.* § 117), **wǭn** (§ 75, 3), **wūn** (§ 75), and then **wun** by shortening; and similarly *once*. The same vowel sound now occurs also in *none* and *nothing*.

2. *broad* is a dialect form which crept into the standard language from those dialects which regularly preserved the ǭ in this word, see index to *ED. Gr.*; and similarly *groat* was often or generally pronounced **grǭt** until about 1800. *hale, raid* beside *whole, road* are northern dialect forms which have crept into the standard language.

ū

§ 77. Through the influence of Anglo-Norman orthography **ou (ow)** was often written for ū from the second half of the thirteenth century, and became general in the fourteenth century, see *EME. Gr.* § 56. This spelling has also been preserved in NE. ME. ū, of whatever origin, has been diphthongized to **au** in the standard language, but in the Scottish and northern dialects it has generally remained down to the present day. It became **uw** in the latter half of the fifteenth century, and then **ou** by about 1500 or soon after. The **ou** then became **au** in the early part of the seventeenth century. It should be noted that the **ou** must have become **au** some time before ME. ǭ (§ 76) and ǫu (§ 89) became **ou**, otherwise they would have fallen together. It should also be noted that the ū must have begun to be diphthongized before ME. ǭ became ū (§ 75), otherwise the two sounds would have fallen together, and then have had the same further development in common. Examples are:—

1. ME. ū = OE. ū (*EME. Gr.* § 56), as *about, brow, brown, cloud, clout, cow, crowd, down, foul, gown, house, how, loud, louse, mouse, mouth, now, out, owl, proud, south, thou, thousand,*

town. *uncouth* has crept into the standard language from
the northern dialects.

2. ME. $\bar{u}$ from early ME. $\breve{u}_3$ = OE. $\breve{u}$ + guttural g (*EME.
Gr.* § 122), as *bow* v., *cowl*, *drought* (OE. drūgoþ), *fowl*, *sow*.

3. ME. $\bar{u}$ from early ME. antevocalic -ǭȝ- (*EME. Gr.* § 114,
2 (*b*)), as *bough*, *plough*, *slough*, which were new formations
from the ME. inflected forms; *enow* (old pl. of *enough*).

4. ME. $\bar{u}$ = the lengthening of OE. u before nd (*EME. Gr.*
§ 73), as *bound*, *found*, *ground*, *hound*, *pound*, *sound* adj. ;
wound pp. (see § 134, 1).

5. French words:— 1. In syllables accented in both
languages, as *abound*, *allow*, *amount*, *announce*, *confound*,
count, *crown*, *devout*, *doubt*, *mount*, *pouch*, *powder*, *renown*,
round, *stout*, *vow*. 2. In syllables accented in English, but
unaccented in French, as *bounty*, *county*, *coward*, *fountain*,
mountain, *vowel*. See *EME. Gr.* §§ 201, 220. The $\bar{u}$-sound
has remained in late French loan-words, as *group*, *rouge*,
route, *soup*.

Note.—1. The ME. $\bar{u}$ has remained undiphthongized after y in
you (*EME. Gr.* § 112, note), and *youth* (*EME. Gr.* § 122, 5).

2. *cucumber* is a spelling pronunciation. It was pronounced
kaukambə until the beginning of the nineteenth century, and was
written cowcumber (O.Fr. co(u)combre).

ü

§ 78. Anglo-Norman $\ddot{u}$ of whatever origin (see *EME. Gr.*
§ 202): The pure $\ddot{u}$-sound did not exist in any of the dialects
of England at the time when the AN. words containing this
sound were introduced. There was a kind of $\ddot{u}$-sound in the
west Midland and some of the southern dialects, but it was
different from the AN. sound, as is evidenced by the subsequent history of the two sounds both in ME. and the
modern dialects (cp. *EME. Gr.* § 57). For AN. $\ddot{u}$ was substituted what seemed to the English ear the nearest equiva-

lent, viz. **iu,** but through the influence of Central French the ū-sound was often pronounced as such by educated speakers in the sixteenth century. This **iu** fell together with the **iu** which arose from older **ęu** in native and AN. words (cp. *EME. Gr.* §§ 112, 209). In the older loan-words it was generally written **u (ui),** and later also **eu (ew), iu (iw),** see § **86** and *EME. Gr.* §§ 112, 116.

§ **79.** The **iu** became **jū** in the standard language during the sixteenth century, but has remained in many of the dialects down to the present day. Examples are:—1. In syllables accented in both languages, as *accuse, amuse, dispute, duke, during, fume, huge, mute, pew, stew, subdue, sue, tube, tune, use* v., *use* sb. 2. In syllables accented in English, but unaccented in French, as *curious, duty, human, music, mutiny, purity, student, stupid, uniform, union, unit.* After **s** the pronunciation fluctuates between **jū** and **ū,** as *pursue, pursuit, suicide, suit.* In *sugar* (AN. sūgre) the **sjū-** has become **šu-** through the intermediate stage **šū-,** and in *sure* (AN. sūr) we have **šuə** beside **šǫə, šǫ̈ə, šǫ̈** (§ **129**). Many dialects have **siu-** in both these words.

§ **80.** After **j** (= **dž**), **l,** and **r** the **jū** became **ū** about the end of the seventeenth or beginning of the eighteenth century, but many of the dialects still have **iu** in this position:—1. In syllables accented in both languages, as *allude, bruise, brute, conclude, fruit, juice, June, jute, lute, plume, prune, rude, salute.* 2. In syllables accented in English, but unaccented in French, as *conclusion, cruel, fluid, frugal, prudent, ruin, rumour, solution.* There is, however, a certain amount of fluctuation between **ū** and **jū** in learned words of this type, as *absolute, allusion, luminous, resolution,* &c.

C. The Diphthongs.

§ **81.** With the exception of **ǫi** all the ME. diphthongs have undergone independent changes in NE. **au** has been

monophthongized to ǭ ; ai (ei) has become ei ; ęu, ęu, iu
have become jū ; ǫu has become ou (§ 89) ; and ǫi has
remained ; for ui, see § 88.

ai (ei)

§ 82. ME. ai (ei) has become ei in NE.   Early ME. ai and
ei fell together in ai (written ai, ay, ei, ey) about 1300
(*EME. Gr.* §§ 107, 205), and from then onwards ai was
mostly written for both old ai and ei, but the spelling of
the old diphthong ei has been preserved in a few words
right down to the present day, as *grey* beside *gray, weigh,
whey*.   The ai became æi about the end of the sixteenth
century at the same time that a became æ (§ 62).   And
then æi became ei in the seventeenth century, and thus fell
together with the ei from ME. ā (§ 69).   This falling together
of the two sounds sometimes gave rise to a being written
for ai, as dalie for dailie, trace sb. for older trayce (O.Fr.
trais) ; and ai for a, see § 69, note 2.   It is sometimes
assumed that the development was as follows :—æi from
older ai became monophthongized to ǣ during the sixteenth
century.   The ǣ was then raised to ę̄ by the end of the
sixteenth or early part of the seventeenth century, and thus fell
together with the ę̄ from ME. ā (§ 69).   And then the ę̄ from
both sources was diphthongized to ei during the seventeenth
century.   Much might be said in favour of this theory, if
the standard language had had its origin in the northern
and north Midland counties, where ME. ai (ei) undoubtedly
became monophthongized at an early period in most of the
dialects of this area, and thus fell together with the normal
development of ME. ā.   But just in that area and the
adjacent areas where the standard language arose, ME. ai (ei)
has generally remained a diphthong down to the present day,
viz. in the south Midland, Eastern, Southern, and south
Western counties, and has not fallen together with ME. ā,
see *ED. Gr.* §§ 43, 48.   From this it may fairly be inferred

that ME. **ai** (**ei**) never became a monophthong in the standard
language. Examples are :—

1. ME. **ai** = OE. **æ** + palatal **g** (*EME. Gr.* § 106), as *brain,
daisy* (OE. **dæges ēage**), *day, fain, hail* sb., pret. *lay, maiden,
main* sb., *may, nail, slain, snail, tail, wain.*

2. Early ME. **ei** = OE. **e** + palatal **g** (*EME. Gr.* § 107, ɪ),
as *blain, braid, flail, laid, lain, lay* inf., *play, rain, say, twain,
way, weigh.*

3. Early ME. **ei** = OE. **ǣ** or **ēa** + palatal **g** (*EME. Gr.*
§ 107, 5), as *clay, gray* (*grey*), *neigh, whey ; hay* (Anglian
hēg).

4. Early ME. **ei** = late OE. **e** before **h**(**h**) or **ht** (*EME. Gr.*
§ 107, 4), as *eight, neighbour* (early ME. **nehhbour**, early OE.
nēahgebūr), *straight.*

5. Early ME. **ei** = ON. **ei** (*EME. Gr.* § 168), as *aye* ' ever ',
bait, greyhound, nay, raise, swain, they.

6. ME. **ai** (**ei**) = O.Fr. **ai** (**ei**) (*EME. Gr.* § 205):—1. In
syllables accented in both languages, as *abstain, aid, aim,
array, assail, avail, chain, claim, complain, defray, delay, detail,
display, entertain, faith, feign, frail, gain, gay, grain, obey,
ordain, pail, pain, pay, praise, rail, ray, reign, remain, stay,
survey, train, vain, vein.* 2. In syllables accented in English,
but unaccented in French, as *acquaintance, dainty, gaiety,
raisin, tailor, traitor,* &c.

§ 83. There are several words which require to be specially
explained :—*height* and *sleight* have regularly preserved the
ME. **ei** in spelling, but have been influenced by *high* and *sly*
in pronunciation, see *EME. Gr.* § 109 ; they are still pronounced **eit** and **sleit** in many dialects. And similarly
either (late OE. **ǣgþer**) and *neither* are still pronounced with
ei in some dialects (cp. *EME. Gr.* § 107, 5), and this would
be the regular pronunciation in the standard language of the
present day, but through some unknown cause the forms
ẹther or **ę̄ther** arose so early as the thirteenth century, and
nẹther or **nę̄ther** in the fourteenth century, and were also

often written **eather** and **neather** in the sixteenth century.
These forms have regularly become ī̆ðə(r), nī̆ðə(r) in standard
NE. (cp. §§ 71–2), and with ī or ē in most of the dialects, see
Index to *ED. Gr.* s.v. The pronunciation with **ai,** now
more common than with ī, is well attested by the orthoepists
of the late seventeenth century, but is of unknown origin.
The pronunciation with **ai** is rare in the dialects. The
regular pronunciation of *key* (OE. **cǣg**) and *quay* (O.Fr. **kai,
kay**) would be **kei** in standard NE., as it still is in most
of the modern dialects, and was also in the standard language
down to the beginning of the eighteenth century. The
pronunciation **kī** has gradually crept into the standard
language from the northern, especially the Scottish dialects,
where the native word is written **kee** so early as the fifteenth
century. The French word was spelled **kay, key** until the
beginning of the eighteenth century, and then began to be
supplanted by Mod. Fr. **quai** which had ousted the old
spelling by the end of the century, although it did not
affect the pronunciation.

au

§ 84. ME. **au,** of whatever origin, was monophthongized
to ǭ through the intermediate stage ǫu about the end of the
sixteenth or beginning of the seventeenth century. Examples
are :—

1. ME. **au** = OE. **a** + **w** (*EME. Gr.* § 110, 1), as *awl, claw,
raw, sprawl, straw, thaw.*

2. ME. **au** = OE. and ON. **a** + guttural **g** = ʒ (*EME. Gr.*
§ 110, 3), as *awe, dawn, draw, fawn* v., *flaw, gnaw, hawthorn,
law, maw, saw* sb.

3. ME. **au** = OE. **a** + **f** = **v** (*EME. Gr.* §§ 110, 1, 242), as
auger, awkward, crawl, hawk.

4. ME. **au** = late Anglian **æ** from older **ea** before **h** and
ht (*EME. Gr.* § 110, 5), as *fought* (ME. **faught**) with **ou**
written for **au** after the analogy of words like *brought* (§ 90)

or with the **ou** from the past participle, pret. *saw, slaughter*.
The u-element disappeared in early NE. before **gh = f** (§ 272),
and then the **a** became **ā** through the intermediate stages
æ, ǣ, as *draught* (*draft*), *laugh, laughter* ; some of the dialects
have also **slaftə(r)**.

5. ME. **au** = late OE. **æ, a,** older **ǣ, ā** before **ht** (*EME.
Gr.* § 110, 6), as *aught, naught,* pret. and pp. *taught.*

6. ME. **au** in French words :—1. In syllables accented in
both languages, as *cause, daub, fraud, pause, paw, sauce ;
fault* (ME. and O.Fr. **faute**), *vault* (ME. **vaute**), see § 55, 5.
2. In syllables accented in English, but unaccented in French,
as *auction, author, autumn, haughty.* 3. In syllables unaccented in both languages the pronunciation varies between
ǭ, o, ə among different speakers, as *authentic, authority.*

The **ǭ** has been shortened to **o** in *cauliflower, laudanum,*
and *sausage.*

§ 85. ME. **au** = Anglo-Norman **au** before nasals regularly
became **ǭ** at the same time as the **au** in native words (§ 84).
Already in ME. there was a certain number of words with **ã**
(= O.Fr. denasalized **ã**, *EME. Gr.* § 185, 1) borrowed from
Central French beside the corresponding AN. words with **au,**
see *EME. Gr.* § 211. In the course of time these borrowings
from or imitations of Central French increased considerably,
and gradually ousted a great many of the **au** forms from the
standard language. In some words still spelled with **au** we
have **ā** beside **ǭ** in pronunciation, as *launch, laundry, staunch,*
and in *aunt* we have the AN. spelling, but only the Central
French pronunciation. In the modern dialects many of the
AN. forms have been preserved which have disappeared from
the standard language, as **džǭm, džǭəm** 'jamb', **ǭnt, ont**
'aunt', &c., cp. *ED. Gr.* § 202. Examples with **ǭ** are :—
1. In syllables accented in both languages, as *brawn, daunt,
fawn* sb., *haunch, haunt, jaunt, lawn, pawn, spawn, taunt,
vaunt.* 2. In syllables accented in English, but unaccented
in French, as *avaunt, gauntlet, jaundice, tawny,* &c.

The following are from Central French, introduced at
various periods :—

1. With **æ,** as *abandon, ample, blandish, brandish, cham-
pion, flank, jamb, lamp, language, languish, lantern, ramp,
ransom,* &c.

2. With **ā,** as *advance, advantage, aunt* (see above), *branch,
chance, chandler, chant, command, dance, demand, example,
grant, plant, sample,* &c.

Note.—au beside a(æ) also occurs in the native word *answer*
from the fourteenth to the seventeenth century.

ęu, iu

§ 86. Early ME. **ęu, iu,** and **ū** (§ 78) all fell together in **iu**
about the end of the thirteenth century (*EME. Gr.* §§ 112,
116, 202, 209).   This falling together of the three sounds in
iu gave rise to a certain amount of confusion in the spelling
of words belonging to these three types, because the **eu, u**
often continued to be written after the sound-change had
taken place.   The result was that old **iu** often came to be
written **eu (ew),** old **ū** (written **u, ui** in early French loan-
words) to be written **eu (ew), iu (iw),** and old **ęu, iu** to be
written **u.**   ME. **ū** has already been dealt with under the
long vowels (§ 78).   Early ME. **ęu, iu** are here treated
together.   The **iu** became **jū** in the standard language during
the sixteenth century, but has remained in many dialects
down to the present day (*ED. Gr.* § 193).   The **jū** then
became **ū** after **ch** (= tš), **j** (= dž), **l,** and **r** about the end
of the seventeenth or beginning of the eighteenth century,
but many of the dialects still have **iu** in this position.   Examples are :—

1. Early ME. **ęu** = OE. **ēow** (*EME. Gr.* § 112, ɪ, 2), as
hue, knew, new, yew; chew (see note) ; *brew, clew (clue), rue,
ruth, truce* (ME. **tręwes**), *true, truth,* the preterites *blew, crew,
grew, threw.*   The preterites *drew, slew* are analogical formations, see §§ 377–8.

2. Early ME. ẹu = AN. ẹu (*EME. Gr.* § 209), as *adieu, due, fuel, view,* and in unaccented syllables, as *curfew, nephew ; Jew, jewel ; blue, crew* sb., *rule.*

3. ME. iu = OE. ī + w (*EME. Gr.* § 116), as *spew, steward, Tuesday* (OE. **Tīwes dæg**).

NOTE.—In some words ME. had double forms, as **sọwen** (**sọwen**) beside **sẹwen** (*EME. Gr.* § 112, note 2) ; NE. *sew* has its pronunciation from the former and its spelling from the latter ; and in like manner beside **chẹwen** ME. had **chọwen** (**chọwen**), and also the dialect form **chawen** (cp. *EME. Gr.* § 113, note), which have become obsolete in the standard language, but are still the usual forms in some of the dialects (*ED. Gr.* § 193).

ẹu

§ 87. ME. **ẹu** remained in early NE. It became **iu** through the intermediate stage **ẹu** in the seventeenth century, and then **jū** in the eighteenth century, with the further change of **jū** to **ū** after **l** and **r**, and thus fell together with the **jū** (**ū**) from ME. **ẹu, iu, ū** (§§ 78, 86), but the two sets of sounds are still kept apart in many of the dialects. Examples are :—

1. ME. **ẹu** from OE. **ǣ** and **ēa** + **w** (*EME. Gr.* § 111), as *dew, few, hew, mew* 'seagull'; *lewd, shrew.*

2. ME. **ẹu** = OE. **ĕow** and **e** + **f** = **v**, as *ewe* (OE. **eowe**), *newt* (OE. **efete**) ; *strew* (OE. **streow(i)an**). Beside **strẹwen** ME. also had **strọwen** and the dialect form **strawen** (cp. *EME. Gr.* § 113, note) which became obsolete in the early NE. standard language, but have survived in some of the modern dialects.

3. In French words, as *beauty, deuce, feud, neuter, pewter.* During the ME. period **flẹume** and **rẹume** regularly became **flẹ̄me** and **rẹ̄me** (*EME. Gr.* § 213, 3), and then later the **ẹ̄** in both words was shortened to **e**, whence *phlegm, realm* which came to be spelled in this manner in early NE. through association with their etymological origin.

NOTE.—NE. *show* from OE. sceáwian (ME. schǫwen) beside *shew* from OE. scéawian (ME. schęwen) are now both pronounced šou in the standard language, but are still kept apart in many of the dialects, see *EME. Gr.* § 111, note.

ǫi, ui

§ 88. ME. ǫi, ui only occurred in French words with the exception of NE. *boy* (ME. boi, boye beside bai, bei) which is of unknown origin. What is written oi in ME. represented two distinct sounds which were kept apart until well on into the eighteenth century:—

1. ME. ǫi = AN. and O.Fr. oi (*EME. Gr.* § 206). The ǫi has regularly remained in NE., as *choice, cloister, coy, employ, exploit, foible, joy, loyal, moist, noise, poise, rejoice, royal, voice, void*, &c.

2. ME. ui which was generally written oi = AN. ui (O.Fr. ǫi, ui), see *EME. Gr.* §§ 207, 210. The words of this type were pronounced with ui in the sixteenth century. The ui then became ai in the late sixteenth or early seventeenth century at the same time that simple u became a (§ 67), but the new diphthong continued to be written oi (oy). This ai-sound then fell together with the ai from ME. ī (§ 73) with the result that i (y) was sometimes written for the oi (oy), as anynte, byle v., pyson for *anoint, boil, poison*. The following and similar words were pronounced with ai down to the early part of the eighteenth century:—*anoint, boil* v., *broil, coil, coin, join, joint, loin, oil, ointment, point, poison, soil, spoil, toil*, but by the middle of the century they generally came to be pronounced with ǫi through the influence of the spelling. This writing of oi for what was ai in sound gave rise to some words being written and pronounced with ǫi which ought historically to have ai from older ī (ȳ), as *boil* sb. (OE. bȳl), *groin* (OE. grȳnd), *joist* (O.Fr. jiste).

ọu

§ 89. ME. ọu (*EME. Gr.* § 113) has generally remained
a diphthong in NE. with change of the first element from
a low-back to a mid-back vowel (§ 58). This ou fell together
in the seventeenth century with the ou which arose from
ME. ǭ (§ 76). Through relying too much upon the testimony
of old writers on NE. pronunciation, some scholars now
assume that ME. ọu was first of all monophthongized to ǭ
which then later became ǭ, and thus fell together with the
ǭ from older ǭ (§ 76), and that then the ǭ in both types of
words was diphthongized to ou in the late eighteenth
century, but the former rather than the latter is more likely
to have been the correct course of development. Examples
are :—

1. ME. ọu = OE. āw, as *blow* (ME. blọ̄wen, OE. blāwan),
and similarly *crow* sb. and v., *know*, shortened to o in
knowledge, mow v., *row* sb., *slow, snow, soul, sow* v., *throw*.

2. ME. ọu = OE. o + guttural g, as *bow* sb. (ME. bọue,
bọwe, OE. boga), and similarly *flown*.

3. ME. ọu = OE. ā + guttural g or final ·h, as *low* adj.
(ON. lāgr), *own* (ME. ọwen, OE. āgen), *dough* (ME. dọugh,
OE. dāh, dāg).

4. Later ME. ọu from older ọu = OE. ōw (*EME. Gr.*
§ 114, ı), as *flow* (early ME. flọwen, OE. flōwan), and
similarly *blow* v. 'bloom', *glow, grow, low* v., *row* v.

§ 90. ME. ọu (*EME. Gr.* § 113, 4, 5) = OE. ŏ before h or
ht, was monophthongized to ǭ at the end of the sixteenth or
beginning of the seventeenth century along with the ọu
from older au (§ 84). This falling together of the two ME.
diphthongs in ǭ sometimes gave rise to ou being written for
au, as pret. *fought* for older faught (§ 84, 4), and au for ou,
as early NE. braught beside *brought*, and similarly with
other words in early NE. Examples are :—*bought, brought,
daughter* (see below), *fought* pp., *ought* 'anything', *nought*

beside the unaccented form *not, sought, thought, wrought.*
The u element of the diphthong disappeared in early NE.
before **gh = f** (§ 272), as **kof** 'cough', **trof** 'trough' beside
the later lengthened forms **kǭf, trǭf**, cp. § 93, 2. Several
of the above words also had **gh = f** in early NE., as **boft** 'bought',
thoft 'thought' (*ED. Gr.* § 359). The early NE. form **dafter**
riming with *after* is still common in some dialects with **ă,**
and points to a ME. dialect form **daughter** (cp. *EME. Gr.*
§ 113, note) beside the regular form **dǫughter**. *daughter* has
been the spelling in the standard language since the sixteenth
century.

2. DEPENDENT CHANGES

§ 91. In a few cases it has been thought advisable to
include under Independent Changes what properly belongs
to Dependent Changes. This applies especially to the history
of **ū** and the ME. diphthongs in NE.

(1) THE LENGTHENING OF SHORT VOWELS BEFORE CONSONANTS.

§ 92. For the lengthening of short vowels before final **·r**
and **r + consonant**, see §§ 107–17.

§ 93. The **æ** from older **a** (§ 62), and **o** were lengthened
in the seventeenth century to **ǣ** (later **ā**) and **ǭ** before voiceless spirants (**f, s, þ**), and voiceless spirants followed by
another consonant, but in the present standard pronunciation
there is considerable fluctuation between **ā** and **æ, ǭ** and **o**
in many of the words belonging to this category : —

1. The **æ** from older **a** (§ 62) was lengthened to **ǣ** in the
seventeenth century, and then the **ǣ** became **ā** in the latter
part of the eighteenth century, as *after, ask, bask, basket, bath,
brass, cast, castle, chaff, clasp, craft, fast, fasten, gasp, glass,
grass, last, laugh* (cp. § 272), *path, rafter, shaft, staff,* and
similarly in French words, as *cask, class, mask, master, pass,
past, plaster, task, vast,* &c. This lengthening of **æ** to **ā**

through the intermediate stage ǣ has not taken place in some words, especially foreign words, as *aspect, bastard, lass, masculine, mass*; æs for ās 'ass' is an artificial pronunciation; *hast* and *hath* are the unaccented forms which have become generalized (§ 69, note 1). The short vowel regularly remained before intervocalic ss, as *classic, passage, vassal*. Forms like *classes, passes* are due to the uninflected forms *class, pass*. In some words the pronunciation fluctuates between æ and ā, as *mastiff, pasture*, &c. In the noun *wrath* (ME. wrappe, OE. wrǣppu), now pronounced rǭþ, the pronunciation is due to the influence of *wroth* (ME. wrǭþ, OE. wrāþ).

2. The o was lengthened to ǭ in the seventeenth century, but in the present standard pronunciation we often have ǭ or o, or both, as *broth, cloth, coffee, cost, croft, cross, doff, dross, frost, froth, gloss, loft, loss, moss, moth, off, often, soft, soften.* The o is especially common in words of more than one syllable, as *foster, gospel, hospital, ostrich*.

§ 94. Lengthening has also taken place before the voiced spirant ð in *father* and *rather*. ME. had the double forms faþer and fāþer; the former has given rise to fāðə through the intermediate stages fæðer, fǣðer in the standard language, and the latter to the dialect forms fę̄ðə, feiðə, feəðə, &c.; and similarly *rather*, and before t in wǭtə 'water' with regular change of ā to ǭ after the w (cp. § 109), see *EME. Gr.* § 102.

(2) THE SHORTENING OF LONG VOWELS.

§ 95. It is almost impossible to lay down any hard and fast rules about the shortening of long vowels in NE., and this applies especially to the shortening which has taken place before single consonants in monosyllables. Shortening regularly took place during the ME. period before nearly all consonant combinations, and also to some extent before single consonants, especially dentals, in monosyllables, see *EME. Gr.* §§ 87–100. The shortenings which took place in ME. have been dealt with under the short vowels (§§ 62–7), but it is probable that some of the shortenings given below also took place before the NE. period began. As we shall see below, the NE. shortenings took place at different periods, and in some categories of words we are able to fix the approximate date. In early NE. the long and the shortened vowels often existed side by side in the same words, and then later one or the other became standardized. When the vowels ẹ̄ and ǭ were shortened in ME. we regu·larly have e and o in NE., but when the shortening took place after they had become ī (§ 71) and ū (§ 75) in late ME. we now regularly have i and a (u) ; and similarly when old ī (§ 73) and ū (§ 77) were shortened in ME. before they began to be diphthongized, we regularly have i and a (u) in NE., but no shortening took place after the diphthongization of the ī and ū. When ę̄ and ǭ were shortened in ME. we regularly have e and o in NE., and also e and o in NE. when the shortening took place before ę̄ and ǭ became ī (§ 72) and ou (§ 76), but no shortening took place after they had become ī and ou. ā was fronted to ǣ in late ME., so that the shortening of ā or ǣ at this period would in either case be æ (§ 62) in NE., but if the shortening took place after ǣ had become ẹ̄ in early NE. we now have e, see § 69.

§ 96. ME. **ā, ai (ei)**: Examples of the shortening of ā before it became ei through the intermediate stages ǣ, ẹ̄ (§ 69) have been given under a (§ 62). The shortening in the colloquial form **weskət** beside **weiskout** 'waistcoat' is quite modern ; for the spelling of this word, see § 69, note 2. Similarly shortenings of NE. ei (§ 82) from ME. ai (ei) are : —əgen beside əgein 'again', əgenst beside əgeinst 'against', *said, says* ; and the early unaccented form *them* from older *theim* (*thaim*).

§ 97. ME. **ę̄**: It is necessary to distinguish between early

and late shortening. When the shortening took place before
ę̄ became ī we regularly have e in NE., but when it took
place after ę̄ had become ī (§ 71) we now have i. For
examples of early shortening, see § 64. Examples of late
shortening are :—pp. bin beside bīn 'been', *breeches, Greenwich : green, grit* (ME. grę̄t, OE. grēot), *nickname* (ME. an
ę̄knāme), *riddle* (ME. rę̄deles, rędeles), *sieve* (ME. sę̄ve),
ship : sheep in the proverb *to lose the ship for a halfpennyworth
of tar*; the shortened forms *hip, sick,* and *silly* occurred
already in ME., see *EME. Gr.* § 99. On *garlic* (OE. gārlēac)
and *rick* (OE. hrēac), see *EME. Gr.* § 35.

§ 98. ME. ę̄ : We have already seen in § 95 that shortening
began to take place in ME. before single consonants in monosyllables, so that we cannot determine with certainty whether
shortening in the following and similar words took place in
ME. or in NE. before ę̄ became ī (§ 72), as *bread, breadth*
(ME. brę̄de), *dead, deaf, death, dread,* pret. *eat* (*ate*), *flesh, fret,
get, head, lead* sb., *let, red, shed* v., *shred, spread, stead, sweat,
thread, threat, tread, wet*; breikfəst beside brekfəst 'breakfast' is a late new formation from *break.* Shortenings which
undoubtedly took place in ME. are given under e (§ 64).
Dissyllabic French words like *measure, pheasant, pleasant,
pleasure, treasure* probably had a short vowel in ME. (cp.
EME. Gr. § 185, 3). There are no examples of the shortening
of ī from older ę̄.

§ 99. ME. ǭ : It is necessary to distinguish between early
and late shortening. When the shortening took place before
ǭ became ū we regularly have o in NE., but when it took
place after ǭ had become ū (§ 75) we now have a (u). For
examples of early shortening see § 66, 3. It is also further
necessary to distinguish between early and late NE. shortening of ū from older ǭ : 1. When the shortening took place
before ME. u became a in NE. (§ 67), and 2. When the
shortening took place after u had become a. In the former
case the u became a at the same time that ME. u became a,

and in the latter case the u has remained. Examples of the
former are:—*blood, brother, does, done, flood, glove, gums,
Monday, month, mother, must, other, rudder, twopence*; and
examples of the latter are:—*book, bosom, brook, cook, crook,
foot, good, hood, hook, look, nook, rook, shook, soot, stood, took.*
In the sixteenth and seventeenth centuries there was great
fluctuation in the above and similar words. Many words
were pronounced with a which now have u, and vice versa.

§ 100. ME. ǭ: The shortening of ǭ generally took place
in ME., but there are a few examples where it took place in
early NE. before the ǭ was diphthongized to ou (§ 76), as
*anon, collier : coal, gone : go, hot, shone, trod (trodden), throttle :
throat.* No shortening took place after the ǭ became ou.

(3) VOWELS BEFORE FINAL ·l(l) AND l+CONSONANT.

§ 101. Between a, o, ǭ and a following final ·l(l) or l+ consonant a glide was developed in late ME. which eventually
became full u-consonant, and then combined with the preceding vowel to form a diphthong of the u-type. It is also
probable that the same kind of glide was developed between
u and a following l+consonant, see § 104.

§ 102. ME. a before final ·l(l) and l+consonant. In this
combination the a became au in late ME., probably in the
second half of the fifteenth century. Although the u was
often not expressed in writing, there are numerous examples
of the spelling au, aw in the late fifteenth century and in
early NE., and a few words still have au, as *baulk, cauldron,
maul,* beside *balk, caldron, mall.* The au then had the same
further development as the old diphthong au (§ 84), that is,
it became monophthongized to ǭ through the intermediate
stage ǫu at the end of the sixteenth or beginning of the
seventeenth century along with the loss of the l in pronunciation before the labials f, v, m, and the guttural k, and
then ǭ became ā before f, v, m in the eighteenth century,

but in the northern and north Midland dialects it has remained down to the present day. Examples are:—

1. *all, ball, call, fall, gall, hall, mall* beside *maul, small, stall, tall, wall.* The accented form šaul, later šǫl (see above), and the unaccented form šæl 'shall' existed side by side down to the eighteenth century, and then the former died out, and šæl came to be used for both the accented and un-accented form. Now šæl is used for the accented form only, and from it has been formed new unaccented forms šəl, šl.

2. *also, altar, bald, exalt, false, halt, halter, malt, palsy, paltry, salt, scald.* The ǭ was shortened to o before ls and lt in the eighteenth century, but in the present standard pronunciation there is a certain amount of fluctuation between o and ǭ, as in fols, solt beside fǭls 'false', sǭlt 'salt'. *scalp,* often written *scaup, scawp* in early NE., is a spelling pronunciation.

3. *balk* beside *baulk, chalk, stalk, talk, walk,* which were often written *tauk, wauk,* &c. in the sixteenth century.

4. *calf, half; calve, halve, salve; almond, alms, balm, calm, palm, psalm,* and with shortening of ā to æ in *salmon* (early NE. saulmon, AN. salmun, saumoun). *palfrey* (O.Fr. palefrei), often written *paulfrey, pawlfrey* in early NE., is now obsolete in the colloquial standard language, and the present pronunciation with ǭ or æ is due to the influence of the spelling; the regular pronunciation would be *pāfri. halfpenny* (*halfpence*) has preserved the old spelling, although the lf disappeared in pronunciation about the middle of the sixteenth century (spelled *hapeney*) with lengthening of the a to ā, which then had the same further development as ME. ā in open syllables (§ 69). In *haulm* beside *halm* the pronunciation with ǭ is due to the influence of the spelling. The regular pronunciation of *qualm* is kwǭm with change of ā to ǭ due to the influence of the preceding w (cp. § 109); the pronunciation with ā is due to the influence of the

spelling. In *almighty, almost* the pronunciation of the initial
vowel with ǭ is due to the influence of *all*.

NOTE.—Late loan-words have not undergone the above sound-
changes, as *album, alcohol, altitude, balcony, heraldic, valve,* &c.

§ 103. Before final ·l(l) and l + consonant o was diphthongized to ǫu in late ME., and then had the same further
development in NE. as earlier ME. ǫu (§ 89). Although
the u was often not expressed in writing, there are numerous
examples of the spelling ou, ow in late ME. and early NE.,
and we still have this spelling in *bowl* (ME. bolle) and *mould*
beside *mold* (ME. mǒlde beside mǭlde 'earth'), see *EME.
Gr.* § 71. Examples are :—

1. *bowl, roll, stroll, toll.*

2. *bolster, bolt, gold* (*EME. Gr.* § 71), *molten, soldier* (ME.
souldeor, O.Fr. soldier).

3. The l disappeared in pronunciation before a labial or
k, as *Holborn, holm, folk, yolk* (OE. g(e)olca).

NOTE.—1. ME. and early NE. wol 'will' + not has become
wount, written *won't* (cp. § 412).

2. The diphthongization of o did not take place before intervocalic l(l), nor in late French loan-words, as *follow, holly; polish,
revolve,* &c.

§ 104. ME. u before l + d or t. The precise process whereby
u before l + d or t has become ou in NE. is uncertain. It is
generally assumed that the u has regularly become ou
through the intermediate stage uw, but this is not borne
out by the modern dialects. Those words belonging to this
category, which have been preserved in the dialects, generally
presuppose a late ME. uw which fell together with old ū
(§ 77), and then had the same further development as old ū.
For this reason it is quite possible that the present standard
pronunciation is due to the influence of the spelling, and is
not a normal development. Examples are :—*bolt* (*boult*)

(ME. **bulte**, O.Fr. **bul(e)ter** 'to sift'), *coulter (colter)* (ME. **cultre**), *poultry* (ME. **pult(e)rie**, O.Fr. **pouletrie**), *shoulder* (ME. **schuldre**, Orm **schulldre**) ; *moult* (ME. **mouten, ou =** ū) with unetymological 1 (§ 55, 5) is undoubtedly a spelling pronunciation.

§ 105. ME. ǭ + ld. In this combination the ǭ became ū towards the end of the fifteenth century, and has regularly remained in NE. (§ 75). There are only four ME. words belonging to this category, viz. **gǭld, mǭlde** 'earth', and the accented forms **schǭlde** 'should', **wǭlde** 'would', beside **gŏld, mŏlde,** and the unaccented forms **schŏlde, wŏlde,** see *EME. Gr.* § 71. **gǭld** and **mŏlde** have been dealt with in § 103. The normally developed forms of **mǭlde, schŏlde, wŏlde** have not survived in NE. The pronunciation **gūld** 'gold' (cp. also the proper name *Gould*) was common until the end of the eighteenth century. From the early NE. accented forms **shūld, wūld** were formed the unaccented forms **shu(l)d** and **wu(l)d** which have now become the accented forms, and from which have been formed the new unaccented forms **shəd** and **wəd.**

§ 106. ME. ǭ + ld (*EME. Gr.* § 71). In this combination the ǭ was diphthongized to ǫu in late ME. (often written **ou, ow** both in late ME. and early NE.), and thus fell together with earlier ME. ǫu, and then had the same further development in common with it (§ 89). Examples are :— *bold, cold, fold, hold, old, scold, sold, told.*

(4) Vowels before Final ·r and r + Consonant.

§ 107. One of the characteristic features of standard NE. is the great influence which the consonant r has exercised upon a preceding vowel or diphthong. The result of this influence has been chiefly of a twofold nature :—

1. Short vowels have been lengthened, and with the exception of o have also undergone a change in their quality,

when both sounds belonged to the same syllable (§§ 108–117),
but have generally remained uninfluenced, when the r(r) is
intervocalic, as *carry, marrow ; herring, very ; spirit, stirrup ;
borrow, origin ; furrow, hurry*.   This differentiation in the
development, which mostly took place in the seventeenth
century, has often given rise to analogical formations, as
stāri 'starry' with ā due to the influence of stā(r), ə̄ring
'erring' : ə̄(r) 'err', stə̄riŋ : stə̄(r) 'stir', and similarly with
many other words.

2. Between a long vowel or a diphthong and r, an ə was
developed partly in the sixteenth and partly in the seventeenth century, although the ə was not expressed in writing
except occasionally after diphthongs, as dę̄ə(r) 'dare',
dę̄əriŋ (§ 119) ; hiə(r) 'hear', hiəriŋ (§ 120) ; bę̄ə(r)
'bear', bę̄əriŋ (§ 122) ; rǭ(r) or rǭə(r) 'roar', rǭring or
rǭəriŋ (§ 125) ; faiə(r) 'fire', faiəriŋ, but faiəri spelled
fiery (§ 123), cp. also *briar, friar* beside *brier, frier* (§ 121) ;
flauə(r) 'flour', but flauə(r) spelled *flower* (§ 126).

In pausa and before a following consonant the r began to
be weakened in the seventeenth century, and in the
eighteenth century it ceased to be pronounced, although it
is always retained in writing (§ 191).   When, however, a
word ends in r and the next word begins with a vowel the
great majority of educated speakers pronounce the r as part
of the following word, as fā rəwei 'far away', kę̄ə rov
'care of', bę̄ə rit 'bear it' (cp. § 190).

ME. a

§ 108. The NE. æ from older a (§ 62) was lengthened to
ǣ in the early part of the seventeenth century before r +
consonant, but before final -r it was not lengthened until
towards the end of the century. Then the ǣ in both
categories became ā in the course of the eighteenth century.
Examples are :—*arm, bark* sb., *cart, hard, park, sharp,*

starling, yard, yarn. French words :—1. In syllables accented in both languages, as *card, chart, depart, large, marble, march, margin, part, remark.* 2. In syllables accented in English, but unaccented in French, as *argument, artist, carpet, garden, garment, market, parcel, pardon, partner. bar, car, jar, scar.*

NOTE.—In ME. and early NE. each of the words *beard* and *fern* had double forms which existed side by side, viz. bẹ̄rd, fẹ̄rn beside the shortened forms berd, fern (OE. bēard, fēarn beside earlier beard, fearn), cp. *EME. Gr.* §§ 63, 68-70. The form bẹ̄rd has regularly become biəd, written *beard* (§ 122), and bĕrd became bəd (§ 112) which was a common pronunciation until well on into the second half of the eighteenth century, and then gradually became obsolete. OE. beard would regularly have become *bād, written *bard (*EME. Gr.* § 59), but this form seems never to have existed either in the standard language or in any of the modern dialects (see *ED. Gr.* p. 323). The form fẹ̄rn became obsolete in the standard language in the seventeenth century, and fĕrn has regularly become fən, written *fern* (§ 112). The form farn from OE. fearn was formerly common in the Scottish dialects, and is still the usual form, pronounced fān, in the northern dialects of England, but there is no indication that it ever existed in the standard language.

§ 109. Through the influence of the w (§ 132) the a in the ME. combination wa· was rounded to o in early NE., and then the o was lengthened to ǭ in the seventeenth century, as *quart, quarter, reward, sward, ward, warm, warn, warp, wart,* cp. § 111.

ME. e

§ 110. ME. e, of whatever origin, became a before r belonging to the same syllable in the fourteenth and fifteenth centuries, although the e was very often retained in writing (*EME. Gr.* § 129). The a then had the same further development as early NE. æ from older a in this position, viz. it eventually became ā through the intermediate stage ǣ, see § 108 ; as *far* (ME. ferre), *star* (ME. sterre), *carve* (ME.

kerve), *dark* (ME. **derk**), and similarly *ajar, char, mar, tar ;*
bark v., *barley, barm* 'yeast', *barn, darling, darn, farthing,*
hart, harvest, marsh, smart, start, starve, yard 'yard-measure' ;
French words, as *farm, garland, garner, marvel, parch,*
parlous, parsley, parson, partridge, tarnish, varnish, &c. In
some words the regular pronunciation has been preserved
with retention of the old spelling, as *clerk* beside *Clark,*
Derby, hearken beside *hark, heart, hearth* beside older *harte,*
harth(e), Hertford beside *hart, sergeant* beside *Sargeant.*

§ 111. Through the influence of the **w** (§ 109) the **a** in the
combination **wa·** was rounded to **o** in early NE., and then
the **o** was lengthened to **ǭ** in the seventeenth century, as
dwarf, thwart, war, warble, wharf, &c.

§ 112. Early NE. **ĕ**, of whatever origin, became **ə** during
the seventeenth century, and was then lengthened to **ə̄**.
Many words, especially French words, which were formerly
pronounced with **ā** (written **a**, and often also **e**), as they still
generally are in the dialects (see *ED. Gr.* § 210), are now
pronounced with **ə̄**, written **e**. This substitution of **ə̄** for
older **ā** was partly due to the influence of the old spelling
with **e** and partly to the reintroduction of the French words
at various dates, especially during the eighteenth century.
Examples are :—*clergy, certain, concern, desert, deserve, fervent,*
herb, kerchief, merchant beside *Marchant, mercy, person,*
sermon, serpent, servant, serve, service, verdict, vermin ; quern,
swerve beside older *quarn, swarve. perfect* for older *parfit* has
come direct from Lat. **perfectus.** French words introduced
into the language after the sound-change of **e** to **a** had taken
place now regularly have **ə̄**, as *avert, emerge, err, eternal,*
prefer, &c.

§ 113. To judge from the history and spelling of *dearth,*
Earl, early, earn, earnest, earth, heard pret. and pp., *hearse,*
learn, pearl, search, yearn, it seems pretty clear that these
words must have had **ĕ** beside lengthened **ę̄** in ME. The **ĕ**
regularly became **a** (see § 110), as in **darth, arne (yarne),**

harde, larne, sarche, &c. These forms died out in the
standard language during the sixteenth and seventeenth
centuries, but have remained in many of the modern dialects
with **ar** or **ā** down to the present day, see Index to *ED. Gr.*
The ę̄ would regularly have become ęə (§ 122) in standard
NE., as it has done in some of the modern dialects, but in
the standard language it was shortened to **e** again in early
NE., and then the **e** became ə, later ə̄, with retention of the
spelling **ea** representing earlier ę̄.

ME. i

§ 114. Before final ·**r** and **r**+consonant ME. **i**, of whatever origin, must have become a kind of sound intermediate
between **i** and **u**, which in native words was sometimes
written **i** and sometimes **u**. The same fluctuation in the
spelling also occurs in early NE., and then later in some
words the **i** and in others the **u** became generalized. The
sound in question became ə about the end of the sixteenth or
early part of the seventeenth century, and was then later
lengthened to ə̄. Examples are:—

1. ME. **i** = OE. **i**, as *birch* (ME. **birche**, OE. **birce**), *whirl*
(cp. ON. **hvirfla**).

2. Late ME. ·**ir**· from older ·**ri**· by metathesis, as *bird*
(early ME. **brid**, later **bird**, **burd**), and similarly *dirt, third,
thirty; burn* (early ME. **brin(n)e**, later **birne**, **burne**), and
similarly *burst*, see *EME. Gr.* § 130.

3. ME. **i** = OE. **y**, as *fir, stir; birth, first, gird, girdle, mirth,
shirt, skirt* (ON. **skyrta**), *thirst; burden, church, churn,
further* v., *furze, hurdle, hurst, murder* v. In some of these
words the difference in spelling may, however, be due to
a difference in dialect, cp. *EME. Gr.* §§ 49, 126.

4. French words, as *Sir; circle, confirm, virgin,* &c. In
firm (ME. **ferme**) and *virtue* (ME. **vertu**) the **i** is due to the
influence of Lat. **firmus, virtus.**

ME. o

§ 115. ME. o before r belonging to the same syllable was lengthened to ǭ in the seventeenth century, as *for, nor, or; corn, fork, former, horn, horse, morning, north, orchard, short, stork, storm, thorn*; in the past participles *borne* (*born*), *forlorn, sworn, torn, worn* ME. had ǭ beside o, see *EME. Gr.* §§ 81, 102, 147. French words:—1. In syllables accented in both languages, as *absorb, cork, corpse, form, order, remorse, scorn, torch*. 2. In syllables accented in English, but unaccented in French, as *corner, enormous, fortune, morbid, mortal, normal, ordinary, organ*.

§ 116. The ǭ before r + d, th, and in some French words before r + other consonants, is regular in the southern standard pronunciation, but the vowel is not so open in the northern pronunciation of the educated classes. The distinction in pronunciation between this and the former category of words (§ 115) also exists in most of the modern dialects, the former being ǭ or ǫə, and the latter ō̧ or ǫə (uə). This difference in pronunciation points to a difference which must have existed in ME. itself. The former category of words doubtless had o, and the latter ō̧ which later became ǭ, cp. *EME. Gr.* §§ 68-9. Examples are:—*board, ford, forth, hoard*. French words:—1. In syllables accented in both languages, as *accord, afford, cord, force, forge, fort, porch, pork, port, resort, sort, sport, support*. 2. In syllables accented in English, but unaccented in French, as *border, porter, portion, portrait*. See § 124.

ME. u

§ 117. Before final -r and r + consonant ME. u, of whatever origin, became ə about the end of the sixteenth or early part of the seventeenth century, and then later it was lengthened to ə̄. Examples are:—

1. ME. u = OE. u, as *burr, cur, spur; curd, curse, hurl, spurn, turf*.

2. ME. **u** in French words, as *dentur, occur; curtain, furnish, hurt, nurse, purchase, surge, turn.*

3. ME. **wur** + consonant = OE. **wyr** + consonant (*EME. Gr.* § 123), as *work* (OE. **wyrcan**), and similarly *worm, worse, worship, wort, worthy,* but we have **iə** in *weird* (OE. **wyrd**), representing a ME. south Eastern form **wẹrd** which crept into the standard language, cp. *EME. Gr.* §§ 57, 69.

4. ME. **wur** + consonant = OE. **weor, wor** + consonant (*EME. Gr.* § 38), as *world, work* sb., *worth ; word.*

§ 118. There is a certain amount of irregularity in the spelling of words which in ME. had **i, e, u** + **r** belonging to the same syllable. The **ir, ur** became **ər** about the end of the sixteenth or early part of the seventeenth century, and then later **er** also partly became **ər,** so that **i, u,** and **e** all fell together in **ə** in the standard language, as also in the modern dialects except the Scottish and the adjacent dialects of England (cp. *ED. Gr.* §§ 56, 76, 107), whence such spellings as *churl* (ME. **cherle, cheerl,** OE. **ceorl**); *flirt* beside earlier *flurt, flert ; her* beside earlier *hir, hur ; kernel* beside earlier *kurnel, kirnel ; sirloin* beside earlier *surloin, serloyn* (O.Fr. **surlonge**); *spurt* beside older *spirt ; urchin* (ME. **irchoun,** O.Fr. **ireçon**); in *virtue* (ME. and O.Fr. **vertu**) the **i** is due to the influence of Lat. **virtus.**

ME. ā

§ 119. ME. **ā** was fronted to **ǣ** in the fifteenth century (§ 69), and then in the sixteenth or early seventeenth century an **ə** was developed between the **ǣ** and the **r,** which combined with the **ǣ** to form the present diphthong **ẹə** (= **æə**) in the standard language and also in many of the dialects, as *bare, care, dare, fare, glare, hare, mare, share, snare, spare, stare* ; French words, as *declare, parent, prepare, rare, scarce, square,* &c.

NOTE. – *are* is the old unaccented form now used both for the accented and unaccented form. The old accented form ẹə(r) became obsolete in the eighteenth century.

ME. ẹ̄

§ 120. ME. ẹ̄ before final ·r and before medial r + vowel. In these combinations an ə was developed between the ī from older ẹ̄ (§ 71) and the r in the seventeenth century, which combined with the ī to form the present diphthong iə, as *here, weary (EME. Gr. § 53); year (EME. Gr. § 64); beer, dear, deer, dreary, leer, steer (EME. Gr. § 65); hear, hearing (EME. Gr. § 66)*. A small number of ME. words had ẹ̄ = WS. ǣ, beside ē̜ = Non-WS. ē, see *EME. Gr. § 52*. After much fluctuation in the early NE. pronunciation and spelling, ẹə (§ 122) in some words and iə in others became the standard pronunciation, as *there, where* which in early NE. were also pronounced with ī, and many of the modern dialects also have iə from older ī in these words (*ED. Gr. § 134); were* beside the unaccented form wə̄(r); *bier*, also written bear(e) from the fifteenth to the beginning of the seventeenth century, when *bier* became the standard spelling, and may be due to imitation of the French form bière; *fear*, also written *fare* in the seventeenth century, which shows that at that time there was also a pronunciation with ẹə (§ 119); *hair* (OE., WS. hǣr, Anglian hē̜r, ME. hē̜r, hẹ̄r) has been influenced by ME. haire (O.Fr. haire) 'hair cloth, a dress made of hair'. All French words have iə, as *appear, arrears, career, cheer, clear, mere, serious, severe, sincere*; and before r + consonant in *fierce, pierce*.

NOTE.—Many of the above words, especially those spelled with ea, are stated as having ẹ̄ beside ī by sixteenth and seventeenth century writers on pronunciation, but it is difficult to determine how far their statements were correct, and how far such writers were merely influenced by the spelling with ea. Even if we assume, as some writers on NE. phonology now do, that ME. ẹ̄ became ę̄ before r some time before it became ī in other positions of the word (§ 71), the fact still remains that in the present standard pronunciation some words have ę̄ə which we should normally expect to have iə, and conversely some words have iə which we should normally expect to have ę̄ə (§ 122). The fluctuation in the development of ME. ę̄ and ẹ̄ is doubtless due to dialectal differences which gradually crept into the standard language in the early NE. period, and that in some words the ę̄ə and in others the iə has become the standard pronunciation, cp. *ED. Gr.* §§ 65, 134, 195.

§ 121. In two English words and a few French words ME. ẹ̄ must have become ī before r in the early part of the fifteenth century, and then the ī had the same further development as old ī, that is, it eventually became aiə (§ 123), as *briar, brier* (early ME. brẹ̄r(e), OE., WS. brǣr, Anglian brēr); *tire* (ME. tẹ̄ren, OE. tēorian); *friar* (ME. frẹ̄re); *quire* (ME. quẹ̄r(e), O.Fr. cuẹr) beside the semi-etymological spelling *choir* (Lat. acc. chorum); *umpire* (ME. noumpẹ̄re, O.Fr. nonper). In *acquire* (ME. acwẹ̄ren, O.Fr. acquerre) the ai from older ī is due to the influence of Lat. acquīro, and similarly *inquire, require*. We also have ai after r in *contrive* (ME. contrẹ̄ven).

ME. ę̄

§ 122. The development of ME. ę̄ in the NE. standard language presents a similar diversity to that of ME. ẹ̄. The ę̄ normally became ẹ̄ towards the end of the fifteenth century, and then the ẹ̄ became ī in the latter part of the seventeenth century (§ 72), but it probably remained before final -r, and then in the seventeenth century an ə was developed between the ẹ̄ and the r, which combined with the ẹ̄ to form the present diphthong ę̄ə. In this manner ME. ę̄, later ę̄ə, fell together with early NE. ę̄ (= æ) from older ā (§ 119), and was often written a from the sixteenth to the eighteenth century, as *bare* 'bear', *pare* 'pear', *sware* 'swear'.

Examples are:—*bear* sb. and v., *pear, swear, tear* v., *wear*
(*EME. Gr.* § 80); *ere* (*EME. Gr.* § 52, 2). But quite a
number of words now have iə which in late ME. and early
NE. must have had ę̄, as *shear, smear, spear ; rear ; ear, near,
tear* sb. Some of these words were spelled with **a** or **ai** in
the sixteenth and seventeenth centuries, which shows that
at that period the pronunciation with ę̄, later ęə, was in
existence, as *share* 'shear', *spair* 'spear' (cp. § 128). See
§ 120 and note.

ME. ī

§ 123. Between the **ai** from ME. ī (§ 73) and **r,** an ə was
developed in the late sixteenth or early seventeenth century,
which gave rise to the present triphthong **aiə,** as *fiery*
(§ 107, 2), *fire, hire, iron, mire, shire, wire* ; and in French
words, as *admire, aspire, desire, expire, squire,* &c.

ME. ǭ

§ 124. ME. ǭ normally became ū towards the end of the
fifteenth century (§ 75), but it probably remained before
final **-r.** According to the sixteenth and seventeenth
century writers on pronunciation, the ǭ must have become ū
before **r** just as in other positions, but not too much
importance can be attached to their statements, because in
the description of sounds all such early writers were often
unduly influenced by the spelling, cp. also § 120, note. We
therefore assume that between the ǭ and the **r,** an ə was
developed in the seventeenth century, which gave rise to the
diphthong ǫə. When preceded by a labial the ǫə normally
became uə, and in the present standard southern pronunciation ǫə beside uə is still often heard, as in *boor, moor, poor.*
Beside uə (ǫə) the standard southern pronunciation now has
also ǭ (ǭə), which probably came into existence in the latter

G

half of the eighteenth century, and has become the standard
pronunciation in all the other words belonging to this
category, as *door* (*EME. Gr.* § 85), *floor, swore, whore*, but the
educated classes of the north and nearly the whole of the
Midlands still pronounce these and similar words with ǫə
(uə), and the modern dialects of England also generally have
ǫə (uə), see *ED. Gr.* § 165. Cp. § 116.

ME. ǭ

§ 125. It is difficult to determine what has been the exact
line of development of ME. ǭ before r in NE. It is probable
that the ǭ became ǭ before r at the same time that it became
ǭ in other positions (§ 76). In this manner the ǭ from
older ǭ fell together with old ǭ before r, and then had the
same further development in common with it, that is, it
became ǫə in the seventeenth century (§ 124). This is still
the common pronunciation of the educated classes in the
north and nearly the whole of the Midlands, and nearly all
the Midland and southern dialects have ǫə or uə. Then in
the latter half of the eighteenth century the ǫə became
ǭ (ǫə) in the standard southern pronunciation. Examples
are :—

1. ME. ǭ from OE. ā (*EME. Gr.* § 51), as *boar, hoar,
hoarse* (ME. hǭrs, OE. hās), *lore, more, oar, roar, sore ; yore*
(late OE. geára from older geára).

2. ME. ǭ from OE. o in open syllables (*EME. Gr.* § 81), as
before, bore pret., *bore* ' to make a hole ', *score, snore*. In the
past participles *borne* (*born*), *forlorn, shorn, sworn, torn, worn*
ME. had o beside ǭ (*EME. Gr.* §§ 81, 102, 147), which
accounts for the fact that ǭ (ǫə) is the standard pronunciation of all educated and of nearly all dialect speakers (cp.
§ 115).

3. French words, as *adore, core, ignore, store* sb. ; *glory,
story*, &c.

ME. ū

§ 126. Between the diphthong which arose from ME. ū (§ 77) and final -r, an ə was developed in the late sixteenth or early seventeenth century which eventually gave rise to the present triphthong auə, as *hour, flour, our, sour.* In some words the ə is expressed by e (§ 107, 2), as *bower, power, shower, tower; flower* and *flour* (*EME. Gr.* § 201) are the same word with modern differentiation in meaning and spelling.

§ 127. ME. ū, of whatever origin, remained in early NE. before r + consonant. In the late seventeenth century an ə was developed between the ū and the r, which gave rise to the diphthong uə, later ǫə. The ǭə then had the same further development as the ǫə from ME. ǭ (§ 124) and ǫ (§ 125) before r, that is, it became ǭ (ǫə) in the standard southern pronunciation in the latter half of the eighteenth century, as *course* beside *coarse* with modern differentiation in meaning and spelling, *court, courtier, discourse, source*; and similarly with the native words *mourn, mourning, sword* (*EME. Gr.* § 38) with short u in OE., which became lengthened to ū in ME. or early NE.; *your* (*EME. Gr.* § 112, note).

ME. ai

§ 128. NE. ei from ME. ai (§ 82) was monophthongized to ę̄ before r about the end of the seventeenth or early part of the eighteenth century, and then between the ę̄ and the r an ə was developed which gave rise to the present diphthong ęə, as *fair, lair, stare, their.* In French words, as *affair, air, chair, despair, fairy, heir, pair, prairie, prayer.*

ME. iu = AN. ū

§ 129. In the combination jū from older iu (§ 78) + final -r the pronunciation now fluctuates between juə, jǫə and jǫə, jǭ, as *cure, endure, mature, obscure, pure, secure*; for *sure*, see § 79.

ME. ęu

§ 130. In the combination jū from ME. ęu (§ 87)+final
-r we now have juə in *ewer* (O.Fr. eawer, ewer), and juə,
joə in *sewer* 'drain' (O.Fr. seuwiere).

ME. ǫu

§ 131. Early NE. ou (§ 89) from ME. ǫu (*EME. Gr.*
§§ 112, note, 114, ɪ)+final -r has become ǫə (ǭ), as *four*, but
we now have ǭ before r+consonant, as *fourteen, fourth*;
in *forty* earlier NE. had short o which has been lengthened
to ǭ again.

(5) The Influence of Labials.

§ 132. ME. a normally became æ about the end of the
sixteenth century (§ 62), but when the a was preceded by w
and not followed by a guttural it was rounded to o some
time before the change of a to æ took place, as *quality,
quantity, quarrel, quarry, squalid, squander, squat, swallow,
swamp, swan, wander, warrant, warrior, was, wash, wasp,
watch, what*; the pret. *swam* is due to the influence of
preterites like *began, ran.* See also §§ 109, 111. But we
regularly have æ when followed by a guttural, as *quack,
swagger, twang, waggon* (*wagon*), *wax*, &c.

§ 133. ME. u preceded by a labial and followed by l(l) has
generally remained in NE. (cp. § 67), as *bull, bullock, full, pull,
wolf, wool*; French words, as *bullet, bullion, pullet, pulpit.*
The pronunciation fluctuated between a and u in the seventeenth and eighteenth centuries in a number of words where
the vowel was preceded by a labial and not followed by l(l),
and some such words with u have been preserved in the
present standard language, as *bush, bushel, butcher, pudding,
push, puss, put, woman, wood.*

§ 134. ME. ū (§ 77), of whatever origin, has remained in
NE. before labials, or when preceded by **w** : —

1. ME. ū = OE. ū, as *coomb* (*combe*), *coop, cooper, droop,
room, stoop* ; and in French words like *troop* (Fr. **troupe**),
tomb (ME. **toumbe**) ; *wound* sb., *wound* (**waund**) pp. is due
to the analogy of past participles like *bound, found,* see
EME. Gr. § 73.

2. ME. ū = OE. ōg (*EME. Gr.* § 114, 2 (*b*)), as *swoon* (cp.
OE. **swōgan**), *woo* (OE. **wōgian**).

The above and similar words have the spelling **oo** for
ou = ū (*EME. Gr.* § 56) after the analogy of words with
oo = ū from ME. ǭ (§ 75). In ME. and early NE. they
were generally spelled with **ou** (**ow**).

(6) Other Changes.

§ 135. In some ME. dialects, especially the northern and
some of the Midland, **i** and **e** before and after certain consonants underwent qualitative changes which are difficult to
define.　The result was that a large number of words, which
in the earlier period had **i** only, came to be written with **e** or
with **e** beside **i,** and conversely some words which in the
earlier period had **e** only came to be written with **i** or **i** beside
e (cp. *EME. Gr.* §§ 127, 131).　This fluctuation in the orthography also existed in the standard language from the
sixteenth to the eighteenth century, and then one or other
of the variants became standardized :—

1. **e** for older **i,** as *clever* (ME. **cliver**), *lemon* (ME. **limon,**
O.Fr. **limon**), *level* (ME. **livel, level,** O.Fr. **livel**), *pepper*
(ME. **piper, peper,** OE. **pipor**).

2. **i** for older **e,** as *hint* (ME. **henten, hinten,** OE. **hentan**),
lizard (ME. **lesard, lisard,** O.Fr. **lesard**), *minnow* (ME.
menow).　Other words which in earlier NE. were often
written with **i** for older **e** are :—*brethren, chemist, get, kettle,
together, yes, yesterday, yet,* &c.

§ 136. In a few words ME. e has become i between r and a following d, n, or t, as *abridge* (ME. abreggen), *gridiron* (ME. gredyrne), *grin* (OE. grennian), *rid* (OE. hreddan); in *pretty* (ME. pretti, pratti) the old spelling with e has been preserved.

§ 137. In the early NE. period there was a tendency for ME. o to become a in some dialects, especially the south Midland, Southern, and south Western (cp. *ED. Gr.* §§ 82–3), and a few words containing this a for o crept permanently into the standard language with the change of a to æ by sound-substitution, as *nap* (ME. noppe), *plat* beside *plot*, *sprat*, *strap* beside *strop*, cp. § 66, note. Many words, which now have o only, had æ beside o in the earlier period of the language.

§ 138. In a few French words e has become æ before tch = tš, and m, as *ambush* (O.Fr. embuscher), *cratch* (ME. crecche, O.Fr. creche), *match* (O.Fr. mesche, Mod.Fr. mèche).

§ 139. o became u before ng in the west Midland dialects during the ME. period, and a few words from these dialects have crept into standard NE. with the regular change of u to a (§ 67), as *among, monger, mongrel* which were formerly often spelled with u, see *EME. Gr.* § 133, cp. also § 66, 2.

§ 140. ME. au was monophthongized to ā before labials, dž, and n + dž about the end of the thirteenth or early part of the fourteenth century (*EME. Gr.* § 213, 1), and then the ā had the same further development as ordinary ME. ā, that is, it has become ei in NE. (§ 69), as *chafe, chamber, flame, gauge* (*gage*), *mavis, safe, sage* 'plant', *sane, wafer* (AN. waufre), *savage* with early shortening; *angel, arrange, change, manger, range, strange, stranger*.

CHAPTER III

THE NE. DEVELOPMENT OF THE ME. VOWELS OF UNACCENTED SYLLABLES

§ 141. From the OE. period down to the present day there has always been a tendency to weaken the vowels in unaccented syllables, and then often for the weakened vowels to disappear, cp. *EOE. Gr.* ch. iv and *EME. Gr.* ch. iv. In dealing with the changes which the accented vowels underwent in the earlier period of the language it is generally possible to fix approximately the date of the changes, but it is practically impossible to do the same with the vowel-changes in unaccented syllables, and for that reason no systematic attempt is here made to deal with the subject chronologically. So much is, however, pretty clear, that to judge from occasional spellings in late ME., and early NE. writings, the changes must have taken place much earlier than is generally assumed. The most radical changes both in spelling and pronunciation have been those which have taken place in syllables which were un-accented in English, but accented in French words, see *EME. Gr.* §§ 215–29. The weakening of vowels in un-accented syllables is generally carried further in everyday words than in learned words or words which rarely occur in colloquial speech. The spelling also has exercised a great influence upon the pronunciation of many words ; and even among educated speakers there is great fluctuation in the pronunciation of certain endings. The dialects, being un-fettered by literary traditions, have carried out the weakening and loss of unaccented vowels far more regularly and con-sistently than the standard language.

§ 142. In dealing with the changes which the vowels of unaccented syllables have undergone in NE., it is necessary to distinguish between formal, solemn speech, and ordinary colloquial speech. In formal and solemn speech the vowels of unaccented syllables are not weakened or omitted to the same extent as in ordinary colloquial speech. This difference is in some measure due to conscious effort at clear enunciation and to the unconscious influence of the written upon the spoken language in formal speech. In ordinary colloquial speech we have also to distinguish between slow and quick utterance, and this is especially the case when the unaccented vowel stands before an l, m, n not followed by a vowel which is pronounced. In the former case we generally have əm, ən, əl, and in the latter case vocalic l, m, n with loss of the ə.

§ 143. From various indications given by the writers on pronunciation in the sixteenth, seventeenth, and eighteenth centuries it is certain that the weakening of vowels to ə and partial loss of such ə must have begun at an early period. As a general rule it may be stated that in the present standard pronunciation palatal or front vowels have become i, and guttural or back vowels have become ə. Before liquids and nasals all vowels have generally been weakened to ə. This ə has generally disappeared in rapid and careless speech when the liquid or nasal is not followed by a vowel which is pronounced. This falling together of final syllables like ·an, ·en, ·in, ·on in ·ən or respectively vocalic ·n has had some influence upon NE. orthography, as in *ribbon* (O.Fr. riban), *beacon* (OE. bēacen), *thousand* (OE. þūsend), *cushion* (O.Fr. coussin), *historian* (O.Fr. (h)istorien) &c. ; and similarly all the endings ·ar, ·er, ·or, ·our, ·ur probably became ·ər or vocalic ·r in early NE., and then later simply ·ə, see § 165.

§ 144. In the standard spoken language the full vowels have often been restored through the influence of the spelling, whereas in the dialects, where there is practically no such influence, the vowels have been regularly weakened, cp. *follow, value,* &c. beside folə, valə, see § 171.

§ 145. In connected speech many words have unaccented beside accented forms. These unaccented forms undergo weakening of their vowels just like the vowels in unaccented syllables. Such words are:—the articles, pronouns, auxiliary verbs, prepositions, conjunctions, and some types of adverbs. In dealing with the vowels of unaccented syllables we shall adopt the following order of treatment:—1. In initial syllables. 2. In medial syllables. 3. In final syllables. 4. Compound words. 5. Unaccented words.

1. INITIAL SYLLABLES FOLLOWED BY THE PRINCIPAL ACCENT

§ 146. In this position the normal development of ME. a, e, i, o, u in NE. is:—a, o, u have become ə ; e has become i ; and i has remained. There is, however considerable fluctuation in the pronunciation. A number of words have æ for ə, as in *ambition, spasmodic* ; some words with inter-consonantal -ar- have ā, and others have ə, as in *barbaric, partake,* but *particular.* Words with the prefixes em-, en-, ex- very often have e beside i ; those with com-, con- often have o̦ beside ə ; those with pro- have o̦, u beside ə, as in *profound* ; and those with o- have o̦ beside ə, and o̦, ou beside ə, as in *obey.* The above deviations from the normal development are due to the influence of the spelling. Examples are :—

a > ə, as *admire, affair, ago, agree, allow, attack ; battalion, career, grammarian, lament, parental.*

o > ə, as *obey, obtain, occasion, official, omit, opinion ; commit, compare, connect ; correct, polite, position, potato, society, tobacco ; profound, pronounce, propose, provide.*

u > ə, as *submit, succeed, suffice, suppose, upon* ; but u has become a (§ 67) in secondary accented syllables, as *umbrella, uphold.*

e > i, as *eleven, emerge, enough, escape ; embark, endure, engage, example, excuse, expect ; before, declare, desire, prepare, preserve, reserve, severe.* But we have ǝ before **r**, as *perform, permit* ; and ǝ beside i before **l**, as *select.*

ME. i has remained, as *improper, improve, insane ; diminish, divide,* but we have ǝ before **r**, as *circumference.* The **ai** in forms like *digest* sb., *digression, dilute, direct,* which formerly also had ĭ, is due to the influence of the spelling ; and poly-syllabic forms like *biography, finality, gigantic, minority, vitality* are due to the influence of the simple forms *biograph, final,* &c.

§ 147. ME. iu = AN. ū (§ 78) has become **jŭ** when it begins a word, and **jŭ** when preceded by a consonant, as *unite ; cupidity, museum, stupidity* ; but we have ŭ in *July* (džŭlai) owing to the dž (§ 80).

§ 148. ǭ from older **au** (§ 84) is generally preserved or only shortened to ǫ, very rarely ǝ, as *audacious, audacity, authentic, autumnal, authority.*

§ 149. Aphesis of initial syllables often took place in ME. and early NE. Many of these aphetic forms have survived in the dialects, which are now obsolete in the standard language, as (*a*)*bout,* (*al*)*low,* (*a*)*mong,* (*ap*)*prentice,* (*a*)*sylum,* (*be*)*cause,* (*e*)*leven,* (*en*)*tice,* (*oc*)*casion.* Many words which had aphesis in the sixteenth and seventeenth century pronuncia-tion now have the full forms through the influence of the spelling, and sometimes both forms have survived with differentiation in meaning, as *live* [**laiv**] : *alive, lone : alone, vantage : advantage, venture : adventure, sample : example, scape-goat : escape, fend : defend, special : especial, spy : espy, squire : esquire, strange : estrange, ticket : etiquette, vie : envy, story : history.*

2. IN MEDIAL SYLLABLES

§ 150. In this position **a, o** have generally become ǝ ; **e** has generally become **i** ; and **i** has generally remained. Examples are :—

a > **ǝ**, as *agreeable, considerable, infamous, magazine, malady,* *relative*, but in a number of words we have i beside ə, as *character, literature, miracle, oracle, spectacle.*

o > ə, as *apologize, monopolize*, but in a number of words we have o̗ beside ə, as *abolition, eloquence, innocence, introduce, opposite.*

u > ə, as *guttural*, *Saturday.*

e > i, as *ancestor, elegant, element, enemy, implement, remedy, telegraph*, but we have ə after ai, as *piety, variety.*

§ 151. ME. i has generally remained, as *animal, citizen, criticism, feminine, infinite, radical*, but in a few words we have ə beside i, as *possible, terrible, unity.* oi has become i in *connoisseur.*

Postconsonantal i generally became j before a following vowel in the late sixteenth or early seventeenth century, and then the combinations sj (tj = sj), zj became š, ž. After other consonants we now have i beside j. The i is especially common after r. dž from dj was formerly also very common, as in *grandeur, soldier, verdure*, but in other words with this combination we now mostly have dj. Examples are:—*clothier, courtier, envious, genial, genius, guardian, opinion, tedious; glorious, historian, imperial, librarian, material; admission, ancient, musician, pension, special ; ambitious, condition, motion, partial, patience* (see § 246); *confusion, occasion, vision* ; but before accented and secondary accented vowels the pronunciation now fluctuates between š, ž + i or j and s, z + i or j, so that in some words we have the former and in others the latter pronunciation ; this fluctuation is due to the influence of the spelling, as *appreciate, negotiate, partiality ; hosier ; association, ecclesiastic, pronunciation ; enthusiasm, physiology.*

§ 152. ME. iu = AN. ü (§ 78) has become ju together with the further change of tj to tš, and the loss of the j after dž, as well as the change of the u to ə before r (§ 143), as *accuracy, annual, regular, regulate, singular, valuable ; century ; injury, prejudice.*

§ **153.** Whatever its origin the vowel in the medial combination vowel + liquid or nasal + vowel has been weakened to ə which in careless speech is lost, and the word is accordingly reduced by one syllable, as *avarice, barbarous; excellent, traveller; evening, halfpenny, listening; average, desperate, difference, every, general, generous, miserable, mystery, several; definite; natural; prisoner, reasonable; history, ivory, memory, timorous, victory; favourite, usurer.*

§ **154.** An interconsonantal vowel often disappeared in ME. and early NE. When the full and the syncopated forms have been preserved they have generally become differentiated in meaning, as *bodkin* older *bodikin, captain* older *capitain, chapter* older *chapiter, damsel* older *damisel, fortnight* older *fourteen-night, goblin* older *gobelin, medicine, partner* older *partener; business* beside *business* 'state of being busy'; *curtsy* beside *courtesy; fancy* beside *fantasy, &c.*

3. IN FINAL SYLLABLES

§ **155.** In treating the vowels of final syllables it is important to make two subdivisions according as :— (*a*) the syllable ends in one or more consonants, or (*b*) ends in a vowel. The general principle of the weakening or loss of vowels in these positions is the same as in initial and medial syllables, viz. guttural or back vowels have been weakened to ə or have disappeared, and palatal or front vowels have been weakened to i. In careless speech the ə disappears in the combinations əm, ən, əl, and then the m, n, 1 become vocalic. In secondary accented syllables the full vowel has generally remained, as in *paragraph, placard; sublet; dialogue, record* sb. ; *empire; window; deluge.*

(A) In Final Syllables Ending in One or More Consonants.

§ **156.** a > ə which in careless speech disappears before 1, m, n, and then the 1, m, n become vocalic, as *Christmas,*

steadfast, trespass ; critical, fatal, general, metal beside the
same word *mettle* with differentiation in meaning, *national,
paternal, radical ; madam ; admittance, balance, distance,
elegant, England, guardian, human, ignorant, librarian, ocean,
pleasant, remnant, servant.*

o, u > ə which in careless speech disappears before
l, m, n, and then the l, m, n become vocalic, as *bullock,
gallop, parrot, purpose ; focus ; gambol, pistol ; awful, graceful;
blossom, bosom, bottom, kingdom ; welcome, wholesome.*

§ 157. ME. e has partly become i, ə, and has partly disappeared.   When the vowel has remained it is ə before
l, n, r (see § 165), and generally i before other consonants :—

1. Before l, as *chapel, cruel, gospel, lintel, quarrel, vessel.*
After the analogy of words ending in -le (*table*, &c.) many
words which in ME. ended in -el came to be written with
-le after the loss of final -e in pronunciation (cp. *EME. Gr.*
§§ 139–42), as *apple* (ME. **appel**), *cattle* (ME. **catel**), and
similarly *bridle, castle, fiddle, riddle, saddle*, &c., see § 17.

2. Before n, as *ancient, happen, heaven, innocent, obedient,
often, patient, present, sentence, stolen, surgeon* (O.Fr. **surgien**),
talent, written, but when the preceding syllable has i we have
i by assimilation, as *chicken, kitchen, linen, women.*   Both in
1 and 2 the ə disappears in careless speech, and then the
l, n become vocalic.

3. Before other consonants, as *basket, closet, college, countess,
goodness, hamlet, heiress, honest, hostess, hundred, kindred,
knowledge, modest, poet, prophet, soonest, twentieth, wicked,
wretched*, but ə after ai, as *diet*, and often ə beside i in
hundred, kindred, and words ending in -less, -ness.

§ 158. ME. e (§ 157) has disappeared in the old adverbial
genitives *hence* (ME. **hennes**), *thence* (ME. **þennes**), *whence*
(ME. **whennes**), *once* (ME. **ǭnes**), *twice* (ME. **twīes**), *thrice*
(ME. **þrīes**), cp. *EME. Gr.* §§ 122, 2, 157 ; and in the inflexional endings of nouns except those ending in a sibilant
(s, z, š, tš, dž), and similarly in the present ending of the

third person singular of verbs (cp. *EME. Gr.* § 146). It has also disappeared in the ending -e**d** of the preterite and past participle of weak verbs except when the present ends in **d** or **t**. Examples are :—*dogs, rooms, caps, cats*, but *faces, glasses, houses, sizes, dishes, watches, bridges; he sends, helps,* &c., but *he misses, rises, wishes, catches, singes ; loved, smiled, helped, shaped,* but *ended, melted,* &c. The vowel has been preserved in a few old past participles which are now used as adjectives, as *aged, beloved, blessed, dogged, learned* ; and in the archaic verbal endings -**est**, -**eth**, as *thou lovest, he loveth.*

§ 159. ME. i has generally remained except before **l** and **n**. Before **l** we have i**l** beside vocalic **l**, but the vowel does not disappear when preceded by **r**, as in *peril*. Before **n** we have i**n** beside vocalic **n** :—

1. Before **l**, as *civil, evil, pupil, subtle* (ME. **sutill**) always with vocalic **l** ; forms like *fertile, hostile* are due to the influence of the spelling.

2. Before **n** : With i, as *discipline, famine, feminine, genuine, ruin*, but in learned words we have ai, as *columbine, feline, pristine* ; with vocalic **n**, as *basin, cousin, garden* (ME. **gardin**), *raisin,* &c., but we have i in *coffin, Latin* due to the influence of the spelling ; both words formerly had vocalic **n**. The word *cushion* (ME. **cuschin**) has -in beside -ən.

3. Before other consonants, as *attentive, attractive, benefice, defensive, heretic, lunatic, malice, profit, punish, satirist, service, stupid, tulip ; definite, favourite, hypocrite, infinite, opposite, requisite,* but we have ai in *appetite, finite, parasite* due to the influence of the spelling. Verbs with a secondary accent on the ending have ai, as *authorize, sacrifice, sympathize.*

§ 160. ME. ā has become i through the intermediate stages ǣ, ẹ̄, ī (cp. § 69). Words of this type were sometimes spelled with i in earlier NE., and in *porridge*, older *pottage*, this spelling has been standardized. But ə beside i is often heard, especially in words ending in -ace, and in nouns and adjectives ending in -ate. Some of the latter

type of words are often pronounced with ei after the analogy
of the corresponding verbs with a secondary accent, which
regularly have ei, as in *advocate, aggravate, animate, intimate,
separate*.   Examples are :—With i, as *cabbage, cottage, courage,
damage, image, orange* ; with ə beside i, as *menace, palace,
preface, purchase, solace ; accurate, fortunate, palate, private,
senate ; advocate, animate, estimate, intimate*.   Forms like
irate, ornate are due to the old-fashioned English pronunciation of words containing Latin ā.

§ 161.   The ME. endings ·oun, ·ous, ·our = ·ūn, ·ūs, ·ūr
(cp. *EME. Gr.* § 201).   These endings remained in early NE.
when they had a secondary accent, but were shortened to
·un, ·us, ·ur when they were unaccented.   The endings
with a secondary accent have not been preserved.   The unaccented endings have now regularly become ·ən, or with
loss of ə vocalic ·n, ·əs, ·ə, as *action, admission, baron, condition, confusion, fashion, lion, million, nation, pardon, passion,
prison, reason, season, wanton ; ambitious, courageous, curious,
dangerous, enormous, envious, famous, gracious, hideous, jealous,
precious, tedious, tremendous ; author, creator, favour, honour,
labour, vigour*.

§ 162.   ME. iu from O.Fr. or AN. ū (§ 78) has normally
become jŭ, as *deluge, refuse* sb., *volume*, &c., but in a few
words it became i with loss of u in early NE., as *biscuit,
circuit, conduit* (cp. § 46), *lettuce, minute* sb.   Before n and r,
iu came to have a double pronunciation in early NE. according as it was unaccented or had a secondary accent.   In
the former case the ·iun, ·iur regularly became ·un, ·ur,
later ·ən, ·ə(r) which were very common in the standard
pronunciation of the seventeenth, eighteenth, and early
nineteenth centuries, but in the present standard pronunciation ə has only been preserved in *figure*.   In the dialects ·ən
or vocalic ·n, and ·ə have been regularly preserved, as in
fǭtən 'fortune', piktə 'picture', mezə 'measure'.   In the
latter case the ·iun, ·iur regularly became ·jŭn, ·jŭr (§ 79)

together with the further change of the combinations dj, tj, sj, zj to dž, tš, š, ž (§ 185), and the weakening of -ŭn, -ŭr to -ən, -ə, as *procedure, verdure ; fortune ; adventure, creature, feature, nature, picture, venture ; censure ; measure, pleasure, treasure.*

§ 163. The normal development of ME. **ai (ei)** is **i**, often written **i** or **e** in early NE. Examples are:—*forfeit* (O.Fr. **forfait**), *harness* (O.Fr. **harneis**), *surfeit* (O.Fr. **surfait**). The **i** when written **ai (eig)** before **n** has also generally remained, as *bargain, captain, certain, chaplain, foreign* (O.Fr. **forain**), *fountain, mountain, sovereign* (O.Fr. **souverain**), but always **ə** in *Britain,* and in certain words all three pronunciations **-in, -ən,** and vocalic **-n** may be heard. When the spelling **-ain** has been changed to **-en** we have **-ən** or vocalic **-n,** as *barren* (ME. **barain**), *dozen* (O.Fr. **dosaine**), and similarly *leaven, sudden, sullen.* Before **l** the normal development is **əl** which in careless speech is reduced to vocalic **l,** as *apparel, arrival, counsel, marvel, travel, victuals,* but we always have vocalic **l** in *battle* (ME. **bataile**).

§ 164. ME. **oi** has regularly become **ə**, as *porpoise, tortoise.*

§ 165. Before **r** all vowels, of whatever origin, have been weakened to **ə** with loss of the **r** in pronunciation, as *popular, vicar* ; the following and other words were formerly written with **-er** : *beggar, briar, cellar, collar, grammar, liar, pedlar, pillar, scholar, sugar, vinegar. baker, manner, mother, prisoner. Yorkshire,* and similarly with other names of counties ending *-shire. author, creator, tailor. favour, honour, vigour. creature, feature, nature ; measure, treasure. comfort, concert, coward, govern, leopard,* &c.

§ 166. Vowels sometimes remain unweakened in learned words, as *syntax, dialect, dialogue, chaos,* &c. Cp. § 155.

(B) In Final Syllables ending in a Vowel.

§ 167. Final **-a** has become **ə**, as *America, drama, sofa, umbrella.*

§ **168.** Final -o is now pronounced ou through the influence of the spelling. In earlier NE. it was regularly pronounced ə, as it still is in most of the dialects, as *grotto, hero, potato, tobacco.*

§ **169.** Final -ī has generally been diphthongized to ai in verbs with a secondary accent, as *crucify, fortify, multiply, occupy, prophesy,* see § 73, 8.

§ **170.** Quite a number of ME. endings of various origin have fallen together in i, written y, in NE. :—

1. ME. -ĭ = OE. -ig (*EME. Gr.* § 138), as *any, body, heavy, holy, many, twenty.*

2. Late ME. -li, -ly = OE. -lĭc(e), ON. -lig-r, -liga, as *freely, gladly, heavenly, surely, truly.*

3. ME. -ĭ = O.Fr. -ĭ (*EME. Gr.* § 199), as *mercy.*

4. ME. -ie = AN. -ie (*EME. Gr.* § 195), as *adversary, envy, February, glory, marry, melody, memory, necessary, story.*

5. ME. -ę̄ = O.Fr. -ę̄ (*EME. Gr.* § 197), as *beauty, bounty, city, pity, poverty.*

6. ME. -ai (-ei) = AN. -eie, Central O.Fr. ę̄e (*EME. Gr.* § 197), generally written -ey after l and n, as *abbey, army, chimney, country, entry, journey, medley, motley, valley.*

7. ME. -ai (-ei) = O.Fr. -ai (-ei) (*EME. Gr.* § 205), as *belfry, very* ; and similarly ME. -ai = OE. -æg (*EME. Gr.* § 106) in the names of the days of the week, as *Sunday, Monday,* &c.

8. In a few learned words the -i is written -e, as *acme, anemone, apostrophe, catastrophe.*

§ **171.** In dealing with the history of the ending -ow, pronounced -ou, it is necessary to take into consideration two types of development which arose in the ME. period : 1. When the w in the ME. combination -we came to stand finally after the loss of the -e, it was vocalized to -u (cp. *EME. Gr.* §§ 134 (*a*), 241, 298). The u-sound remained in late ME. and early NE., but during the early NE. period it came to be written -ow, and then later the -ow was pronounced -ou through the influence of the spelling. 2. In

ME. an o was often developed between a liquid and a following w from older ʒ, which combined with the w to form the diphthong ǫw, as in borǫwen 'to borrow', folǫwen 'to follow', see *EME. Gr.* § 152, 2. Early NE. had accordingly forms like bōru, folu beside borow, folow, and these double forms are well attested by the early writers on NE. pronunciation. Both the -u and the -ǫw would normally have become -ə in the present standard pronunciation, just as they have in most of the dialects, but we now have the pronunciation -ou in both types through the influence of the spelling. Examples are:—With ME. w = OE. w, as *arrow, meadow, narrow, shadow, sparrow, widow, yellow*; ME. w from older ʒ, as *borrow, follow, hallow, hollow, morrow, sorrow; fellow* (ME. fĕlowe, fĕlawe, ON. fēlagi), *window* (ME. windowe, ON. vindauga).

§ 172. ME. -iu (*EME. Gr.* §§ 202, 209) has normally become -jŭ (cp. § 79), as *ague, nephew* (ME. nevew), *sinew, value,* but *issue* and *virtue* have išū, išjŭ, vətšŭ beside isjŭ, vətjŭ (§ 185).

4. COMPOUND WORDS

§ 173. For practical purposes compound words may be conveniently divided into three classes:—

1. Old compounds in which the second element has been entirely obscured through the loss of accent, as *Clifton : town* (OE. tūn), *Cobham : home* (OE. hām), *daisy* (OE. dæges ēage), *garlic* (OE. gārlēac), *kindred* (OE. -ræden), *Maldon : down* (OE. dūn), *stirrup* (OE. stig-rāp). In words of this type the vowel in the second element has regularly been weakened according to the rules which prevail for the unaccented syllables of simple words.

2. Compounds in which the second element is not consciously associated with the independent simple word. In these compounds the second element is unaccented, and the stem-vowel has been weakened according to the rules which

prevail for the unaccented syllables of simple words, as *breakfast, cupboard, Englishman, kingdom, madam, Plymouth, Yorkshire.*

3. Compounds in which the second element is consciously associated with the independent simple word. In compounds of this type the stem-vowel of the second element does not lose its accent and accordingly remains unweakened, as *footstep, fortnight, likewise, newspaper, weekday, workhouse* (Yks. dial. **wākəs**). Compounds with **-ful** fluctuate between **-ful** and **-fəl, -fl** with vocalic l in adjectives, as *beautiful, careful,* but nouns always have **-ful,** as *basketful, handful.*

Sometimes the same word which forms the second element of compounds has double forms according as it is unaccented or accented, as *brimstone,* but *milestone ; holiday,* but *holy day ; somebody,* but *anybody ; Sunday,* but *weekday ; waistcoat,* but *petticoat.*

5. UNACCENTED WORDS

§ 174. In ordinary connected speech the more important words of a sentence are accented and the less important are unaccented. The more important words in an ordinary sentence are:—Nouns, adjectives, principal verbs, certain pronouns, such as *this, that* when used demonstratively, *who, what, which,* and *both,* and most adverbs. The less important words are:—the articles, most pronouns, auxiliary verbs, prepositions, conjunctions, and some adverbs. When words of the latter kind are unaccented they undergo the same kind of weakening as the vowels in the unaccented syllables of nouns, adjectives, and principal verbs.

§ 175. In the course of the history of the language it has sometimes happened that the old accented form of a word has entirely disappeared, and then the old unaccented form has come to be used as the accented form from which a new unaccented form has often been formed, as ME. **ich : i** which

later became the accented form ī = NE. *I*; NE. *ous (OE.
ūs): as 'us': dial. əz; *it* (OE. **hit**); *have : I've*; early NE.
šǭl : šæl : šəl (šl). In other cases the old unaccented form
has disappeared, and then the old accented form has come
to be used for both, as in *by, my* beside older **bĭ, mĭ**. The
old accented beside the unaccented form has often been
preserved, as in **ðī** beside **ðĭ, ðə** 'the'; **æt** beside **ət** 'at';
woz beside **wəz** 'was'. When both forms have been preserved they have sometimes been differentiated in meaning,
as *also : as, than : then, off : of, too : to*. Examples of the
various types of words are :—

ei : ə 'a'; æn : ən and vocalic n 'an'; **ðī : ði, ðə**, formerly
also **ð'** 'the'.

hī : **hi, i,** early NE. also **a** (= ə) 'he'; **hiz : iz** 'his'; **him :
im**; **šī : ši** 'she'; **wī : wi** 'we'; **hə̄ : (h)ə** 'her'; **as : əs**
'us'; **ji** 'ye' : **i** in *willy nilly*; **ðei : ðe** 'they'; **ðem : ðəm,
ðm** 'them'.

bī : **bi** 'be'; **bīn : bin** 'been'; **æm : əm, m** 'am'; **iz : z**
'is', but **s** after voiceless consonants, as in **it's**; **ǎ : ə** 'are'
beside the old accented form in **eint** 'are not'; **wǫz : wəz**
'was'; **wę̄ə : wə̌** 'were'; **hæv : həv, əv, v** 'have' beside
the old accented form in *behave*; **hæz : həz, əz, z** 'has';
hæd : həd, əd, d 'had'; **kæn** 'can' : **kən, kn** with vocalic
n; **kud : kəd** 'could'; **dū : du, də** 'do'; **mast** 'must' :
məst, but **məs** before consonants; **šæl** 'shall' : **šəl**, and **šl**
with vocalic **l**; **šud : šəd** 'should'; **wil : wəl, əl, l** 'will';
wud : wəd, d 'would'.

æt : **ət** 'at'; **fǭ, fǭə : fə, fǫ** 'for'; **ov** 'of' : **ǫv, əv, ə**, but
f before voiceless consonants; **tū : tu, tə** 'to'; *doff, don* for
do off, do on.

ænd : **ənd, ən** 'and'; **æz : əz** 'as'; **nǭ, nǭə : nə, nǫ** 'nor';
ðæn : ðən 'than'; **ðæt** 'that' demonstrative pronoun : **ðət**
relative pronoun and conjunction.

nought : not beside **nt** after vowels, as *can't, don't, shan't*,
but with vocalic **n** after consonants, as *didn't, isn't*.

§ **176.** Some words have become unaccented through being used before proper names, as *Sir* which is now used independently : *sire ; madam : dame ; mister : master ;* sən(t), sin(t) : seint 'saint'.

CHAPTER IV

THE NE. DEVELOPMENT OF THE ME. CONSONANT-SYSTEM

§ **177.** ME. had the following consonant-system (see *EME. Gr.* §§ 13–21, 24) :—

		Labial	Inter-dental	Dental	Guttu-ral	Pala-tal
Explosives	{ voiceless	p		t	k (c)	
	{ voiced	b		d	g	
Spirants	{ voiceless	f	þ	s(c), sch	ȝ (gh)	ȝ (gh)
	{ voiced	v (u)	þ	s (z)	ȝ	ȝ
Nasals		m		n	n	
Liquids				l, r		
Semi-vowels		w				ȝ (y)

To the above must be added the aspirate **h** and the affricataé **tš** (written ch, cch, tch, § 274), **dž** (written g, gg, j, § 278). As the ME. consonants have not undergone many sound-changes in NE. we shall not make separate headings for the independent and dependent changes.

THE SEMI-VOWELS.

w

§ **178.** ME. **w** has generally remained initially before vowels, and in the combinations **d, t, th,** and **s + w,** as *wait, war, warm, waste, water, wish, wolf, word ; dwarf, dwell ; twelve, twig ; thwack, thwart ; sweet, swell, swim,* but the **sw** is written **su** in French words, as *assuage, persuade.*

§ **179.** The ME. combinations **kw, gw,** written **qu, gu,** have also generally remained, as *banquet, conquest, equal, liquid, marquis, quaint, quality, quarter, queen, question, quick, quiet, require ; anguish, distinguish, languish, language.* In some of the above words ME. and early NE. had forms with and without **w.** The forms with **w** have usually been generalized, but we still have **k** in *conquer, liquor, quoit* (cp. *EME. Gr.* § 254), and **gw** beside **g** in *languor.* Late French loan-words regularly have **k,** as *bouquet, etiquette, quay,* &c.

§ **180.** In the initial combination **wr·** the **w** ceased to be pronounced in the seventeenth century, as *wrack, wrap, wreath, wrench, wretch, wrist, write, wrong.*

§ **181. w** disappeared between a consonant and a back rounded vowel in late ME. or early NE., although it has mostly been retained in writing, as *so, thong ; sword, two ; who, whose, whom* with **wh·** from older **hw·** (§ 284). In forms like *swollen, swoon, swoop, swore, swum, swung,* formerly often written and pronounced without the **w,** the **w** has been restored through the influence of the spelling and related forms. Initial **w·** has disappeared before **ū** from older **ō** (§ 75) in *ooze* (ME. **wǭse**), and a **w·** has been added in *woof* (ME. **ǭf**) from association with *weave, web, weft.*

§ **182. w** regularly disappeared in early NE. in the initial syllable of the second element of compounds, but in the present standard pronunciation it has generally been restored again through the influence of the spelling, except in proper names, as *answer* (OE. **and·swaru** sb., **and·swarian** v.), *boatswain* (**boutswein** beside **bousn**), *coxswain* (**kokswein** beside **koksn**), **heipəþ** 'halfpennyworth', *housewife* beside *hussif, huzzif, threshold* (OE. **þerscwold**) ; *Chiswick, Greenwich, Southwark, Warwick,* &c. In the dialects the **w** in the compounds with *-ward(s, -worth* has regularly disappeared (*ED. Gr.* § 247), as **ǭkəd(z, forəd(z, ǭpəþ** 'halfpennyworth', **penəþ** 'pennyworth', but in the standard language the **w** has been restored again in such compounds except in *toward(s,* which is pronounced without and with **w**, as *awkward, back-ward*(s, *forward*(s, *pennyworth*, &c.

§ 183. **w** has disappeared in the unaccented forms of *will, would*, as *I'll, he'll, he'd* 'he would', &c.

j = i·Consonant

§ 184. ME. initial **j**, written ȝ, **y** (*EME. Gr.* §§ 255, 292), has remained in NE., and is now always written **y**, as *yard, year, yearn, yellow, yes, yesterday, yet, yield, yoke, young, youth.*

§ 185. Early NE. **sj, zj**, and **tj** have become **š, ž, tš**, as *admission, ancient, gracious, nation* (ME. **nācioun**), *noxious, pension, social, special, sugar, sure ; confusion, division, measure, occasion, pleasure, treasure, usual, vision ; creature, feature, fortune, future, mixture, nature, venture, virtue.* Forms like *assume, pursue, suet, suit ; piteous, Tuesday, tune* are due to the influence of the spelling. The normal development of **dj** is also **dž**, as in *soldier, verdure,* **edžukeit** beside **edjukeit** 'educate'. Through the influence of the spelling we now generally have **dj** (di), but in the eighteenth century **dž** was common in many or all of the words which now have **dj** (di), as *duke, India, odious,* &c. ; many of the dialects still have **dž** in such words (cp. *ED. Gr.* § 296). On the loss of the **j** after **l, r, dž, tš**, as in *allude, blue, clew ; brew, brute, rule, shrew ; Jew, juice, June ; chew*, see §§ **80, 86–7.**

The Liquids.

l

§ 186. ME. **l** has generally remained in NE. both initially, medially, and finally, as *labour, ladder, lamb, language, large, lesson, long, loud ; blame, clean, clear, England, fellow, follow, glad, glory, golden, help, malady, melt, milk, old, place, salt, silver, sleep, swallow, wild ; ale, all, deal, fall, hill, isle, meal,* *nail, owl, pull, sell, shall, soul, steal, tell, will, wool,* but in unaccented syllables we regularly have vocalic l after consonants, as *apple, battle, cradle, meddle, noble, people, riddle, table.*

§ 187. l disappeared in the combination lnt in the seventeenth century, as *shan't, won't.* It has also disappeared in the originally unaccented forms *should* and *would* (§ 105). For the loss of l before labials and k, see §§ 102–3.

§ 188. Through the influence of Latin an etymological l was often restored about the time of the revival of learning (cp. § 55, 5), as *assault* (ME. **assaut**), *fault* (ME. **faute**), and similarly *cauldron, falcon, herald, realm, scaffold, scald, soldier, vault,* &c. (cp. *EME. Gr.* § 208); *chronicle* (O.Fr. **chronique**), and similarly *participle, principle, syllable,* &c. An unetymological l has been inserted in *moult* (ME. **moute**, Lat. **mūtāre**), and in *could* after the analogy of *should* and *would.*

r

§ 189. ME. r was a trilled consonant in all positions of the word, as it still is in the Scottish dialects and in those of small parts of Dur., Cum., and Wm. (*ED. Gr.* § 260). In some of the southern parts of England it had begun to be weakened before consonants, especially s, and sometimes omitted in writing, in late ME. and early NE., as is evidenced by such early spellings as **Dos(s)et** 'Dorset', **wosted** 'worsted'; and in two names of fishes the forms without r became standardized in the fifteenth and sixteenth centuries, viz. *bass* (late ME. and early NE. **bace, base,** OE. **bærs**) and *dace* (ME. **darse,** O.Fr. **darz, dars**). In the standard language it is now untrilled and preserved only before vowels which are pronounced.

§ 190. It has been preserved initially and medially before vowels, and also finally when the next word in the same sentence begins with a vowel, as *read, reason, red, rich, room,*

*round, run, write, wrong; borrow, bring, bury, carry, courage,
crown, fresh, grass, green, marry, merit, pray, priest, secret,
sparrow, story, tree, trouble, vary, very, weary; I hear it.* After
the analogy of such combinations as *far away, fear it*, it is
very common to insert an **r** in such combinations as *idea of
it* even among educated speakers in the south Midland and
southern counties.

§ 191. Medially before consonants, and finally in pausa,
and when the next word in the sentence began with a consonant, the **r** began to be weakened in the standard language
in the early part of the seventeenth century, and in the
eighteenth century it ceased to be pronounced, although it
is always retained in writing, as *arm, bark, bird, burn, burst,
court, earth, hard, horse, large, learn, search, short, source, turn,
word; better, care, err, far, father, fire, flower, honour, more,
nature, nor, order, poor, pure, star, sure, tower; I hear them,*
but *I hear it.* See §§ **108–31.**

§ 192. *bridegroom* (OE. **brȳd-guma**) is due to association
with *groom.* *cartridge* is a corruption of French **cartouche.**
colonel, a late sixteenth-century French loan-word, has been
the usual English spelling since about 1650. The earlier
form was *coronel* (O.Fr. **coronel**); the present pronunciation
represents the latter form with loss of the second **o.**

The Nasals.

m

§ 193. ME. **m** has generally remained in all positions of
the word, as *make, man, money, mother, my; brimstone,
chamber, common, company, damage, sermon, simple; climb,
comb, lamb; aim, beam, claim, come, fame, name, room, time.*
For final vocalic **-m** in unaccented syllables see § 156.

§ 194. **m** has become **n** by assimilation in *ant* (OE. **æmete,**
modern dialects **emmet**), and in *scant* (ON. neut. **skammt**).

n

§ 195. ME. initial and medial n has generally remained in NE., as *name, night, noble, noise, nut ; gnaw, knee, know ; answer, aunt, bench, chance, cleanse, dinner, enemy, envy, friend, ground, honey, honour, send, singe, snow, strange, wonder*.

§ 196. Medial n has been regularly assimilated to ŋ before g, k in accented syllables, but has remained in unaccented syllables. There are, however, many exceptions to this sound-law owing to new formations in different directions, and there is also much fluctuation among different speakers. Regular forms are:—with ŋ, as *concourse, congregate, congress, conquer, handkerchief* (hæŋkətšif), *incubus, syncope* ; with n, as *concoct, concur, encamp, encounter, incapable*. With n beside ŋ, as *concave, concord, concrete, income, increase* sb., *inquest* ; with ŋ beside n, as *congratulate, increase* v., &c.

§ 197. In a few words a medial n has been inserted before dž and g in unaccented syllables. This insertion of n began to take place in late ME. and early NE. Examples are:— *messenger* (ME. messager), and similarly *harbinger, nightingale, passenger, popinjay, porringer, scavenger*.

§ 198. Late ME. final -n has generally remained in NE. Examples are:—(a) In accented syllables, as *begin, chin, green, hen, man, moon, queen, reign, sign, slain, son, town, vine, wine* ; (b) In unaccented syllables, as *barren, chosen, drunken, heathen, heaven, swollen, token, written*, see *EME. Gr.* §§ 147, 247. For vocalic n, see § 156.

§ 199. Final -n often disappeared in late ME. and early NE. in unaccented monosyllables when the next word began with a consonant, as *a : an*, formerly also *i' : in, o' : on* ; and in some words with later differentiation in syntactical usage, as *my : mine, no : none*.

§ 200. Final -n disappeared after l and m by assimilation

in late ME. and early NE., as *kiln* (often with spelling pronunciation kiln), *mill* beside *Milner, autumn : autumnal,
column, condemn, damn : damnation, hymn : hymnal, solemn :
solemnity.* It has also disappeared in the medial unaccented
syllable of *handicap* = *hand-in-cap.*

§ 201. In a few words—mostly French loan-words—final
-n has become -m in unaccented syllables, as *flotsam* (O.Fr.
floteson), *random* (O.Fr. randon), and similarly *jetsam,
ransom, vellum, venom ; seldom* (ME. selden).

§ 202. n has become m by assimilation in *anthem* (OE.
antefn), *hamper* (O.Fr. hanaper). We also have m for older
n in *lime-tree* (older *line-, lind-*).

§ 203. In a few words an n has been added or lost through
a false division of words, as *a newt* for *an ewt* (ME. ewte,
OE. efete), *a nickname* for *an ickname* (ME. ēkenāme), for
the nonce = ME. for þen ǫnes). *an adder* for *a nadder* (ME.
nadder, naddre, OE. nǽdre), and similarly *apron, auger,
umpire.*

ŋ

§ 204. ME. guttural ŋ has remained in accented syllables,
as *among, anguish, anxious, bring, drink, England, finger,
hunger, ink, language, long, sing, think, tongue, uncle.*

§ 205. Guttural ŋ from older ŋg (§ 270) became dental n
in final unaccented syllables in early NE., as is evidenced by
such early spellings as *fardin, standyn* for *farthing, standing,*
and conversely *chicking, gudging* for *chicken, gudgeon* ; and by
all the modern dialects. Many educated speakers still preserve the dental n, but through the influence of the spelling
the guttural ŋ began to be restored again in the early part
of the nineteenth century, and has now become the regular
pronunciation with most educated speakers, as *evening,
living, morning, walking,* &c.

THE LABIALS.

p

§ 206. ME. **p** has generally remained in NE. in all positions of the word, as *palace, path, penny, pillow, place, please,
plough, plum, poverty, present, price, priest; apple, chapter,
company, depart, repent, simple, space, speak, weapon; drop,
help, lamp, lip, sheep, sleep.*

§ 207. **p** has become **b** by assimilation in *cupboard,
raspberry.* It has also become **b** in *cobweb* (ME. **coppewebbe**),
lobster (OE. **loppestre**), *pebble* (OE. **papol-stān**); and similarly in some dialects and even among educated speakers in
depth and *baptist.*

§ 208. A **p** was developed between **m-t** in late ME., but
it is now not pronounced by all educated speakers, as *empty*
(OE. **æmtig**), *consumption, prompt, tempt,* see *EME. Gr.*
§ 251. An etymological **p** has been inserted in *bankrupt*
(older *bankroute*), and *receipt,* see § 55.

§ 209. The **p** before n, s, t, and ph = f in Greek words
was probably never pronounced in English, as *pneumatic,
psalm* (OE. **sealm**), *psalter* (OE. **saltere**), *Ptolemy, sapphire.*

b

§ 210. ME. **b** has generally remained initially, medially,
and also finally except after **m,** as *bath, battle, bear, bind,
black, blind, branch, bring; labour, marble, table; crib, ebb,
rib, robe.*

§ 211. Final **b** disappeared after m in early NE., as *climb,
comb, dumb, lamb, oakum* (OE. **ācumba**), *womb.* After the
analogy of words like *lamb,* a **b** has been added in *crumb*
(OE. **crūma**), *limb* (OE. **lim**), *numb* (ME. **nume**), *thumb* (OE.
þūma), cp. *EME. Gr.* § 251.

§ 212. The development of a **b** between **m-l, m-r,** took
place during the ME. period, as in *bramble* (OE. **brēmel,**
gen. **brēmles**), *slumber* (OE. **slūmerian**), and similarly
embers, nimble, shambles, thimble. A **b** was also developed in

O.Fr. in these positions, whence *chamber, humble, member, number, tremble* (*EME. Gr.* § 251). The form *plumber* (**plamə**) is due to *plumb*.

§ 213. b has become p in *gossip* (OE. **godsibb**), *purse* (Fr. **bourse**).

§ 214. At the time of the revival of learning an etymological b, which was never pronounced, was inserted in a few words, as *debt* (ME. **dette** : Lat. **dēbita**), *doubt* (ME. **doute** : Lat. **dūbitāre**), *subtle* (ME. **sutill, sotill** : Lat. **subtīlis**). See § 55.

f

§ 215. ME. f occurred initially and finally both in native words and loan-words. In native words it also occurred medially when doubled and in combination with voiceless sounds, and in loan-words between voiced sounds. The f has remained in NE., and is written ph in Greek words, as *face, father, fault, find, flesh, flour, foot, fortune, freeze, friend, full, pheasant, philosopher, phlegm, phonetics ; brief, chief, deaf, half, loaf, mischief, roof, stiff, thief, wolf; after, gift, offer* (OE. **offrian**) ; *afraid, confess, defend, orphan, profit, prophet.* Formerly ph was often pronounced p before th in words like *diphtheria, diphthong, naphtha,* and is still so pronounced by some people.

§ 216. f became v in late ME. and early NE. through loss of stress in **ov, əv** ' of ', and then the v generally disappeared before words beginning with a consonant, as is still the case in the modern dialects, but in the standard language the v has been restored again except in a few stereotyped forms like *o'clock, Will o' the wisp.*

§ 217. f has disappeared in **heipəni** ' halfpenny ', and *huzzy* (ME. **hūs-wīf**) from earlier *huzzif, hussif* (§ 182).

§ 218. *vane* (OE. **fana**), *vat* (OE. **fæt**), and *vixen* (OE. **fyxen**) are Ken. and southern dialect forms which have crept into the standard language, see *EME. Gr.* § 236.

v

§ 219. In early ME. v was generally written u between vowels, and then later v. In the seventeenth century the v became fully established in all positions of the word. In early NE. final -v was written -ue, whence the present spelling with -ve. The ph for v in *nephew* (ME. neuew) is a pseudo-learned spelling. v, which occurred in ME. native words between vowels, and between l, n, r and a vowel, has remained in NE. In French loan-words v occurs initially, medially between voiced sounds, and finally. Examples are :—*anvil, avenge, cover, even, evil, fever, harvest, heavy, liver, river, serve, seven, shovel, silver, travel*; and in plurals like *staves, wives, wolves*. When ME. v has become final in NE. through the loss of final -e in pronunciation, it has regularly remained, as *alive, delve, give, have, live, move, prove, serve*; on forms like *five, glove, grave, twelve*, see *EME. Gr.* § 267. French loan-words with initial v are :—*valour, vanish, very, voice*, &c.

§ 220. Forms like *leafy, roofs, wolfish* are new formations with f direct from *leaf, roof, wolf*. After the analogy of forms like *grief : grieve*, to *believe* was formed *belief* (ME. bilēve). The -ff in *sheriff* (ME. schir-rēve, OE. scīr-gerēfa) is due to the analogy of *bailiff*. The first element of *lieutenant* had the double forms *leef-, lieu-* in ME., we now have the pronunciation from the former and the spelling from the latter form.

§ 221. Intervocalic v disappeared in late ME. and early NE. in unaccented forms like *e'en* 'even', *e'er* 'ever', *ne'er* 'never', *o'er* 'over'; they are now only used in poetry, but in the dialects they are still very common.

The Dentals.

t

§ 222. ME. t has generally remained in NE. in all positions of the word, as *table, take, tell, time, tongue, touch, travel, tree, twelve, twig; battle, better, bottom, daughter, fortune, history, letter, little, nature, pity, sister, stone, street, strong, study; bite, doubt, eat, eight, faint, foot, gift, honest, hunt, kept, last, sent, sit, slept, theft.*

§ 223. In late ME. and early NE. **th** was sometimes written for **t** in Latin and Greek words borrowed from French (see *EME. Gr.* § 269, note 2), and then later the **th** came to be pronounced **þ** through the influence of the spelling, as *anthem, apothecary, authentic, author, authority, enthusiasm, panther, theatre, theme, throne,* but the old pro- nunciation has been preserved in *Anthony, Thames, Thomas, thyme.* In the combination **sþ** the pronunciation fluctuates, as in **æsmə, æsþmə, æstmə** 'asthma', and similarly *isthmus,* but only **t** in **estə** 'Esther'. A **t** is now written in some French loan-words which in ME. had **c = s**, as *nation* (ME. **nācioun**), *patient* (ME. **pācient**), &c., see § 246.

§ 224. **t** has become **d** in *card* (O.Fr. **carte**), *diamond* (O.Fr. **diamant**), *jeopardy* (O.Fr. **jeu parti**).

§ 225. Intervocalic **t** became **r** in *porridge* (O.Fr. **potage**) in the sixteenth century. This change of intervocalic **t** to **r** when the first vowel is short is very common in some dialects, e. g. in Yks. dialects, as *a mer im* 'I met him', but *a mīt im* 'I meet him'.

§ 226. *fifth* (ME. **fifte**), *sixth* (ME. **sixte**), *eleventh* (ME. **ellefte, ellevende**), *twelfth* (ME. **twelfte**) are new formations after the analogy of forms like *fourth* (ME. **fourþe**) which regularly have **th**, see *EME. Gr.* § 366. The forms *fift, sixt,* &c., were in regular use until the seventeenth century, and still are so in the dialects.

§ 227. **t** disappeared in pronunciation in the late sixteenth and early seventeenth centuries between **s, f** and a following **l, m,** or **n,** as *bristle, bustle, castle, chasten, chestnut, christen, Christmas, epistle, fasten, listen, moisten, often, soften, thistle, whistle.* Forms like *beastly, justly,* &c., are due to the influence of the simple word. In earlier NE. there was a general tendency for interconsonantal t to disappear in pronunciation in words where it is now often restored again by 'careful' speakers, as in *bankruptcy, facts, perfectly, roast-beef, waistcoat, wristband*, &c., but the t is rarely, if ever, pronounced in *mortgage*. It has disappeared in ordinary colloquial speech in the combinations ltš, ntš, as *belch, filch, milch-cow; bench, drench, quench*, although here again some 'careful' speakers pronounce the t, see § 277.

§ 228. A t has been developed after s in *against, amidst, amongst, hoist, whilst*; and between s and r in *tapestry* (O.Fr. tapisserie). Final t has disappeared after l, n in *anvil* (ME. anvilt), *craven* (ME. crāvant).

d

§ 229. ME. d has generally remained in all positions of the word, as *dance, daughter, day, deep, doom, doubt, dress, drink, dwell; children, needle, riddle, saddle, sudden; bind, bird, field, friend, good, hold, made, mild, odd, second, wind.*

§ 230. In native words single d became ð between a vowel and a following vocalic r in late ME. or early NE., as *father* (ME. fader), and similarly *gather, hither, mother, tether, thither, weather, wither, whither*, but in loan-words we have d, as *consider, powder*, &c., and late NE. formations also preserve the d, as in *feeder, leader, rider*. In the dialects this sound-change has also regularly taken place in words which had -dd- in ME., as blaðə, bleðə (ME. bladder, bledder), foðə (ME. fodder), and similarly in *adder, ladder*, &c.; and in French words like *consider, powder*, see *ED. Gr.* § 297.

§ 231. d has become t after voiceless consonants in the preterite and past participle of weak verbs, as *asked, fetched, hoped, laughed, wished*, &c., see § 390.

§ 232. In ordinary colloquial speech interconsonantal d has disappeared in various combinations where it is now often restored again by 'careful' speakers:—Between l or n + ž, as *bilge, bulge, indulge; change, danger, hinge, singe, strange*, see § **280**.   Between **n** and **z**, as *almonds*, *hands*, *pounds*, *stands*.   Between **n** and various other consonants, as *grandfather*, *grandmother*, *grindstone*, *groundsel*, *handful*, *hand-kerchief*, *handsome*, *landlord*, *landscape ;* *bread and butter*. **zdt** has become **st** in *I used to go*.

§ **233**. Final **-d** has been lost after **n** in *lawn*, older *laund;* *groin* (ME. **grīnde**), *wood-bine*, older *-binde*.

§ **234**. A **d** has been developed after final **-n** in *bound*, older *boun* (ON. **būenn**), *pound* v. (OE. **pūnian**), and similarly *astound*, *hind* ' farm servant ', *lend*, *sound* sb.

þ

§ **235**. ME. **þ**, which occurred initially, medially when doubled, and finally, has generally remained in NE.   In the fourteenth century **th** gradually came to be used beside **þ**, but the **þ** continued to be written beside **th**, especially initially, throughout the ME. period.   Examples are :— *thank*, *thing*, *think*, *thong*, *three*, *thunder ; breath*, *health*, *hearth*, *moth* (OE. **moþþe**), *mouth*, *oath*, *path*, *tooth*, *youth*.   But we have **th = t** in a few words, as *Thames*, *Thomas*, *thyme*, see § **223**.

§ **236**. Initial **þ** became voiced at an early period in pronominal forms and forms derived from them (cp. *EME. Gr.* § 236).   This voicing of **þ** was due to the loss of accent in these words.   Examples are :— *than*, *that*, *those*, *the*, *then*, *there*, *thence*, *they*, *them*, *their*, *this*, *these*, *thither*, *thou*, *thee*, *thy*, *thine*, *though*, *thus*.   The **th** in *with* is generally voiceless among educated speakers of Scotland, Ireland, and the north of England ; in the other parts of England it is generally voiced.

ð

§ **237**. ME. **ð**, written **þ**, which only occurred medially between voiced sounds, has generally remained in NE., as *brethren*, *brother*, *either*, *fathom*, *feather*, *heathen*, *lather*, *leather*, *other, wether, whether.* The **th** is voiceless in late loan-words, as *atheist, catholic, ether, method, sympathy.* Forms like *bethink, earthen, nothing,* &c., have þ through the influence of the simple word.

§ 238. When ME. medial ð has come to stand finally or before final -e, which is unpronounced in NE., it has generally remained after long vowels, and similarly in the plural of nouns, but has become voiceless after short vowels, and similarly in the plural of nouns. Examples of ð are :— *bathe, bequeath* (ME. biquēþen), *booth* (ME. bōþe), *breathe, seethe, smooth* (ME. smōþe), *soothe, scythe ; baths, mouths, oaths,* &c. Examples of þ are :—*froth* (ME. froþe), *health* (ME. helþe, *EME. Gr.* § 91, 2), and similarly *pith, tenth, twentieth,* &c. ; *deaths, smiths,* &c. ; in *cloths* we have double forms with differentiated meaning, viz. klōþs, kloþs 'kinds of cloth ', and klōðz 'pieces of cloth '. When final -e disappeared at an early period in ME., the ð has become þ in NE., as *both* (late ME. bōþ, older bōþe), and similarly *beneath, earth, fourth,* see *EME. Gr.* §§ 139, 238.

ð has become d before liquids, as *Bedlam* : older *Bethlehem, fiddle* (OE. fiþele), *rudder* (ME. roþer), *spider* (ME. spīþre), *swaddle* (ME. swaþlen).

§ 239. The normal development of OE. rþ = rð in ME. was probably **rd**, but throughout the ME. period and far into the NE. period **rd** and **rð** existed side by side in most of the words belonging to this category, and then in some words the **rd** and in others the **rð** became standardized. The dialects also have (r)d beside (r)ð, but not necessarily in the same words as in the standard language, e. g. all the dialects have d in *farthing*, and many dialects have ð in *burden, murder.* Examples with d in the standard language are :—*afford* (OE. geforþian), *burden* (OE. byrþen), and similarly *murder*, see *EME. Gr.* § 275 ; and examples with ð are:—*farthing* (ME. ferþing), and similarly *further, northern, worthy.*

The Sibilants.

§ 240. ME. s had a twofold pronunciation in native words:—1. It was voiceless initially, medially when doubled, and in combination with voiceless consonants, and finally in early ME.   2. It was voiced (= z) medially between voiced sounds, and in late ME. also finally after vowels in unaccented syllables, cp. *EME. Gr.* § 276.   This distinction has generally been preserved in NE.   In late ME. and early NE. an attempt was sometimes made to distinguish the two sounds in writing after the analogy of French orthography, as *hence* (late ME. hens), *ice* (ME. īs), *mice* (ME. mīs), but *freeze* (ME. frēsen), *glaze* (ME. glāsen), *hazel* (ME. hāsel).

§ 241. In some French loan-words we now write s (ss) where in French they have or formerly had c, ç, as *lesson* (Fr. leçon), *mason* (Fr. maçon), *sausage* (Fr. saucisse), *search* (O.Fr. cercher) ; and in other words we write -ce where in French they have -s, as *defence* (Fr. défens), *pace* (Fr. pas), *palace* (Fr. palais).   In loan-words initial s- is sometimes written c-, sc-, or sch- before palatal vowels, as *cease, certain, city ; scene, scent, scissors ; schism, schismatic ;* and also sc medially, as *crescent, irascible, nascent.*

s

§ 242. ME. s has remained initially, as *save, cease, certain, city, scarce, scent, school, scorn, sea, send, sentence, serve, siege, sign, skin, sleep, small, snow, son, soul, space, speak, split, spread, stand, strange, study, swear, swim.*

§ 243. It has also remained :—

1. In the medial or final combinations sk, sp, ss, and st, as *ask, bask, escape, task ; gospel, grasp, hospital, wasp, whisper ; blossom, gossip ; arrest, best, estate, first, last, master, sister.*

2. Medially after consonants, as *answer, consult, curtsy, gipsy, hansom, insect, mercy, person, pursuit* ; and after the

loss of d, t before l, m, n, as *castle, Christmas, groundsel*
(graunsl), *fasten, listen,* but we have z beside s in *mistletoe.*

3. Initially in the second element of compounds, as
asunder (OE. on sundran), *besides, besiege, forsake, handsome,
himself, seaside, unseen,* &c.

4. The final s in prefixes before consonants and mute
c = s, as *discover, disdain, mischief, misfortune, misuse*
(misjūz); *excuse, expect, explain; exceed, excell, excess.*

5. In French loan-words with intervocalic s, ss (also
written c, sc, ss in older French), and in Latin and Greek
loan-words, as *assault, basin* (O.Fr. bacin), *deceive, December,
decide, descend, essay, lesson, mason* (O.Fr. masson), *medicine,
necessary, passage, research* (O.Fr. recerche), *resource* (Fr.
ressource), *sausage* (AN. saussiche), *vessel; absent* adj.,
absent v., *asylum, basis, crisis, criticism, designate, desolate,
episode, morose, parasite, philosopher, prosody, thesis,* &c. See
§§ 250, 253.

§ 244. Medial s has become z before voiced consonants
and syllabic m, as *criticism, dismal, enthusiasm, gooseberry,
gosling, grisly, husband, muslin, raspberry* (rāzbəri), *schism,
Tuesday, wristband* (rizbænd, rizbənd).

§ 245. ME. final ·s, and the medial ·s-, ·ss· which became
final in NE. through the loss of final ·e in pronunciation,
and now written ·s, ·ss, ·se, ·ce, has generally remained, as
abuse sb., *basis, curious, hideous, this, Thomas, thus, us, yes;
axe, vex, wax; ass, bless, dress, grass, pass; base, case, cease,
chase, false, goose, horse, house, lease, mouse, sense, use* sb.,
*verse; advice, balance, defence, device, face, fleece, ice, lace, mice,
niece, rejoice, service.* Preterites like *chose, rose* are due to the
levelling out of the s = z of the present and past participle.

§ 246. Early NE. sj has become š (written s, sh, ss, c,
sc, and t), as *anxious* (ænɪɔ(k)šəs), *Asia, conscience, fashion,
issue, mansion, mission, ocean, passion, special, sugar, sure.*
In the endings ·tion, ·tial, ·tious, ·tient, ·tience the
writing with t is etymological (§ 55, 7), O.Fr. regularly

had -cioun, &c., as in **condicioun, nacioun,** &c. Examples
are :—*condition, nation, portion ; essential, partial ; ambitious ;
patient ; patience.*

§ 247. In a few words the final -s has disappeared through
being regarded as a plural ending, as *pea* (ME. pḗse), *riddle*
(OE. rǣdels), and similarly *burial, cherry, girdle.*

§ 248. From *isle* the s has been introduced into *island*
(OE. īegland), and also into *aisle* (Fr. **aile**), see § 55.

z

§ 249. In native words initial z- did not occur in the
ME. standard language, but we now have it in a few foreign
words, as *zeal, zephyr, zeppelin, zero, zest, zinc, zone,* &c.

§ 250. ME. intervocalic z has generally remained both in
native and French simple words, as *besom, busy, chosen, daisy,
dizzy, frozen, hazel,* pl. *houses, lazy, risen, thousand.* Forms
like *fleeces, glasses, horses* beside *houses* are new formations
made direct from the singular. French words :—1. With
the accent in front of the z, as *citizen* (AN. **citeseyn**), *cousin,
dozen, music, physic, pleasant, present* adj., *reason, scissors*
(ME. **cisoures**), *season, usage, visit,* &c. 2. With the accent
after the z, as *desert* v., *deserve, desire, desist, dessert* (Fr.
dessert with z), *museum, present* v., *preserve, preside, resign,*
but *re-sign, result, resume,* &c. From the above and similar
examples it will be seen that the z, which arose from original
simple s in French itself, has been preserved independently
of the position of the accent in NE. A few words now
have z, which formerly had s, as they still have in French ;
they originally belonged to the type of words dealt with in
§ 243, 5, but they are now pronounced with z after the
analogy of words like *deserve, desire,* &c., as *discern* (Fr.
discerner), *possess* (Fr. **posséder**), *resemble* (Fr. **ressembler**),
resent (Fr. **ressentir**) ; and also in *absolve, observe* (Fr. **ob-
server** with s), although the z is not intervocalic.

§ 251. The normal development of the s in the prefix dis-
before vowels is z, just as it is in modern French des = Lat.
dis-. We now, however, generally have s through the influence of the pronunciation of Latin dis- in compounds, as
*disabuse, disadvantage, disagree, disappear, disavow, disembark,
disembody, disincline, disobey, disoblige, disown*, but many, if
not all, of the above words were pronounced with z in earlier
NE., as is still so in *disaster, disastrous*, and *disease*; and
some words still have the old pronunciation with z beside
the new ˉwith s, as *disable, disarm, dishonour, dishonest,
disorder, dissolve.*

§ 252. Nearly all the NE. words containing the Latin
prefix ex- were introduced into English from French. The
x in these words is now generally pronounced gz before
accented vowels, as in *exámine, exért, exist*, but ks after
accented vowels, as in *éxecute, éxercise, éxodus*. In French
the ks regularly became gz before vowels, and the position
of the accent was unconnected with the change, so that in
French we not only have gz in words like *examiner, exister*,
but also in words like *executer, exercer, exode*. This change
of ks to gz is well attested by early French writers on pronunciation, and there can hardly be any doubt that the
French loan-words, which now have gz, had it before they
were introduced into English. A small number of words in
which the accent has been thrown back on to the first
syllable are now pronounced with ks through the influence
of the usual English pronunciation of Latin ex-, and even
here the old beside the new pronunciation exists in *exile*
(égzail beside éksail), *éxigence*, and in some words we also
have ks beside gz before accented vowels, as in *exhále,
exhilarate, exiguous, exúde*, &c. Other examples are :—
1. With gz, as *exact, exaggerate, exaggerátion, exalt, exaltátion,
example, examinátion, exasperate, exasperátion, executor, ex-
emplar, exemplify, exemplificátion, exempt, exertion, exhaust,
exhibit*, but *exhibition* with ks, *exhort*, but *exhortátion* with gz

and **ks,** *exonerate, exoneration.* 2. With **ks,** as *execrable, execrate, execution, exorcise.*

§ 253. In earlier NE. there was, as there still is, some fluctuation in the pronunciation of the s in words ending in ·ison, ·sity, ·sive, ·sory, ·sy. In earlier NE. all or most of the words belonging to this category were pronounced with z or with z beside s, as some of them still are. This fluctuation was doubtless due to a conflict between the Latin and the French pronunciation of the s (cp. § 243, 5). In some words the former with s, and in others the latter with z, has been standardized, according as they were felt as being of Latin or French origin ; and in a few words we still have the double forms, as *comparison, garrison,* but *orison, venison; animosity, curiosity, generosity ; decisive, expensive ; compulsory, illusory,* but *advisory ; courtesy, jealousy,* but z beside s in *heresy, poesy ;* and z in *pansy, posy, quinsy.*

§ 254. ME. z has remained after liquids and m, as *clumsy, damsel, Jersey, palsy.*

§ 255. ME. medial z, which became final in NE. through the loss of final ·e in pronunciation, has remained, as *abuse* v., *advise, blaze, cause, cheese, choose, cleanse, close* v., *devise, ease, eaves, exercise, freeze, furze, gaze, glaze, graze, noise, nose, please, praise, prize, raise, refuse, rise, seize, size, sneeze, Thames, use* v., *wheeze.* The s for z in verbs like *curse, practise, promise, purpose* is due to the influence of the corresponding nouns which regularly have s. Forms like *wise* (ME. **wīs**) have z from the old inflected forms.

§ 256. The ME. unaccented ending ·es became ·ez (= NE. ·iz, often written ·ys in early NE.) during the ME. period (*EME. Gr.* §§ 146, 276, 1). This ending occurred in the genitive singular of nouns, the plural of nouns, and the present third person singular of verbs. The i from older e has remained in NE. after the sibilants s, z, š, ž, but disappeared after other consonants, and then the z remained after vowels (cp. *EME. Gr.* § 330) and voiced consonants,

but became s after voiceless consonants, as *glasses* (glāsiz),
horses, foxes; roses (rouziz), *sizes; dishes* (dišiz), *fishes;*
crutches (kratšiz), *churches; ages* (eidžiz), *bridges; days*
(deiz), *seas, trees; dogs* (dogz), *hills, lambs; doves* (davz),
names, robes, tongues; books (buks), *cats; dukes* (djūks), *ropes*;
and similarly in verbs, as *blesses* (blesiz), *chases; rises*
(raiziz), *chooses; banishes* (bænišiz), *finishes, wishes; grudges*
(gradžiz), *judges; does* (daz), *plays, sees; bids* (bidz), *begs,*
steals; lives (livz), *loves; helps* (helps), *seeks, sits; bites*
(baits), *writes.* In adverbs which were naturally isolated
from the inflectional system, the e in the old genitive
ending -es disappeared much earlier than in nouns and verbs,
whereby the dissyllabic forms became monosyllabic, and the
final -s accordingly remained, and was later generally written
-ce to indicate that it was voiceless (see *EME. Gr.* §§ 122, 2,
145–6, 157), as *else* (early ME. elles, later els), *hence* (early
ME. hennes, later hens), and similarly *once, twice, thrice;*
since, thence, whence. A somewhat similar process took
place with the nouns *dice* and *pence,* in which the fourteenth-
century plurals dys, dyse, dyce and pens came to be felt
as collectives, and not as ordinary plurals.

§ 257. Final -s became -z during the ME. period in unaccented words, as *as, has, hers, his, is, ours, theirs, whose,*
yours, but it has become voiceless again in combination with
voiceless consonants, *it's = it is* or *has, what's = what is* or
has. z has also become voiceless in the phrase *I used to*
(jūstə) *go,* beside *I used* (jūzd) *it.*

§ 258. Early NE. zj has become ž, as *confusion, division,*
measure, occasion, pleasure, usual, vision, see § 185. Forms
like *enthusiasm, Parisian, physiology* with zi are due to the
influence of the spelling.

š

§ 259. ME. š, written sch, sh, ssh, and ss, has remained
in all positions of the word, as *shade, shall, shame, sheep, ship,*

*short, shoulder, shrine, shroud ; ashes, bishop ; blush, English,
fish, fresh, wash, wish.* The ME. š from older ss after i in
French words has also remained, as *abash* (O.Fr. **esbahiss-**),
anguish (O.Fr. **angoisse**), *cash* (O.Fr. **caisse**), and similarly
ambush, bushel, crush, cushion, lash, parish, radish, usher, and
in many verbs like *establish, finish, flourish, punish.* In late
French loan-words it is written **ch,** as *champagne, charade,
machine.*

The Gutturals.

k

§ 260. ME. **k** has generally remained in NE. So far as
can be determined **k** was always guttural in ME. and early
NE., but in the early part of the seventeenth century it
became differentiated into a palatal and a guttural **k**
according as it was followed at that time by a palatal or
a guttural vowel (cp. § 266). This palatalization of the **k**
gave rise to the development of a **j**-glide between the consonant and the following palatal vowel. From the seventeenth down to the early part of the nineteenth century,
writers on English pronunciation often draw attention to
the palatal **k**, which they generally write **ky** or **cy,** as **kyan,
cyan** [kjæn], **skyirt, kyind,** &c. This palatal pronunciation of **k** disappeared in the standard language during the
nineteenth century, but it is still preserved in some dialects,
see Index to *ED. Gr.*

§ 261. In NE. the k-sound is written **c, k, ck, ch, q, qu**
(**-que**), **x = ks.** It is written **c** before guttural vowels (*coat*),
l, r (*clean, cream*), and final **t** (*act, insect*), but **k** before palatal
vowels (*keep*), after **n, l, r** (*blank, milk, dark*), and finally after
long vowels (*seek*). It is written **k** before palatal vowels,
because if written **c** it might be mistaken for **c = s.** In
O.Fr. **c = k** became differentiated into **ts,** later **s,** before
palatal vowels (whence **c = s** in many NE. words) and

c = k before guttural vowels. It is written ck medially
and finally after old short vowels (*ticket, back*); final -ik was
formerly often written -ik, -ic, -ick, -ique in foreign words,
but now only -ic except in recent loan-words like *critique*.
In French loan-words it is often written qu initially and
medially (*quay, conquer*); through the influence of the
spelling this qu = k has come to be pronounced kw in
some words, as *banquet, marquis, quote*. It is written q in
the combination qu = OE. cw (*EME. Gr.* § 252), as *queen,
quick*; and ch in Greek loan-words, as *archangel, chaos, Christ,
echo, epoch, monarch, stomach, sepulchre.* Other examples of
the k-sound are:—*cage, calf, catch, cause, claim, come, cool,
cow, craft, creep, cure, kettle, king, quarter, question, quoit;
scale, scrape, sky; cricket, doctor, escape, etiquette, fickle, fact,
liquor, occasion, pocket, second, secret, uncle, vixen, wicket; ask,
attack, critique, dark, make, milk, music, neck, ox, prick, public,
take, talk, work, yoke.*

§ 262. k in the initial combination kn- ceased to be pronounced in the seventeenth century, as in *knee, knight, knit,
know.*

§ 263. Early NE. had *ake* v. (= OE. acan, ME. āken)
beside *ache* sb. (= OE. æce, ece, ME. āche, ēche, cp. § 274),
but through the mixing up of the noun with the verb in the
eighteenth century, we now have the spelling of the noun in
the verb, and the pronunciation of the verb for both.

§ 264. Medial k has disappeared in āst ' asked '; it disappeared in the preterite and past participle of *make* during
the ME. period (*EME. Gr.* § 250), and formerly also in
ta'en ' taken ', which is still common in the dialects. It has
also disappeared in *blackguard* [blægād].

§ 265. An etymological k, written c, has been inserted in
a few words, as *indict* (early NE. indite), *victuals* (O.Fr.
vitailles) ; and through the influence of the spelling it is
now pronounced in *verdict* (ME. and early NE. verdit). Cp.
§ 55.

g

§ 266. ME. g has generally remained in NE. So far as
can be determined g was always guttural in ME. and early
NE., but in the early part of the seventeenth century it
became differentiated into a palatal and a guttural g according as it was followed at that time by a palatal or a guttural
vowel (cp. § 260). This palatalization of the g, gave rise to
the development of a j-glide between the consonant and the
following palatal vowel. From the seventeenth down to the
early part of the nineteenth century writers on English pronunciation often draw attention to the palatal g, which they
generally write **gy,** as **begyin, gyarden, gyet, guyide**
'guide'. This palatal pronunciation of g disappeared in
the standard language during the nineteenth century, but it
is still preserved in some dialects, see Index to *ED. Gr.*
Although the present pronunciation of *girl* is generally gə̄l, it
is also pronounced giəl or geəl by some people, and this may
be a remnant of the palatal pronunciation of the g.

§ 267. In NE. the g-sound is generally written g (gg),
rarely **gu, gh.** It is written **gu** in some French loan-words
before **e, i,** and also **a.** The **u** was used in the French
orthography to show that the g was an explosive and not
dž (§ 42). After the analogy of the spelling in French
words it was introduced into a few native and ON. words,
as *guess, guest, guild, guilt, tongue.* The spelling with **gh**
was very common in early NE., especially in Caxton's
works. It was introduced by Caxton from the Netherlands,
where it was used to express the voiced spirant ꝫ. It has
been preserved only in *aghast, ghastly, gherkin,* and *ghost.*
Examples are :—*gate, gay, gift, give, glad, glass, go, goat, goose,
grammar, grass, green, guard, guarantee, guerdon, guide, guise,
bargain, eager, figure, sugar, tiger, vigour, waggon ; dog, drag,
egg, fatigue, frog, intrigue, league, plague, stag, vague.*

§ 268. g in the initial combination **gn·** ceased to be pronounced in the seventeenth century, as in *gnarl, gnash, gnat, gnaw*.

§ 269. In French orthography **gn** was used to express palatal n′ (cp. *EME. Gr.* § 210). In loan-words the **gn** has been retained in writing, but an ordinary **n** has been substituted for it in pronunciation, as *assign, benign, campaign, condign, deign, ensign, feign, impugn, reign, sign*; after the analogy of *reign* a **g** has been introduced into *foreign* (O.Fr. **forain**), *sovereign* (O.Fr. **souverain**). Through the influence of the spelling the **g** is now pronounced in some words, as *assignation, recognize, signal, signet*, &c.

§ 270. Final ·ŋg became ·ŋ in late ME., as in *among, bring, hang, long, sing, strong, tongue* (cp. § 205). Medial ŋg has remained before vowels and voiced consonants, as *anger, angle, angry, anguish, England, finger, hunger, hungry, language*; also in the comparative and superlative of adjectives, as *longer, longest, stronger, strongest*. Forms like *hanging, singer, singing, wrongly*, &c., are due to the influence of the simple forms *hang, sing, wrong*.

Palatal χ

§ 271. Palatal χ occurred in ME. before **t,** and finally, and was written ȝ, **gh**, see *EME. Gr.* §§ 307-8. It disappeared in pronunciation in late ME. or early NE., although the **gh** has been preserved in writing down to the present day, as *fight, knight, light, might, night, right, plight, sight* (cp. *EME. Gr.* § 46); *eight, height, straight, weight* (cp. *EME. Gr.* §§ 107, 4, 109); *high, nigh, thigh* (cp. *EME. Gr.* § 109). After the analogy of such words **igh** was often written for **i** in early NE., and this spelling has been preserved in *delight* (ME. **delite**) and *sprightly* (early NE. *spritely*).

Guttural χ

§ 272. ME. guttural χ occurred chiefly before **t**, and finally,
and was written **h, ʒ** in early ME., and then later **gh**, see
EME. Gr. §§ 307–8. In NE. the writing of **gh** has remained
except in *draft, dwarf*, although the sound itself has either
disappeared or become **f**. In late ME. or early NE. a labial
glide was developed before the. χ, and then the labialized χ
became **f** in the sixteenth century, but beside the labialized
χ there must also have existed the χ without labialization,
which ceased to be pronounced in the standard language in
the late sixteenth or early seventeenth century. And then
during the seventeenth and early part of the eighteenth
century one or other of the two developments became
standardized in the various words belonging to this category.
A similar twofold development has also taken place in the
dialects, which often have **f** where the standard language
does not have it, as **daftə** 'daughter', **doəf, duəf** 'dough',
druft 'drought', **slaftə** 'slaughter', **þruf, þrif** 'through'.
After a great deal of fluctuation in earlier NE., the standard
language now has **f** finally after short vowels, but **gh** unpronounced after long vowels and diphthongs, as *chough,
clough, cough, enough, rough, tough, trough ; dwarf* (OE.
dweorh, ME. **dwergh, dwerf, dwarf**) ; but *bough, dough,
plough, slough* 'bog' (cp. *EME. Gr.* § 114), *though, through ;
furlough*, older *vorloffe, forloff, furloff*, which was borrowed
from Dutch in the seventeenth century, is a spelling pronunciation. Before **t** the development with labialization
has been standardized in *draft* (*draught*), and *laughter* which,
however, may be a new formation from *laugh* (§ 93, 1). In
all other words of this type the development without labialization has been standardized, as *aught, bought* (early NE. also
boft), *brought, daughter* (earlier NE. also *dafter*), *drought,
fought, naught, ought, slaughter, sought, taught, thought* (early

NE. also *thoft*). After the analogy of words like *aught*, gh
has been inserted in *haughty* (early NE. *hautie*).

§ 273. χ became k before the voiceless spirants f, s during
the ME. period, as *heifer* (ME. hekfore, OE. hēahfore) from
early NE. *hekfer* by assimilation of the medial consonants ;
hough (hock) is a back-formation from ME. hogh-sinewe, OE.
hōh-sinu.

The Affricatae tš, dž.

tš

§ 274. ME. tš from OE. palatal c (*EME. Gr.* §§ 282-3)
was written ch after the analogy of O.Fr. orthography.
Instead of the writing chch for double tš after short vowels
ME. had cch which in late ME. came to be written tch,
whence spellings like NE. *flitch* (OE. flicce), *witch* (OE. wicce).
After the analogy of such forms we now have tch for old
single tš in *ditch* (OE. dīc), *pitch* (OE. pic). In early French
loan-words we have tš, but in late ones š, as *chair, chandler,
chance, chief,* but *chaise, chandelier, machine.*

§ 275. ME. tš has generally remained in all positions of
the word, as *chalk, change, chapel, charge, charity, charm, cheap,
cheese, cherish, child, choose, church ; achieve, archbishop* (OE.
ærce-, ęrce-biscop), *butcher, duchess, kitchen, merchant, mischief, orchard, purchase, wretched ; beech, catch, coach, crutch,
each, much, preach, search, speech, such, teach, torch, which,
wretch.*

§ 276. It has become dž after an unaccented vowel, as
cabbage (ME. cabache), *sausage* (AN. saussiche), *spinach*
(O.Fr. (e)spinache), and similarly *Greenwich, Harwich, knowledge, partridge ;* and before an accented vowel in *ajar,* older
on chár (OE. on cierre).

§ 277. The t in the combinations ltš, ntš probably disappeared in the course of the sixteenth century in simple
words, but it is now sometimes restored again by ' careful '

speakers through the influence of the spelling, as *belch, filch, milch-cow ; bench, branch, drench, French, lunch, luncheon, quench, wrench*, cp. § **227**. In proper names like *Colchester, Manchester, Winchester* the **tš** has been preserved through the influence of the simple word *Chester*.

dž

§ **278.** dž was written **g** (**gg**) and **j** in ME. and corresponded to OE. palatal **cg** (also written **cge, cgi**) and O.Fr. **dž** (written **j, g** initially and **g, gg, j** medially, *EME. Gr.* §§ 296–7). **dge** came to be written for **gg** in late ME., whence NE. *bridge, edge,* &c. After the analogy of such words **dge** came to be written in words which never had **gg,** as *badge, judge, lodge,* &c. In NE. **dž** is written **dge** finally after short vowels, and **ge** after long vowels and diphthongs, and in words of more than one syllable. In early French loan-words we have **dž**, as *image, page*, but in later ones **ž**, as *prestige, rouge.*

§ **279.** ME. dž has generally remained in NE. in all positions of the word, as *gem, general, gentle, join, joy, justice, major ; cudgel, legend, majesty, religion, suggest ; edge, hedge, midge, ridge, pledge, wedge ; age, charge, college, courage, large, pigeon, siege.*

§ **280.** The d in the combinations **ldž, ndž** has disappeared in ordinary colloquial speech, but through the influence of the spelling it is often restored again by ' careful ' speakers, as *bilge, bulge, divulge, indulge ; angel, change, danger, hinge, orange, plunge, singe, strange,* cp. § **232.**

h

§ **281.** In native words ME. initial h has regularly remained in standard NE. before accented vowels and **jū** from older **iu** (§§ **86, 1, 87, 1**), and also in the dialects of Scotland, Ireland, and Northumberland, but in the other dialects of England

it has disappeared except perhaps in those of north Durham
and north Cumberland (*ED. Gr.* § 357), as *hand, help, house ;
hew, hue.* Initial h was not pronounced in O.Fr. (AN.) native
words (*EME. Gr.* § 302), and consequently when such words
were introduced into English there was much fluctuation in
the pronunciation both in ME. and early NE.   The h is now
pronounced in many words in which it was generally unpronounced in ME., as *habit* (ME. abit), *herb* (ME. erbe,
herbe), and similarly *haste, hermit, homage, horrible, host,
hotel, huge, human, humble,* &c., but the h is still not pronounced in *heir, honest, hour, hostler,* also written *ostler.*

§ 282. Initial h is generally or often not pronounced in
unaccented syllables, as *heróic,* but *hero ; histórian, histórical,*
but *history ; heréditary.*   In the colloquial language it is also
omitted in the unaccented forms of pronouns, and in the
auxiliary verb *have* (§ 175), as *he, him, his, her, 'em* (ME. hem,
OE. heom) ; the unaccented form *it* supplanted the accented
form *hit* (OE. hit) so early as the fifteenth century.

§ 283. Medial h is generally not pronounced in the second
elements of compounds which are no longer felt as such, as
Durham, forehead, household, neighbourhood, shepherd, &c., but
when the second element is consciously associated with the
independent simple word, the h is generally pronounced, as
boathouse, buttonhole, moorhen, somehow, &c.   It is generally
or often unpronounced between an accented and unaccented
vowel, as *annihilate, vehement, vehicle,* but generally pronounced before an accented vowel, as *apprehend, behave, dis-
hearten, prehensible, upheave ;* in French loan-words like *exhibit,
exhort* the h was never pronounced in English.

§ 284. Except before ǭ (§ 75), OE. χw (written hw) became
voiceless w (written wh) in the Midland and southern dialects
during the ME. period, but remained in the northern dialects,
and was generally written qu, qv, quh (*EME. Gr.* § 303).
Before ǭ, later ū, the w disappeared in pronunciation in late
ME. or early NE., whence the present NE. forms *who* (hū),

whom, whose (§ **181**). The voiceless **w** became voiced during
the eighteenth century, and thus fell together with old **w**
before vowels, as *what* (**wot**), *wheat, when, where, which, white,
why*, &c., but through the influence of the spelling many
Midland and southern speakers now pronounce the voiceless
w again in these and similar words. In the north the
voiceless **w** never became voiced, and is accordingly pronounced as such both by educated and dialect speakers.
whole (ME. hǫǫl, OE. hāl) is a dialect form which crept into
the standard language at an early period. The **wh** was pronounced in the standard language in the seventeenth and
eighteenth centuries, and is still pronounced with **w** in
many dialects. In *whore* (OE. and ME. hōre) there is no
evidence beyond the spelling to show that the **wh** in this
word was ever pronounced either in the standard language
or the dialects, although it is reasonable to suppose that it,
like *whole,* is an old dialect form.

ACCIDENCE

CHAPTER V

NOUNS

§ 285. OE. nouns have two numbers : singular and plural, as in NE. ; three genders: masculine, feminine, and neuter ; four cases: nominative, accusative, genitive, and dative ; and the vocative which is like the nominative. They are divided into six declensions : 1. The **a**-declension containing masculine and neuter nouns. 2. The **ō**-declension containing feminine nouns. 3. The **i**-declension containing masculine, feminine, and neuter nouns. 4. The **u**-declension containing masculine and feminine nouns. 5. The **n**- or weak declension containing masculine, feminine, and neuter nouns. 6. Nouns whose stems originally ended in a consonant other than ·n, and comprising masculine, feminine, and neuter nouns. The normal case-endings of the six declensions were :—

	1.	2.	3.	4.	5.	6.
Sing.						
N.	–, ·e, ·u(·o)	–, ·u(·o)	–, ·e	–, ·u(·o)	·a, ·e	–, ·u(·o)
A.	–, ·e, ·u(·o)	·e	–, ·e	–, ·u(·o)	·an, ·e	–, ·u(·o)
G.	·es	·e	·es, ·e	·a	·an	–, ·e, ·es
D.	·e	·e	·e	·a	·an	–, ·e
Plur.						
N.A.	·as, –, ·u(·o)	·a(·e)	·as, ·e(·a), ·u(·o)	·a	·an	–, ·e, ·as, ·ru(·o)
G.	·a	·a(·en·a)	·a	·a	·en·a	·a, ·ra
D.	·um	·um	·um	·um	·um	·um, ·rum

§ 286. In passing from OE. to ME. all the vowels were weakened to e, and final -m became -n. The result of this weakening was that many case-endings fell together, and that in some instances different declensions fell entirely together, e. g. the second and fourth declensions. After this weakening had taken place the -e of the nominative singular in the fifth declension supplanted the -en of the oblique cases of the singular. At a later stage final -e disappeared or ceased to be pronounced, cp. *EME. Gr.* §§ 139–42, 153–4. The case-endings of prime importance for the subsequent history of the inflexional endings in ME. and NE. are:—

1. The genitive singular ending -es which occurs in the first declension, the masculines and neuters of the third declension, and the neuters and nearly all of the masculines of the sixth declension. 2. The nominative and accusative plural ending -es from older -as which occurs in the masculines of the first and third declensions, and in some of the masculines of the sixth declension.

§ 287. In late OE. and early ME. the genitive ending -es gradually began to be extended to those declensions to which it did not originally belong, and similarly with the plural ending -es. During the ME. period the s-genitive and s-plural were gradually extended to all the declensions with the few exceptions which will be dealt with below. After the s-plural had been extended to the nominative and accusative of all declensions it gradually supplanted the old genitive and dative, that is to say the nominative and accusative came to be used for the genitive and dative. During the ME. period the ending -es became -ez (= NE. -iz, often written -is, -ys in late ME. and early NE., cp. *EME. Gr.* §§ 134, 143), and the vowel disappeared except after the sibilants s, z, š, ž, and then the -z remained after vowels and voiced consonants, but became -s after voiceless consonants, see §§ **158, 256.** The present rule for the retention or omission of the i from older e had become fully

established in the sixteenth century, although through the
influence of tradition we still continue to write ·es or ·s.

1. THE PLURAL OF NOUNS

§ 288. From what has been stated in the previous paragraphs we thus arrive at the following general rules for the
formation of the plural of nouns in NE. :—

1. Nouns ending in a voiced sound other than z, ž form
their plural in ·z, as *dogs* (dogz), *hills, lambs, pens; doves*
(davz), *apples, names, tongues; days* (deiz), *pianos, trees.*

2. Nouns ending in a voiceless sound other than s, š form
their plural in ·s, as *books* (buks), *cats; dukes* (djūks), *ropes.*

3. Nouns ending in one of the sibilants s, z, š, ž form
their plural in ·iz, as *glasses* (glāsiz), *cases, horses, palaces,
foxes; roses* (rouziz), *sizes; crutches* (kratšiz), *churches; ages*
(eidžiz), *bridges.*

§ 289. ME. native nouns ending in the voiceless spirants
f, s, þ regularly changed these to the corresponding voiced
spirants v, z (written s), and ð (written þ), cp. *EME. Gr.*
§§ 237, 327. But this rule has not been rigidly preserved in
the present standard language, because in some nouns the
plural is now formed direct from the singular, and in
others the singular has been formed direct from the
plural :—

1. Regular plurals are: *calves, halves, knives, leaves, lives,
loaves, shelves, thieves, wives, wolves,* &c. New plurals formed
direct from the singular are: *beliefs, dwarfs* beside earlier
NE. *dwarves, cliffs, hoofs* beside earlier NE. *hooves, roofs;*
French loan-words not being subject to the interchange
between f and v regularly have f, *chiefs, proofs, safes, strifes.
glove* (ME. glōf) with v from the old inflected forms. A few
nouns still have the regular beside the new plurals, as
scarves, wharves beside *scarfs, wharfs;* and *staves* beside *staffs*
with differentiated meaning.

2. *house*, plural *houses* (**hauziz**), is the only noun of this type which has preserved the old formation of the plural. All the other nouns now form their plural direct from the singular, as *glasses* (**glāsiz**), and similarly *asses, crosses, horses, lasses, masses*, &c.

3. Regular plurals are: *baths* (**bāðz**), *mouths, oaths, paths, wreaths*, &c., but in these and similar nouns the dialects generally have **þs** (*ED. Gr.* § 378). New plurals formed direct from the singular are: *births* (**bə̄þs**), *deaths, hearths, heaths, months. clothes* (**klouðz, klouz**) is the old plural of *cloth*, and *cloth* has now two plurals with differentiated meaning: **klǭþs** 'kinds of cloth', and **klǭðz** 'pieces of cloth' (§ 238).

§ 290. By referring to paragraph 170 it will be seen that the NE. ending **·y**, preceded by a consonant, arose from various ME. sources, and that one of those sources was **ie** which only became **y** when final, and not when followed by a consonant, whence the preservation of the **ie** in the writing of the NE. plural of nouns ending in **·y**, as *bodies, cities, flies, ladies*, &c. Nouns ending in **·y** preceded by the vowels **a, o** preserve the **y** in the plural, as *boys, days, plays, toys*, but when the preceding vowel (**e**) is unpronounced earlier NE. had the plural ending **·ies** beside **·eys**, as *journies, vallies* beside the present spelling *journeys, valleys*.

§ 291. In two words late ME. had double plurals which have now been differentiated in meaning, viz. *dice : dies, pens* (Chaucer **pens**) : *pennies* (§ 256), cp. also the double plural ending in *two sixpences* (ME. **sixpens**).

§ 292. The foreign nouns ending in **·o** follow the general rule of forming their plural in **·z**, written **·s**, as *pianos*, but the plural ending of a few such nouns is now written **·es** = **·z** after the analogy of native words like *foes, toes* where the **·e** was added to the singular in early NE. to indicate that the **o**, now pronounced **ou** (cp. § 76), was long, as *cargoes, heroes, potatoes, tomatoes*.

§ 293. In early OE. the monosyllabic neuter nouns with a long stem-syllable belonging to the a-declension had no nominative and accusative plural ending, but in late OE. and early ME. the plural ending -es was extended analogically to most of the nouns belonging to this category, cp. § 285 and *EME. Gr.* 331. A number of such nouns, especially those denoting collectivity, weight, measure, and time, generally remained uninflected in the plural in ME. and early NE., and *deer, sheep, swine*, and *pound* in *a five-pound note* still remain uninflected. Partly after the analogy of such words and partly for other reasons a considerable number of nouns, which were originally masculine, feminine, or neuter, now have or can have the singular and plural alike. This is especially the case with nouns denoting collectivity, mass, weight, measure, &c., as to shoot wild-fowl, grouse, snipe, &c.; to catch fish, mackerel, pike, salmon, &c.; nouns used collectively are often treated as plurals, as *cannon, cattle, cavalry, infantry, poultry*, &c.; nouns preceded by a numeral, as *three foot wide, ten stone weight, a two year old horse, three score*, and similarly *brace, bushel, couple, dozen, gross, hundredweight, mile, pair, pound, ton*, &c.; *fortnight* (OE. pl. niht) and a *twelvemonth* (OE. pl. mōnaþ) are old uninflected plurals preserved in compounds. For a full and learned treatment of nouns which have the singular and plural alike, see *On the origin and history of the unchanged plural in English*, by E. Ekwall, Lund, 1912.

§ 294. French loan-words ending in -s (-ss) often had the singular and plural alike in ME. and early NE., as *corpse* (ME. corps, cors), *verse* (ME. vers), *duchess, princess*, but they now form their plural in the ordinary manner.

§ 295. OE. had a large number of masculine and feminine nouns belonging to the n- or weak declension, and also three neuter nouns. Through the gradual spreading of the s-plural to this declension very few of the old plurals in -en remained in the standard language of the fourteenth century,

e. g. Chaucer has only **flęęn** 'fleas', **hǫsen, oxen, pēsen**
'peas', **ȳen** 'eyes'; in a few words he has weak and strong
forms side by side, as **aschen, bęęn, fǫǫn** 'foes', **tǫǫn** 'toes'
beside **asches, bęęs, fǫǫs, tǫǫs**, and in the old strong noun
schǫǫn beside **schǫǫs** 'shoes'. The only old weak noun
which now has the plural in -**en** is *ox*, pl. *oxen*, besides the
archaic form *hosen*; earlier NE. had a few other plurals in
-**en**, as *eyen, shoon, housen, peasen*, &c., and the dialects still
have quite a number of such plurals, see *ED. Gr.* § 379.

§ **296.** With the exception of the double plural forms
brethren and *children*, and some of the nouns which in OE.
formed their plural by umlaut, all the nouns belonging to
what is generally called the ' Minor Declensions ' took the
s-plural in ME., as *books* (ME. **bǫkes**, OE. **bēc**), *goats* (ME.
gǫtes, OE. **gǣt**), *nights* (ME. **niȝtes, niȝt**, OE. **niht**) ; *months*
(ME. **mǫn(e)þs**, OE. **mōnaþ**) ; *brothers* (ME. **brǭþęres**, OE.
brōþor, brōþru), *mothers* (ME. **mǫdres**, OE. **mōdor, mōdru**) ;
friends (ME. **frēndes**, OE. **frīend, frēond, -as**) ; *calves* (ME.
calves, OE. **cealfru**), *lambs* (ME. **lambes**, OE. **lambru**), see
EME. Gr. §§ 345-52. The only nouns preserved in NE.
which now form their plural by umlaut are : *feet* (OE. **fēt**):
foot, geese (OE. **gēs**) : *goose, lice* (OE. **lȳs**) : *louse, men* (OE.
men) : *man, women* (OE. **wimmen, wīfmen**) : *woman* (§ 133),
mice (OE. **mȳs**) : *mouse, teeth* (OE. **tēþ**) : *tooth*, and the archaic
biblical form *kine* (ME. **kȳn, kīen** with -**n**, -**en** from the
weak declension, OE. **cȳ**) beside the new formation *cows*
which does not occur until the early part of the seventeenth
century ; many of the dialects have preserved the old plural
kye (OE. **cȳ**). *brother* had three plural forms in ME., viz.
the ordinary plural **brǭþęres; brḗþer** formed after the
analogy of words like pl. **tēþ : tǫþ** ; and **brḗþęren** formed
from **brḗþer** with -**en** from the weak declension (*EME. Gr.*
§ 350) ; in NE. *brothers* and *brethren* have been differentiated
in meaning. *child* had two plural forms in ME., viz. **childre,
childer** (OE. **cildru**) beside **children** with -**n** from the weak

declension ; the former is now the general form in the
dialects of England, and the latter in the standard language.

§ 297. In a few words the old singular has come to be
regarded as a plural, as *alms* (ME. almess, OE. ælmesse),
eaves (OE. efes), *riches* (O.Fr. richesse). In the following
words the old singular came to be regarded as a plural, and
from which a new singular has been formed :—*asset* (ME.
assets), *burial* (OE. byrgels), *cherry* (OE. cieres, cires),
gentry (O.Fr. genterise), *girdle* (OE. gyrdels), *pea* (OE. pise,
piosa), *riddle* (OE. rædels), *shuttle* (OE. scytels). On the
other hand a few old plurals have come to be regarded as
singulars, as *amends* (O.Fr. amende), *chess* (O.Fr. esches,
pl. of eschec 'king'), *means* (ME. mẹne, O.Fr. meien), *news*
(probably a translation of Fr. nouvelles) ; *bellows, gallows*
beside the double plurals *bellowses, gallowses* which are now
obsolete in the standard language, but still very common in
the dialects ; *bodice* an old plural of *body* beside the new
plural *bodies* with differentiated meaning, *invoice* (Fr. envois)
beside the new plural *invoices, quince* (pl. of ME. quine),
truce (ME. trew(e)s), cp. § 240.

2. THE GENDER OF NOUNS

§ 298. In OE. the gender of nouns did not depend upon
their meaning as in NE. ; thus mūþ 'mouth' was masculine,
nosu 'nose' feminine, and ēage 'eye' neuter; wīfman
(wimman) 'woman' was masculine, wīf and mægden
'maiden' neuter. The gender of a noun depended in a great
measure upon the declension to which it belonged or upon
the suffix which it contained ; thus all nouns which formed
their plural in ·as were masculine, all nouns belonging to
the ō-declension were feminine, all nouns which formed
their plural in ·u (·o) were neuter, and so also were generally
the nouns which had no special plural ending, all nouns
whose singular ended in ·a were masculine. And in like

manner nouns containing the suffixes ‑aþ(‑oþ), ‑dōm, ‑els,
‑ere, ‑hād, ‑ing, ‑ling, and ‑scipe were masculine; those
containing the suffixes ‑en (= OHG. ‑in), ‑estre, ‑nes(s),
‑ræden, ‑þo (‑þ), ‑ung, and ‑wist were feminine; and those
containing the suffixes ‑en (= Goth. ‑ein), ‑et(t), ‑incel,
and ‑lāc were neuter.

§ **299.** When the gender of nouns depends upon the
declension to which they belong or upon the suffix which
they contain, such nouns are said to have grammatical
gender. During the ME. period grammatical gender in
nouns disappeared almost entirely. This loss of grammatical
gender did not take place concurrently in all the dialects.
The process began much earlier in the northern than in the
other dialects. Even in the OE. period both the gender
and declension of nouns fluctuated considerably in the
Northumbrian as compared with the other dialects. It had
almost entirely disappeared in the Midland dialects by the
end of the twelfth or early part of the thirteenth century,
in the south-western dialects by the middle of the thirteenth
century, and in the south-eastern dialects, including Kentish,
in the latter part of the fourteenth century, so that by about
the end of the fourteenth century grammatical gender had
become almost entirely lost in all the dialects. This loss of
grammatical gender in nouns was due to various causes :—
1. The gradual breaking up of the OE. system of declensions
through the weakening of all the vowels in unaccented
syllables to e and in part to the eventual loss of the e in
writing or pronunciation. 2. The loss of inflexions in the
definite article, adjectives, and demonstrative pronouns,
which also led to the confusion between masculine and
feminine suffixes. 3. The loss of the association of gender
with suffixes. The result of all these changes was that
natural gender came to be substituted for grammatical
gender, so that in NE. we have the general rule that nouns
denoting the male sex of persons or animals are masculine,

those denoting the female sex of persons or animals are feminine, and those denoting inanimate objects or abstract ideas are neuter. But we still have a kind of specious grammatical gender in personified words, such as *sun* (masculine) and *moon* (feminine), reversing the OE. gender in these words. This personification of inanimate objects is very common in all the dialects.

3. THE CASES OF NOUNS

§ **300.** By referring to paragraph **287** it will be seen that with few exceptions the ending of the genitive singular and of the whole of the plural had become alike in pronunciation during the ME. period, viz. ·**es** (= ·**iz**) after sibilants, ·**s** (= ·**z**) after vowels and other voiced consonants, and ·**s** (= ·**s**) after other voiceless consonants. And this is still the general rule in the standard language of the present day, although we now distinguish them in writing by the orthographical device of writing ·'**s** for the genitive singular, ·**s**' for the genitive plural, and ·**s** for the ordinary plural, as *prince's, princes', princes ; judge's, judges', judges ; king's, kings', kings ; aunt's, aunts', aunts ;* but *man's,* pl. *men's.*

§ **301.** Genitives without ·(**e**)**s** in those types of nouns which did not have it in OE. are occasionally found throughout the ME. period, and a few such genitives are still preserved in NE., as *Friday, Lady day* beside *Thursday, the Lord's day ; bridegroom* beside *bridesmaid.*

§ **302.** During the ME. period the preposition **of** came to be used before the nominative and accusative singular to express the genitival relationship, and was used at first with those nouns which did not naturally have ·**es** in the genitive singular. Apart from a few isolated phrases like *out of harm's way* the genitive is now restricted to personal beings, and in other cases the preposition *of* is used.

§ **303.** After masculine nouns, especially proper names,

the possessive pronoun *his* was occasionally used in OE.
instead of the ordinary genitive ending -es. This mode of
expressing the genitive became very common from about
1400 to the middle of the eighteenth century, as ' we ȝesawon
Enac his cynryn' (Ælfric, *c.* 1000); 'amang þe king his
cnihtes' (Laȝamon, *c.* 1205); 'to play with a chyld his
brouch'(Trevisa, *c.* 1387); 'to forsake syr Sathanus his werkus
everychon' (Audelay, *c.* 1426); 'themperor Augustus his
daughter' (Spenser, 1579); 'Sejanus his Fall', the title of
one of Ben Jonson's plays; 'and this we beg for Jesus Christ
his sake' (Prayer Book, 1662); 'King Edward the Fourth,
his death' (Walpole, 1767); for other early examples, see
N. E. D. sub *his*. And in like manner the possessive pronoun
for *her* was used very early after feminine nouns or nouns
referring to females as a substitute for the genitive ending,
as ' Nilus seo ea hire æwielme is neh þæm clife' (K. Ælfred,
Orosius, c. 893); 'Here begynnyth the wyf of bathe hire
tale' (Camb. MS. of Chaucer, *c.* 1435); 'Elizabeth Holland
her howse, newlie made in Suffolk' (*State Papers*, 1546);
'presuming on the Queen her private practice' (Fuller, 1655),
see *N. E. D.* sub *her*. The plural **hiera** 'their' also occurs in
OE. as a substitute for the genitive ending, as ' Affrica and
Asia hiera landȝemircu onginnaþ of Alexandria' (K. Ælfred,
Orosius, c. 893). *their* began to be used as a substitute for
the genitive plural ending in the sixteenth century, as
'Vntyll the vtopians their creditours demaunde it'
(Robinson's translation of More's *Utopia*, 1551); 'The House
of Lords their proceedings in petitioning the King' (Pepys,
Diary, 1667), see *N. E. D.* sub *their*. The *his, her, their* are
still often written by semi-educated persons on the fly-leaf
of books, especially of family Bibles, &c. The origin of the
use of *his, her, their* after nouns as a substitute for the
genitive ending is not certain. The usual explanation is
that it originally started out from the genitive singular
ending (-es) of nouns ending in a sibilant, where the -es,

later written ·is, ·ys (= ·iz), came to be regarded as the un-accented form of the possessive pronoun *his* (= iz), and then from nouns of this type it was extended to those which did not end in a sibilant. And then after the analogy of this construction *her, their* came to be similarly used. From the OE. examples given above it will be seen that this explana-tion can hardly be the right one, because the construction with the pronouns for *her, their* occurs even earlier than with *his.*

§ 304. In late ME. and early NE. the genitive ending was often omitted in nouns ending in a sibilant, especially in those denoting animate objects, e. g. in Shakespeare : 'Ceres blessing' (*Temp.* IV. i. l. 117) ; 'I did command your Highness letters' (*Lear,* II. iv, l. 29) ; 'our mistress ornaments are chaste' (*Lucrece,* l. 322). From the seventeenth century onwards the genitive of such nouns has generally been expressed either by ' or 's, the former being generally used in polysyllabic words, and the latter in monosyllabic and dissyllabic words, but in both types the pronunciation is the same, as *Augustus' chariot, Socrates' wife ; James's, judge's, justice's ;* but the old pronunciation has been preserved in a few isolated phrases like *for conscience, goodness,* or *Jesus sake,* beside *for God's sake.*

§ 305. In ME. and also until well on into the NE. period nouns ending in ·f (written ·f, ·fe) regularly changed the f into v in the inflected forms (cp. *EME. Gr.* §§ 237, 327), but except in the isolated forms *calveshead, calvesfoot* we now form the genitive singular direct from the uninflected form, as *calf's, thief's, wife's, wolf's* : gen. plural *calves', thieves', wives', wolves'.*

CHAPTER VI

ADJECTIVES

1. THE INFLEXION OF ADJECTIVES

§ 306. OE. adjectives were declined according to the strong or weak declension (*EOE. Gr.* § 269), and had eleven different endings for expressing the various numbers, genders, and cases. After these endings had been weakened down in late OE. and early ME., the form of the masculine nominative singular had become generalized for the whole of the singular, and the form of the nominative accusative plural had become generalized for the whole of the plural before the end of the first half of the thirteenth century, so that in standard ME. the following was the general scheme for the inflexion of adjectives :—

(*a*) Monosyllabic adjectives ending in a consonant remained uninflected throughout the singular, and had ·e throughout the plural, as brǭd ' broad ', glad, pl. brǭde, glade.

(*b*) Adjectives which ended in a vowel in OE. or which came to end in a vowel in ME. remained uninflected throughout the singular and plural.

(*c*) Dissyllabic adjectives including past participles ending in a consonant remained uninflected throughout the singular and plural through the loss of the old final ·e in the plural, as bitter, litel, bounden, cursed, &c., see *EME. Gr.* § 142. Earlier NE. still preserved the old distinction between the singular and plural in *enough* (ME. inough, OE. genōh), pl. *enow* (ME. inowe, OE. genōga, ·e), and in the dialects it has been preserved down to the present day.

§ 307. In the colloquial language the final ·e had ceased to be pronounced in all forms before the end of the four-

teenth century, but in poetry it often continued to be pronounced until the fifteenth century, and then later it also
generally disappeared in writing just as it did with nouns.
This entire loss of inflexional endings in adjectives is one of
the most marked characteristics of the English language as
compared with any other of the Germanic languages. See
EME. Gr. §§ 353–5.

2. THE COMPARISON OF ADJECTIVES

§ 308. In OE. the comparative and superlative were
declined according to the weak declension except that the
neuter nominative accusative singular had the strong beside
the weak form in the superlative, but in ME. they came to
remain uninflected just as they still are in NE.   In OE. the
comparative had or had not umlaut in the stem-syllable
according as the ending ·ra corresponded to Germanic ·izŏ
or ·ōzŏ, and similarly in the superlative ·est = Germanic
·ist· beside ·ost = Germanic ·ōst·, see *EOE. Gr.* § 291, as
eald ' old ', ieldra, ieldest; grēat ' great ', grīetra, grīetest;
lang ' long ', lengra, lengest; but earm ' poor ', earmra,
earmost; glæd ' glad ', glædra, gladost; lēof ' dear ',
lēofra, lēofost.   The ·ra and ·ost regularly became ·re
(·ere) and ·est in late OE. and early ME. (*EME. Gr.* §§ 148–9),
so that in ME. the comparative was generally formed by
means of ·re (·ere), later ·(e)r, and the superlative by ·(e)st,
as harder, hardest : hard ; clēner, clēnest : clēne ' clean '.
The ·(e)r, ·(e)st have been regularly preserved in NE. for the
formation of the comparative and superlative, as *harder,
hardest : hard ; wiser, wisest : wise ; narrower, narrowest :
narrow ; simpler, simplest : simple.*   In monosyllabic adjectives
ending in a single consonant preceded by a short vowel the
consonant was doubled in the comparative and superlative
in late ME. in order to indicate that the stem-vowel was
short.   This rule has also been preserved in NE., as *gladder,*

gladdest : glad ; thinner, thinnest : thin.   On the -i- in forms
like *happier, happiest : happy ; holier, holiest : holy,* see § 170.
The comparative and superlative *farther, farthest : far* are
new formations with -th- from *further, furthest ;* the old
forms *farrer, farrest* were common in the standard language
down to the seventeenth century, as they still are in the
dialects.

§ 309. In OE. and ME. a certain number of adjectives
had umlaut in the comparative and superlative (§ 308), but
in the language of the present day only scanty fragments
have been preserved, viz. *elder, eldest* with differentiated
meaning beside the new formations *older, oldest ; elder* was
still sometimes used in the seventeenth century with its old
meaning.   *near* (ME. **nẹre**, OE. **nēahra, nēarra**) is properly
the comparative of *nigh* (ME. **nīȝ**), and is now used as the
positive to which a new comparative *nearer* has been formed,
and a superlative *nearest* beside the old superlative *next* (OE.
nīehst) ; *near* with its old comparative meaning was still
occasionally used in the seventeenth century.   Forms like
gretter (OE. **grīetra**), *grettest* (OE. **grīetest**) : *great* (OE.
grēat) ; *lenger, lengest : long ; strenger, strengest : strong,* beside
the new formations *greater, greatest ; longer, longest ; stronger,
strongest,* are also occasionally found in the sixteenth century.

§ 310. In early ME. long vowels were regularly shortened
in the comparative, and then the short vowel was often
extended to the superlative, and sometimes even to the
positive, as **gretter, grettest : grẹt** 'great'; **hotter, hottest :
hǫt** 'hot'; **latter, last : lāte** 'late'; **stiffer, stiffest : stīf**
'stiff', but in later ME. the comparative and superlative
were generally formed direct from the positive as they still
are in NE., as *greater, greatest : great ; later, latest : late,* beside
the old forms *latter, last* with differentiated meaning, see
EME. Gr. §§ 50, 359.   On shortened forms like *hot, red,
stiff,* &c., see §§ 95–100.

§ 311. A few adjectives in NE. as in ME. and OE. form

their comparatives and superlatives from a different root
than the positive, but being regularly developed from the
corresponding ME. forms they require no special comment:
—*better, best : good ; worse* beside the archaic double comparative *worser, worst : bad, evil, ill ; more, most : much ; less*
beside the double comparative *lesser, least : little.* Early NE.
also had *badder, baddest : bad.*

§ 312. During the ME. period the comparative and superlative of adjectives began to be formed by placing the
adverbs *more, most* before the simple adjective. This mode
of forming the comparative and superlative was at first used
irrespectively of the length of the adjective. During the
earlier NE. period the present rule for forming the comparative and superlative of monosyllabic adjectives, and of
adjectives of more than two syllables, became fairly well
established, viz. the former taking the suffixes *-er, -est,* and
the latter having *more, most* placed before them. For dissyllabic adjectives no hard and fast rule has been established
beyond that those ending in *-er, -le, -ow,* and *-y* have *-er, -est,*
and those ending in *-ed, -ful, -ing, -ish, -ive,* and *-st* have
more, most. Of the other dissyllabic adjectives custom has
gradually settled quite arbitrarily which of them take *-er,*
-est, and which of them take *more, most.* In earlier NE. it
was not uncommon to add *more, most* pleonastically to the
comparative and superlative, as *more better, best ; more harder,*
hardest, cp. also *most unkindest cut of all* (Shakespeare). Such
forms are still very common in the dialects, and are generally
used to express special emphasis.

§ 313. In a certain number of OE. words the comparative
was originally formed from an adverb or a preposition, with
a superlative in ·um·, ·uma, cp. Lat. optimus 'best', sum-
mus 'highest'. The simple superlative suffix was preserved
in OE. forma = Goth. fruma, ME. þe forme 'the first',
from which was formed in ME. the new comparative former.
In prehistoric OE., as in Goth., to ·um· was added the

ordinary superlative suffix -ist-, which gave rise to the
double superlative suffix -umist-, as Goth. frumists 'first',
hindumists 'hindmost'. In OE. -umist- regularly became
-ymist-, later -imest-, -emest-, -mest-, as inne 'within',
innera, innemest, see *EOE. Gr.* § 293. In ME. the ending
-mest came to be associated with mḛst, mǭst 'most',
whence such ME. forms as formḛst, formǭst beside formest
'foremost', inmǭst, innermǭst, utmǭst, uttermǭst, &c.,
and NE. forms like *foremost, hindmost, inmost, upmost, outmost*
beside the older form *utmost* with differentiated meaning;
and late new formations like *endmost, topmost*, &c.; with
-*most* added to OE. words ending in -*er*, as *aftermost, under-
most;* and to original comparatives in -*er*, as *bettermost,
furthermost, innermost, lattermost, lowermost, nearmost, upper-
most, outermost* beside the older form *uttermost* with differentiated meaning.

3. NUMERALS

A. Cardinal Numerals.

§ 314. Apart from the regular phonological changes the
cardinal numerals have undergone few changes in passing
from ME. to NE. The following are the most important
changes to be noted:—

ME. ǭn (OE. ān), but ǭ before words beginning with
a consonant, was used as a numeral; and the early shortened
form an (*EME. Gr.* § 101), but a before words beginning
with a consonant, was used as the indefinite article. In
NE. *one,* pronounced wan (§ 76, note 1), beside the normally
developed form in *alone, atone, only,* is used both before
words beginning with a vowel and with a consonant. The
indefinite article is now pronounced æn beside the unaccented
form ən before words beginning with a vowel, and ei beside
the unaccented form ə before words beginning with a consonant. NE. *two,* pronounced tū (§§ 75, 3, 181), and the

isolated form *twain* (§ 82) are regularly developed from ME.
twǭ, twein(e) = the OE. masculine form twēgen. The
shortened form ten beside the normal form tēne existed
already in ME. (cp. *EME. Gr.* § 92, 1), and the normally
developed form tēne has been regularly preserved in the
NE. cardinals *thirteen* to *nineteen*. The cardinals *four* to
nineteen could be inflected in ME. when they stood after the
noun or were used alone. Two of these inflected forms
have been generalized in NE., viz. *five* (ME. fīf, fīve), and
twelve (ME. twelf, twelve). In OE. the decades, hundred
and þūsend, were nouns and governed the genitive case. In
ME. they were almost exclusively used as adjectives as in
NE. In NE. they can, however, be used as nouns when not
preceded by another cardinal numeral, as in *the seventies,
hundreds or thousands of people were there.*

B. Ordinal Numerals.

§ 315. In passing from ME. to NE. most of the ordinal
numerals have undergone analogical changes besides the
regular phonological changes. Some of these analogical
changes began to take place during the ME. period (cp.
EME. Gr. § 365). From about the end of the thirteenth
century onwards the French form secounde came to be
used beside the English form ǭþer. In NE. the old meaning
of *other* has been preserved in the phrase *every other day.*
From fēo(we)rþa ' fourth ' onwards the suffix -þa (ME. -þe)
was used in OE. after voiced sounds, and -ta (ME. -te) after
voiceless sounds for the formation of ordinals from cardinals,
and an -n regularly disappeared before the -þa, as seofoþa
(ME. sevefþe) formed from seofon (ME. seven), beside
fīfta, siexta, en(d)le(o)fta, twelfta = ME. fifte, sixte,
ellefte, twelfte. We now form all the ordinals from *fourth*
onwards by the addition of -th to the corresponding cardinal,
as *fifth, sixth, seventh, tenth, eleventh, twelfth, thirteenth,* &c.,

but in earlier NE. the forms *fift*, *sixt*, *twelft* were still
common, e. g. in the titles of two of Shakespeare's plays we
have: 'The Life of King Henry the Fift'; 'King Henry
the Sixt'. In many dialects the ·t-forms have been extended
to all ordinals after *third*, cp. *ED. Gr.* § 400. In *eighth*
(ME. eiȝteþe, OE. eahtoþa) th is now written for older **tth**;
eighth has been the common spelling since the seventeenth
century, but from the thirteenth down to the nineteenth
century the ordinal form is often identical with that of the
cardinal. In ME. the decades of the cardinals ended in ·i,
and those of the ordinals in ·iþe, as **twenti, twentiþe**, where
the final ·i is now regularly written ·y (cp. § 170), but in
earlier NE. it was also often written ·ie. From the sixteenth
century onwards the ordinals of this type have been formed
from the corresponding cardinals with this spelling ·ie,
whence the present spelling *twentieth*, *thirtieth*, &c., which
are now pronounced **twenti·iþ, þɔti·iþ**, &c., through the
influence of the spelling. ME. **hundred** and **þousend** had
no ordinal forms just as in OE., so that NE. *hundredth* and
thousandth are new formations.

CHAPTER VII

PRONOUNS

1. PERSONAL

§ 316. The old accusative forms **mec, þec, ūsic, ēowic** of
the first and second persons singular and plural had been
supplanted by the old dative forms **mě, þě, ūs, ēow** ' you '
in late OE., so that the old datives were used to express
both cases in ME. also. And in ME. the old accusative
forms of the masculine and feminine and the old accusative

plural forms of the third person were supplanted by the old
dative forms. The old genitives (OE. mīn, þīn, pl. ūre,
ēower ; his, hiere (hire), pl. hiera, hira, heora) lost their
genitival meaning in fairly early ME. except in isolated
phrases like ūre nǭn 'none of us ', ūre aller ' of all of us '.
The old genitival meaning came to be expressed by the
preposition *of* and the dative of the personal pronouns.
The old dual forms nom. wit, ʒit ; acc. dat. unc, inc ; gen.
uncer, incer gradually disappeared in the latter half of the
thirteenth century (*EME. Gr.* § 371). In OE. and ME.
most of the personal pronouns had accented beside unaccented forms, and this distinction has been preserved in
NE., but many of the present accented forms correspond to
the ME. unaccented forms from which new unaccented
forms have been made, see below.

A. The First and Second Persons.

§ 317. Singular: The ME. accented form was ich, but
also ic until the beginning of the thirteenth century, and
the unaccented form was i which is the common form in
Chaucer both for the accented and the unaccented form.
He rarely used ich. From i a new accented form ī was
formed in late ME. or early NE., which has regularly
become ai (§ 73) written *I*, and is now used for both the
accented and the unaccented form, but the old unaccented
form i has been preserved in many of the modern dialects in
interrogative and subordinate sentences. The old accented
form ich was in use throughout the ME. period in the
southern and south-western dialects. The forms ich (uch,
utchy) along with the contracted forms ch'am, &c., were
formerly used in the modern dialects of Dor., Som., and
Dev., and these forms are still used by old people in a small
district of Som. close to Yeovil on the borders of Dor.
Contracted forms were also common in the Elizabethan

dramatists in the speech of rustics, as in *King Lear*, *chill*
'I will', *chud* 'I would'. Accusative and dative ME. mę
beside unaccented me = NE. mī (§ 71) beside mi.

ME. nom. þū, written þou, beside the unaccented form þu,
acc. dat. þě. þū, þę regularly became ðau (§ 77), ðī (§ 71)
in early NE., written *thou, thee*. In the Elizabethan period
thee was often used for *thou*, just as it still is among Quakers.
thou and *thee* are used in the Bible, in liturgical language,
and in poetry, but in the ordinary standard language they
became obsolete in the eighteenth century. They have,
however, been preserved in their various dialect forms in
most of the dialects of England, to express familiarity or
contempt, but they cannot be used to a superior without
conveying the idea of impertinence. The ME. unaccented
form with elision of the vowel was also common in earlier
NE., as *th'art*. Plural forms began to be used beside the
old singular forms at an early period. From the thirteenth
century onwards ӡē̆ (yĕ) began to be used for þou as the
pronoun of respect in addressing a superior, and in the
form ī (generally written ee) it has survived in most of the
south Midland and southern dialects down to the present
day. During the fourteenth century you also came to be
used for both þou and þē, and then in the fifteenth century
yē also came to be used for the accusative þē and you.

§ 318. Plural: Nom. ME. wę beside unaccented we =
NE. wī beside wi written *we* ; acc. dat. ME. ūs written ous
beside unaccented us. The accented form ous, which would
have become *aus in pronunciation (§ 77), has not been
preserved in NE. ; it was supplanted by the old unaccented
form us (= NE. as § 67) in late ME. or early NE., and
from this a new unaccented form əs, written *us*, has been
made.

Nom. ME. ӡę̄ (yę̄) beside unaccented ӡĕ (yĕ) = NE. yī
beside yĭ; acc. dat. ME. ӡọu (yọu) = yū (*EME. Gr.* § 112,
note 1) beside unaccented ӡŭ (yŭ). The accented form yọu,

which would have become *yaú written *you* (§ 77), has not
been preserved in NE. ; it was supplanted by the lengthened
form of yŭ after the time when ME. ū became diphthongized
in early NE., and then from this a new unaccented yŭ,
written *you*, was made. *you* began to be used for *ye* so early
as the fourteenth century, and conversely *ye* began to be
used for *you* in the fifteenth century, although the old
distinction between the nom. and acc. dat. was generally
preserved until about the middle of the sixteenth century.
The old distinction between them is regularly preserved in
the 1611 edition of the Bible, but in Shakespeare they are
used indiscriminately without any distinction of case or
number. Except in poetry *ye* became extinct in the standard
language in the second half of the seventeenth century. It
is still often used in poetry, and in many of the dialects it is
still used for both the nom. and acc. dat.

B. The Third Person.

§ 319. Masculine singular: Nom. ME. hē beside unaccented hĕ = NE. hī (§ 71) beside hi, i; ME. had also the
unaccented forms ha, a (still preserved in the modern dialects
in the form ə) which are still found in the Elizabethan
dramatists, as 'A' shall not tread on me', *Coriolanus* v. iii,
l. 127. ME. acc. dat. him = NE. *him* beside unaccented
him, im. The OE. acc. hine had become extinct in standard
ME. by the early part of the fourteenth century, but it is
still in common use in the modern dialects of the south
Midland, southern, and south-western counties in the form
ən, generally written en, un, and is used of inanimate as well
as of animate objects.

§ 320. Feminine singular: In ME. the nominative was
expressed by several different forms in the various dialects
(see *EME. Gr.* § 375), but the east Midland form schē
gradually became the standard form during the ME. period,
which has regularly become NE. šī (§ 71) beside unaccented

ši written *she.* ME. acc. dat. **hir(e)** beside **her(e)**, often
written *hir* (*hur*) in early NE., has regularly become **hɜ**
beside unaccented **hə, ə,** written *her,* in the present standard
language, see §§ 112, 175.

§ 321. Neuter singular: ME. nom. acc. **hit** beside unaccented **it**; it began to appear so early as the twelfth
century, and in the fifteenth century supplanted the old
accented form in the standard language. From the old unaccented form a new unaccented form **t** was formed in early
NE., as *'tis* ' it is '. The old accented form **hit** is still used
in the modern dialects of Scotland and Northumberland.
The ME. dat. **him** has been supplanted by the acc. **it**
in NE.

§ 322. Plural: The ME. plural forms were partly of
native and partly of Scandinavian origin, viz. **h**-forms
beside **þ**-forms (see *EME. Gr.* § 376), but before the end
of the ME. period the **h**-forms had generally been ousted by
the **þ**-forms, so that in late ME. we have nom. **þei (þey)** =
NE. **ðei** beside unaccented **ðe** (§ 175) written *they* ; acc. dat.
þeim (þeym) beside unaccented **þem**. The old accented acc.
dat. form was often used until well on into the sixteenth
century, and then became obsolete. The old unaccented
form has now become the accented form, and from it a new
unaccented form **ðəm**, written *them,* has been made. An old
unaccented **h**-form (ME. **hem**, OE. **him, hiom, heom**) has
been preserved in the colloquial standard language and the
dialects in the form **əm** generally written *'em.*

2. REFLEXIVE

§ 323. When the personal pronouns were used reflexively
in OE. the word **self** (declined strong and weak) was often
added to emphasize them, as **ic self** beside **ic selfa**, acc.
mec selfne, gen. **mīn selfes**, dat. **mě selfum,** and similarly
hě self beside **hě selfa**, acc. **hine selfne**, dat. **him selfum** =
ME. **him selfen**, NE. *himself* ; or with the dative of the

personal pronoun prefixed to the nominative **self,** as **ic mĕ
self,** pl. **wĕ ūs selfe,** and similarly in early ME. From the
early part of the thirteenth century new forms began to
appear. In the first and second persons singular the form
self came to be regarded as a noun and then the possessive
pronoun was substituted for the dative of the personal pronoun, as **mī self, þī self** beside older **mĕ self, þĕ self,** and
then in the early part of the fourteenth century this new
formation was extended to the plural also, as **our(e) self(e),**
selve(n); ȝour(e) self(e), selve(n) beside older **wĕ ūs
selve(n); ȝĕ ȝou selve(n).** And then towards the end of
the fifteenth century the present s-plurals *ourselves, yourselves*
came into existence and eventually became the standard
forms. This change in the formation of the reflexive pronouns did not take place in the third person so early as in
the first and second persons. **his selve(n), þeir selve(n)**
beside older **hem selve(n), þem selve(n)** did not begin to
appear until the first half of the fourteenth century. The
new formations **his selve(n),þeir(e) selve(n)** disappeared in
the standard language about the end of the fifteenth century,
but they have remained in the dialects down to the present
day. The s-plural *themselves* came into existence about 1500
and during the first half of the sixteenth century became the
standard form. From the form alone it cannot be determined whether the **hire** in ME. **hire self** and the *her* in
NE. *herself* represent the old dat. acc. or the old possessive.
The present NE. forms accordingly are: *myself, (thyself),*
himself, herself, itself, pl. *ourselves, yourselves, themselves.*
Beside the accented forms we also have in the standard
colloquial language the unaccented forms **mĭself, həself**
(**əself, əself**), **ðəmselvz.**

§ 324. In ME. as in OE. the reflexive pronouns were often
expressed simply by the acc. dat. forms of the personal pronouns, and this manner of expressing them was also common
in earlier NE., as it still is in the modern dialects.

3. POSSESSIVE

§ 325. In OE. and early ME. the possessive pronouns
mīn, þīn, and ūre ' our ' were declined in the singular and
plural, all genders, like an ordinary strong adjective, but
before the end of the ME. period they had become in-
declinable ; the other possessive pronouns were expressed
by the genitive of the personal pronouns, see *EME. Gr.*
§ 378. In NE. as in ME. we have to distinguish between
the conjunctive and disjunctive use of the possessive pronouns.

A. CONJUNCTIVE.

§ 326. From the twelfth century onwards the ME. conjunctive forms mīn, þīn were used before a following word
beginning with a vowel, and mī, þī when the next word
began with a consonant, but at that early period the -n was
retained in the oblique cases, in the plural, and when the
pronoun followed the noun. From the end of the sixteenth
century the forms *my* and *thy* came to be used also before
words beginning with a vowel or h, although it was not
consistently carried out by Shakespeare and his contemporaries. In the seventeenth century there was much
fluctuation in the use of *my, mine ; thy, thine,* but apart
from poetical licences *my, thy* have been the ordinary forms
in prose since the latter part of the seventeenth century.
The unaccented form mĭ is now seldom used except in the
combinations *milord, milady.* ME. his, hir(e), her(e) = NE.
his (hiz, unaccented iz), *her* (hə̄, unaccented hə, ə). The old
neuter form *his* was preserved down to the seventeenth
century, and is common in the Bible, as ' And the earth
brought forth grass, and herb yielding seed after his kind ',
Genesis i. 12. Beside this old form *his* the new form hit
beside it came to be used in the fourteenth century,

especially in the west Midland dialects, and remained in
common use until the early part of the seventeenth century,
cp. 'The hedge-sparrow fed the cuckoo so long, that it had
it head bit off by it young', *King Lear*, i. iv, ll. 234-5, and
in the northern and most of the Midland dialects it has
remained down to the present day. Towards the end of
the sixteenth century from *it* a new form *its* was formed with
s from *his*. This form *its* does not occur in the 1611 edition
of the Bible, although in the modern reprint of this edition
its has been substituted for *his*, cp. *Leviticus* xxv. 5 ; *its* is
also not found in Spenser, rarely in Shakespeare and Bacon,
but more frequently in Milton, and is common in Dryden.

ME. our(e), ȝour(e) = NE. *our, your* with uə(ǫ) for auə
in pronunciation through the influence of *you* (§ 318). In
early ME. *their* was expressed by þeir (ON. þeir(r)a) in the
northern dialects, and by her(e), hir(e) in the Midland and
southern dialects. By the latter half of the fifteenth century
þeir had spread to all the dialects, whence NE. *their*.

B. DISJUNCTIVE.

§ 327. In OE. and early ME. the disjunctive and the
conjunctive possessive pronouns were alike in form. The
differentiation in form first began to appear in the northern
dialects towards the end of the thirteenth century, and had
gradually spread to all the dialects by about 1500, although
in some southern writers the old forms are found until well
on into the seventeenth century.

§ 328. The ME. disjunctive forms were : mīn, þīn, his ;
the possessive pronouns ending in ·r(e) took a new genitive
ending ·es, as hires (heres), ūres (oures), ȝǫures, heres
(þeires). These new formations began to appear in the
northern dialects towards the end of the thirteenth century,
whence they gradually spread to the Midland dialects in the
latter part of the fourteenth century. From these forms are

regularly developed the NE. forms *mine, thine, his, hers, ours, yours, theirs*. The conjunctive form *its* is not used disjunctively.

4. DEMONSTRATIVE

§ 329. The OE. simple demonstrative masc. sě, fem. sēo, neut. þæt was used to express the definite article *the* and the demonstrative *that*. It was declined in the singular and plural, all genders, and had ten different forms for expressing the various numbers, genders, and cases. s-forms only occurred in the masculine and feminine nominative singular, all the other forms began with þ-, see *EME. Gr.* § 380. For sě, sēo a new nominative þě was formed partly in late OE. and partly in early ME. with þ- from the inflected forms. The old inflected forms began to be lost from about the middle of the twelfth century, so that already in early ME. the uninflected form þě had come to be used as the definite article for all cases and genders of the singular. And before Chaucer's time this uninflected form þě had also come to be used as the definite article for all cases and genders of the plural as well. In NE. þě has regularly become ðī (§ 71) beside unaccented ði before words beginning with a vowel, and ðə before words beginning with a consonant. After þě had become exclusively used as the definite article the old neuter form þat came to be used exclusively as a demonstrative pronoun with the plural þǭ (OE. þā), just as we find them so used in Chaucer and his contemporaries. In early NE. þǭ was completely supplanted by þǭs (= OE. þās), which was originally the plural of the OE. word for *this*, whence NE. *that*, pl. *those*. It should be noted that the old instrumental singular OE. þȳ has been preserved in NE. in the form *the* before comparatives, as *the more the merrier, the sooner the better*, and that the old ending of the neuter of the definite article survives in *tone* (OE. þæt ān), and *tother* (OE. þæt ōþer) in all the modern dialects.

§ **330.** The OE. forms for *this*, plural *these* were : sing. masc. þĕs, fem. þīos (þēos), neut. þis, pl. þās for all genders. This pronoun had nine different forms for expressing the various numbers, genders, and cases, see *EME. Gr.* §§ 382–3. The late OE. weakened inflected forms were preserved in early ME., but during the ME. period they gradually disappeared, so that by the time of Chaucer the old neuter form þis had come to be used for all cases and genders of the singular. Already in early ME. the old plural form þǭs (OE. þās) came to be used for all cases of the plural, but before the time of Chaucer this form had been supplanted by the new formation þēse, which was formed from the old nominative singular þēs (= OE. masc. þĕs, fem. þēos) by the addition of ·e after the analogy of the adjectival plural in ·e (§ 306). Then þǭs came to be used exclusively as the plural of þat. Whence NE. *that*, pl. *those ; this*, pl. *these*.

5. RELATIVE

§ **331.** In OE. the relative pronoun was expressed by the relative particle þe alone or in combination with the personal or the simple demonstrative pronoun, and for the third person also by the simple demonstrative pronoun alone, see *EOE. Gr.* § 312. This manner of expressing the relative pronoun became obsolete in early ME. From the thirteenth century onwards it was generally expressed by the uninflected old demonstrative neuter þat for the singular and plural of all genders, or by which (pl. which(e)), þe which, and the oblique forms whǭs (whǭs), whǭm (whǭm) of the interrogative for the genitive and dative. The nominative form *who* did not come into common use until the sixteenth century. At first it did not always relate to persons, but could also relate to animals and inanimate objects, but now *who* and *whom* relate only to persons, whereas *whose* can

relate to inanimate objects as well as to persons. *which* now
relates to neuter antecedents, but formerly it could relate to
masculine and feminine antecedents, cp. 'Our Father, which
art in heaven'. In ME. as also in NE. *that* relates to persons
and inanimate objects, but it cannot now be combined with
a preposition, as it could be formerly, cp. 'I am possess'd of
that is mine', *T. Andronicus*, I, l. 408. The old interrogative
neuter form *what* has been used as a relative pronoun since
the thirteenth century ; formerly it could refer to persons as
well as to inanimate objects, whereas now it only refers to
the latter, but in the modern dialects it can still refer to
persons, as *the man what did that*.

6. INTERROGATIVE

§ 332. The NE. interrogative pronouns *who, whose, whom,
what*, and *which* are regularly developed from the corresponding ME. forms. The OE. instrumental form hwȳ (hwī)
has been preserved in the NE. interrogative adverb *why*.
The old interrogative pronoun *whether* ' which of two ' was in
common use down to the seventeenth century, but it is now
only used adverbially. In the sixteenth and seventeenth
centuries *who* was often used for *whom*, as it still often is in
the standard colloquial language ; in the dialects *whom* is
hardly ever used. *whose* is now used of persons only, except
occasionally in poetry, but formerly it could also be used of
inanimate objects. In ME. just as in NE. *what* can be used
as a neuter singular interrogative pronoun and as an interrogative adjective, but in ME. it was only used as an interrogative adjective before the singular of masculine, feminine,
and neuter nouns, whereas in NE. it is used also before
plural nouns, as *what men ?, what things ?*

CHAPTER VIII

VERBS

§ 333. In treating the history of the ME. verbs in NE. we shall generally follow the same order as that adopted in the *EME. Gr.* §§ 388–443, viz. we shall divide the verbs into three main groups : Strong, Weak, and Minor Groups.

§ 334. The chief characteristic differences between the ME. and NE. verbal forms are :—

1. The loss of personal endings in both strong and weak verbs. The normal ME. endings in the Midland and southern dialects were :—

A. The Present.

Indic.	E.M.	W.M.	S. and S.E.
Sing.	-e, -est, -eþ	-e, -es(t), -es	-e, -(e)st, -(e)þ
Pl.	-en	-en (-es)	-eþ

Subj. Sing. -e, pl. -en in all dialects.
Imper. Sing. —, -e, pl. -eþ.
Pres. Part. M. -ende, S. -inde (later -inge, -ing).
Inf. -en.

B. The Preterite.

Indic. { Strong verbs sing. —, -e, —,   pl. -en
       { Weak ,,   ,, -e, -est (-es), -e   pl. -en
Subj. strong and weak verbs sing. -e, pl. -en.
Pp. : strong verbs -en, weak verbs -ed (-d), -t.

The personal ending -e disappeared or ceased to be pronounced during the ME. period, cp. *EME. Gr.* §§ 139–42, 153–4, and the ending -est became obsolete in the ordinary

standard language in the eighteenth century at the same time
as the personal pronoun *thou* (§ 317), although the old second
pers. singular is still often used in liturgical language and
poetry. The standard ME. ending of the third pers. singular
was ·eþ, and ·eth (·ith) remained the general or predominant
ending in prose literature during the greater part of the sixteenth century, but ·es beside ·eth was not uncommon in
poetry, and in the colloquial language it had become the predominant ending in the early part of the sixteenth century.
From the colloquial and poetical language it gradually
passed into that of the prose and during the seventeenth
century became general except in formal and stilted language.
In ME. this ending properly belonged to the West Midland
and northern dialects. From the former it gradually spread,
probably aided by the common verbal form *is*, to the
other dialects, and eventually became the standard ending,
whence the present endings ·(e)s = iz after sibilants, z
after other voiced consonants and vowels, and s after other
voiceless consonants, see §§ 158, 256. The n in the plural
ending ·en regularly disappeared in the standard language
during the ME. period, and then the plural came to be like
the first pers. singular in form (cp. *EME. Gr.* § 147), but the
old ending ·e(n) was sometimes preserved as an archaism
until well on into the sixteenth century, and in some of the
Midland dialects it has been preserved right down to the
present day. The southern plural ending ·eþ was also
sometimes used in the standard language of the late ME.
period, and was still often used by many writers until well
on into the NE. period.

In early ME. the present participle had the ending ·and
in the northern dialects, ·ende in the Midland, and ·inde (later
·inge, ·ing) in the southern. The ending ·ing(e), which was
due to the influence of the old endings ·inge, ·ing (= OE.
·ung, ·ing) of verbal nouns, had become the standard ending
by Chaucer's time. This substitution of the old verbal noun

ending for the participial ending in the standard language
arose from the loss of the preposition on through the intermediate stage ǝ in such combinations as on strīking(e) beside
strīkende. That this is the origin of the NE. ending of the
present participle is clearly seen by the fact that the present
participle takes the prefix ǝ· down to the present day in all
the Midland, except the north Midland, southern, south-
eastern, and south-western dialects, see *ED. Gr.* § 437. The
n in the infinitive ending ·en regularly disappeared during
the ME. period, and then the infinitive came to be like the
first pers. singular in form, cp. *EME. Gr.* § 147. The ME.
ending ·en of strong past participles has generally remained
in NE. except in class III, where it has only been preserved in
isolated forms now used as adjectives (§ 348). The ME.
prefix i·, y·, older ʒe· = OE. ge· in the past participle
generally disappeared in later ME., but it was sometimes
retained in poetry until well on into the NE. period, and it
has been preserved in the form ǝ· in many of the south
Midland and south-western dialects right down to the
present day.

2. The great process of levelling and analogical formations
which have taken place in the preterite and past participle of
strong verbs.

3. The great number of ME. strong verbs which have
become weak in NE., especially in classes II, III, VI,
and VII.

A. STRONG VERBS

§ 335. Before beginning to classify the strong verbs it will
be useful to state here in a connected manner some of the
changes which these verbs have undergone during the NE.
period :—

1. With the exception of *was : were* all strong verbs have

lost the old distinction between the preterite singular and plural. Either the singular form has come to be used for the plural, as *we rode* (§ 336), or the plural form has come to be used for the singular, as *I found* (§ 353), or a new preterite has been formed from the past participle, as *I, we bore* (§ 359). In the northern dialects the preterite singular had begun to be levelled out into the plural already at the beginning of the fourteenth century, whereas in the Midland and southern dialects the old distinction between the stem-vowels of the singular and plural was generally preserved throughout the ME. period, but even in Chaucer the singular was sometimes levelled out into the plural. On the other hand the form of the plural was sometimes levelled out into the singular in the Midland and southern dialects, as sēt(e) sēt(e), pl. sēten sēten beside northern sat, pl. sat(e).

2. In earlier NE. the preterite was often used for the past participle in all classes of strong verbs, and in a few verbs this has now become the standard form, as *abode, shone; sat; held.*

3. Another characteristic feature in NE. strong verbs is the remarkable influence which the past participle has exercised on the formation of new preterites, as *bore, spun, got,* &c. This influence was already great in ME. in the verbs of class II, whence *chose, froze* (§ 345).

4. In the fourth and fifth classes of verbs a new type of preterite arose in late ME. whereby the a in those verbs which normally had this vowel was lengthened to ā, and then the ā was often extended analogically to class I, as **drave, wrate** (§ 338), and to class II, as **chase, fraze** (§ 345).

5. The ME. ending ·en, (·n) of the past participle has generally been preserved except in class III, where it has only been retained in isolated forms now used as adjectives, as *bounden, molten,* &c., see § 348.

The Classification of Strong Verbs.

Class I.

§ 336. The principal parts of strong verbs belonging to this class normally had:—

OE.	ī	ā	i	i
ME.	ī	ǭ	i	i

ME. ī, ǭ have regularly become **ai** written **i** (§ 73), **ou** written **o** (§ 76), and the short **i** of the past participle has remained. The pret. singular had come to be used for the plural already in late ME. and early NE. Only a small number of the verbs originally belonging to this class have preserved the normally developed preterite and past participle in the standard language of the present day, viz. *ride, rode, ridden*; and similarly *arise, drive, rise, smite, stride, write*, but even in these verbs there was great fluctuation in the formation of the preterite and past participle in earlier NE., see below.

§ 337. From the sixteenth down to the eighteenth century the regular pret. singular was often used for the past participle, as *abode, arose, drove, rode, shone, smote* beside the early shortened form *smot(t), stroke* 'struck', *strove, throve, wrote*; and in the two verbs *abide, shine* the new past participles *abode, shone* with early shortening (§ 100) have become the standard forms.

§ 338. After the analogy of preterites like *brake, spake* beside *broke, spoke* in the fourth class of verbs (§ 359) new preterites like *drave, rade, smate, strade, strake, strave, thrave, wrate* beside *drove, rode*, &c., were formed in the early part of the sixteenth century. Preterites of this type were very common in the sixteenth century, and are also found in the

1611 edition of the Bible.   After the early part of the seventeenth century they occur chiefly in poetry, but they are
still common in many of the modern dialects.

§ 339. In early NE. a new preterite was often formed
from the past participle, especially in the seventeenth
century, as *bit, rid (ridde), ris* (= **riz**), *slid, strick* ' struck ',
strid, writt (writte); and then later these new preterites came
to be used also as past participles, as *bit, rid (ridde), slid,* &c.,
beside *bitten, ridden,* &c. In two verbs these new formations
have become the standard forms, viz. *bite, bit, bit* beside
bitten; slide, pret. and pp. *slid* beside the weak form *slided*
(§ 340).

§ 340. Already in ME. a few of the verbs belonging to
this class had weak beside strong forms in the preterite and
past participle (cp. *EME. Gr.* § 397), and such forms were
not uncommon in earlier NE., as *abided, drived, shined,
strided, thrived* beside the regular strong forms *abode, abidden ;
drove, driven,* &c. ; and a few verbs have such double forms
in the present standard language, as *thrived* beside *throve,
thrived* beside *thriven,* and similarly with the archaic verbs
rive, shrive so far as they are still used in literature. The
following verbs are now always weak : *bide* (one's time),
glide, gripe, slide (pret. and pp. *slid* beside *slided*), *writhe.*

§ 341. From the sixteenth century onwards the old weak
verbs *chide, hide* have had strong beside weak past participles,
viz. *chidden, hidden* beside *chid, hid. strive* (O.Fr. **estriver**)
became a strong verb during the ME. period and has
remained as such in NE.

§ 342. The present normally developed parts of *strike*
would be *strike, stroke* (= **strouk**, § 76), *stricken* which was
the most common form down to about 1600, and which is
still preserved in the phrase *stricken in years. stroke* (= **strǫk**)
was the common preterite form in the sixteenth century,
but from about 1600 it began to be supplanted by *strook*
(= **strǫk** of uncertain origin, but well attested in the modern

dialects, see *E. D. D.* s. v.) and *struck*. From the seventeenth century onwards the commonest form of the preterite and past participle has been *struck*, which seems to be an early shortening of **strōk** after the **ǭ** had become **ū** (§ 75). From the fifteenth down to the nineteenth century this verb has had at one time or another various formations of the preterite and past participle, viz. pret. *stroke, strook, struck, strick, strake, strack* beside weak *striked, straked*; pp. *stricken, strick, stroke, strooken, strucken, struck* beside weak *striked, straked*. In the standard language the only forms now used are: pret. *struck*, pp. *struck* beside the isolated form *stricken*.

Class II.

§ 343. OE. had a considerable number of verbs which belonged to this class, but some of them became obsolete during the ME. period. NE. has preserved eighteen of the OE. verbs and of these fifteen have become weak, and only three have remained strong, viz. *choose, freeze*, and *fly*, but even *choose, freeze* often had the weak preterites and past participles *choosed* (*chused*), *freezed* from the sixteenth to the eighteenth century. Some of the old strong verbs became weak or had weak beside strong forms already in ME. In the standard language the following verbs are now always weak : *brew, chew, lie* 'tell lies', *rue, seethe*; with shortening of the vowel in the preterite and past participle : *cleave, creep, flee, lose, shoot*; verbs which in OE. and ME. had **ū** in the present : *bow, brook*; and *shove, suck, sup* with early shortening of the **ū** (§ 67, 4), see *EME. Gr.* § 402. Some of these verbs had strong beside weak preterites and past participles in earlier NE., and a few isolated strong past participles now used as adjectives have been preserved down to the present day, as *cloven : cleave, forlorn : lose, sodden : seethe*. For other old strong forms see below. The preterite

of *seethe* is now always *seethed*, but in the sixteenth and
seventeenth centuries *sod* formed from the old past participle
was very common. The preterite and past participle of *flee*
is now always *fled*, but in earlier NE. *fleed*, formed direct
from the present, was also common.

§ 344. The principal parts of strong verbs belonging to
this class normally had:—

OE.	ēo	ēa	u	o
ME.	ę̄	ę̄	u (ǭ)	ǭ
NE.	ee (= ī § 71)	ea (= ī § 72)		o (= ou § 76)

There is not a single NE. verb which has preserved what
would have been the regularly developed parts, and *freeze* is
the only strong verb which now has **ee** in the present. In
addition to *creep*, *flee*, *seethe* late ME. and early NE. had
presents like *cheese* (*chese*) ‘to choose’, *sheete* ‘to shoot’ which
became obsolete in the sixteenth century, *leese* (*lese*, *lees*,
lease) ‘to lose’ which became obsolete in the seventeenth
century; the old spelling *cleeve* was regularly preserved
until the sixteenth century, and then it became mixed up
with the old weak verb *cleave* (= OE. **cleofian**), whence the
modern spelling *cleave*. In ME. three verbs had **ǭ** (cp. § 75, 2)
beside **ę̄** in the present, viz. **chǭsen, lǭsen, shǭten** beside
chę̄sen, lę̄sen, shę̄ten. The latter presents were gradually
supplanted by the former, whence NE. *choose* (formerly also
written *chose*) beside *chuse* (§ 71, note) from the sixteenth
down to the nineteenth century, *lose* (formerly also written
loose), and *shoot* (formerly also written *shote*, *shout*). In
earlier NE. what is written *choose* often rhymes with French
words like *abuse*, *muse*, *refuse*, which seems to indicate that
it sometimes had the pronunciation of the form *chuse*, still
common in some dialects.

§ 345. In early ME. the preterite plural regularly had **u**,
but later the verbs of this class generally had **ǭ** from the
past participle, and then in early NE. the **ǭ** was levelled out

into the singular, whence the NE. preterites *chose, froze* beside the past participles *chosen, frozen* with s, z for older r from the present, see *EOE. Gr.* §§ 115–16. The pret. singular would now regularly have ea (= ī) from older ę̄ (§ 72), and a few old forms like *chese, cleve* were in common use until the beginning of the sixteenth century, and then became obsolete. Besides the strong preterites *chose, froze,* early NE. had also a few others, as *clove* beside *cleft* (*cleved, cleaved*), *crope* beside *crept,* and from the seventeenth down to the nineteenth century also *creeped.* From these old strong preterites new weak preterites were sometimes formed in early NE., as *cloved, frozed,* but they never became very common. After the analogy of preterites like *brake, spake* beside *broke, spoke* in the fourth class of verbs (§ 359), new preterites like *chase, clave, fraze* beside *chose, clove, froze* were formed in early NE., but they had become obsolete in the standard language by about 1600, although this type of preterite has been preserved in some dialects down to the present day.

§ 346. In ME. the principal parts of *fly* were :—flīen, pret. sing. fleiჳ (flę̄ჳ, OE. flēah), pl. flǫwen (flǭჳen), pp. flǫwen (flǭჳen, OE. flogen). NE. *fly* and *flown* are regularly developed from the corresponding ME. forms. The new preterite *flew* came into existence in the fifteenth century, and was formed after the analogy of preterites like *blew* beside pp. *blown* in the seventh class of verbs (§ 384) due to the past participles being alike in formation. In the seventeenth and eighteenth centuries this new preterite was often used for the past participle, and in the sixteenth and seventeenth centuries a new past participle *fline* (*flyen*) was often formed direct from the present. The principal parts of *flee* and *fly* were often mixed up in early NE., just as they were in ME. (cp. *EME. Gr.* § 401), with the result that in the sixteenth century *flew* was sometimes used as the preterite of *flee.*

Class III.

§ 347. This was by far the largest class of strong verbs in OE. It included the strong verbs containing a medial nasal or liquid + consonant, and a few others in which the stem-vowel was followed by two consonants other than a nasal or liquid + consonant (*EOE. Gr.* § 339). Those OE. verbs which survived in ME. generally remained strong, but in NE. all the verbs containing a liquid + consonant have now become weak.

§ 348. In early NE. the preterite, whether old or a new formation, was often used for the past participle, as *bound*, *drunk* (*drank*) beside *bounden*, *drunken*, and then later the old past participle in *-en* was supplanted by it, so that in the present standard language the old past participle has only been preserved in isolated forms now used as adjectives, as *bounden*, *drunken*, *molten*, *shrunken*, *sunken*, and *swollen*.

§ 349. In ME. the verbs of this class are subdivided into three groups :—

(*a*) Those which have i in the present, a(o) in the pret. singular, and u(o = u) in the pret. plural and past participle.

(*b*) Those which have ī in the present, a (o) in the pret. singular, and ū (ou = ū) in the pret. plural and past participle.

(*c*) Those which have e in the present, a in the pret. singular, o (u) in the pret. plural, and o in the past participle ; and a few others. See *EME. Gr.* §§ 403–6.

Group (*a*).

§ 350. This group includes the ME. verbs containing a nasal + consonant other than d or b. The principal parts of the verbs belonging to this group had :—

OE.	i	a (o)	u	u
ME.	i	a (o)	u, o (= u)	u, o (= u)

All the NE. verbs of this group regularly have **i** in the present, and **u** (formerly also written **o**, § 67, 1) in the past participle. In some verbs the ME. vowel of the pret. singular has been levelled out into the plural, as sing. and pl. *drank*; and in other verbs the vowel of the pret. plural has been levelled out into the singular, as sing. and pl. *spun*, *swum*. In earlier NE. the old pret. singular was often used for the past participle, as *began*, *rang* beside the regular forms *begun*, *rung*. In one verb the form of the past participle has come to be used for the present, as *run*, *ran*, *run*. This verb was **rinnen (rennen)** in ME., and *rin* (*ren*) remained in common use down to the sixteenth century. The form *run* (also written *ron*) came into existence in the latter part of the fifteenth century, and then in the seventeenth century *rin* (*ren*) became obsolete. The pret. *ran* was often used for the past participle from the sixteenth down to the nineteenth century.

§ 351. In the sixteenth, seventeenth, and eighteenth centuries there was a great deal of fluctuation between **a** and **u** in the preterite. In the standard language of the present day some verbs have generalized the **a**, and others the **u**. The following verbs have generalized the **a** : *begin*, *began*, *begun* ; and similarly *drink*, *shrink*, *sink*. In ME. the verbs *sing*, *spring*, and *ring* (originally a weak verb) regularly had **o** in the pret. singular, but they now have **a** after the analogy of preterites like *began*, *drank* (§ 63). The following verbs have generalized the **u** in the preterite, as *cling*, *clung*, *clung* ; and similarly *fling*, *sling*, *slink*, *spin*, *sting*, *stink*, *string* (originally a weak verb), *swing*, *win* (pret. and pp. written *won*), *wring*. The verbs *dig* and *stick* are old weak verbs which passed over into this class in the sixteenth century. From the sixteenth down to the eighteenth century *stick* also had a pret. *stack* which is still common in some dialects. The pret. *dag* is also common in some dialects, but it does not seem ever to have existed in the literary language.

§ 352. In earlier NE. many of the above old strong verbs
had weak beside strong preterites and past participles,
especially from the sixteenth down to the eighteenth
century, as *clinged, runned, shrinked, slinged, slinked, stinged,
stinked, swimmed, swinged, wringed*, beside the old strong
forms given above.

Group (*b*).

§ 353. This group includes the ME. verbs containing
a nasal + d or b. The principal parts of the verbs belonging
to this group had :—

ME.   ī   a (o)   ū (ou = ū)   ū (ou = ū)

ME. ī and ū have regularly become ai (written i) and au
(written ou) in NE., see §§ 73, 77. The pret. singular with
a (o) occurs occasionally in early NE., as *band* (*bond*), *fand*
(*fond*), see § 63, but already in late ME. the stem-vowel of
the plural began to be levelled out into the singular, and
this gradually became the normal form in early NE., as
bind, bound, bound; and similarly *find, grind*. The regular
preterite and past participle of *wind* would be *wūnd* (written
wound); *wound* (= waund) is a new formation after the
analogy of *bound*, &c., see § 134, 1. From the sixteenth
down to the nineteenth century *grind* had a weak beside
a strong pret. and pp. *grinded* beside *ground*.

§ 354. *climb* with weak pret. and pp. *climbed* had become
fully established by the beginning of the seventeenth
century, but from the late ME. period down to the seventeenth century this verb had a great variety of other forms.
In the sixteenth and seventeenth centuries the present was
often written *clime* rhyming with *time*, to which a preterite
clame was formed in the fifteenth century. From the
fifteenth down to the seventeenth century there was also
a present form *climme* (*clim*) rhyming with short ĭ, which
had a strong pret. *clamme* (*clam*), pp. *clum* (ME. clumben) in

the fifteenth and sixteenth centuries, and a weak pret. and pp. *climmed* in the sixteenth century. The old strong pret. *clomb* (also used as pp.) corresponding to ME. clǫmb (*EME. Gr.* §§ 72, 404) was not uncommon down to the seventeenth century, and it still occurs occasionally as an archaism.

Group (c).

§ 355. This group includes the ME. verbs containing a liquid + consonant, and a few others containing two consonants other than a liquid + consonant. The principal parts of the verbs belonging to this group generally had :—

e   a   u (o)   o

The verbs of this group regularly had **u** in the pret. plural in early ME., but later they generally had **o** from the past participle, and in late ME. the **o** was often levelled out into the pret. singular. With the exception of *fight* all the ME. verbs belonging to this group have become weak in NE., viz. *bark, burn* (*EME. Gr.* § 130), *burst* (*EME. Gr.* § 130), *carve, delve, help, melt, smart, starve, swallow* (*EME. Gr.* § 406), *thrash (thresh), warp, yell, yelp, yield.* Even before the end of the ME. period some of them had become entirely weak, others had weak beside strong preterites and past participles ; and nearly all of them had become predominantly weak by the first half of the sixteenth century. Just a few old strong preterites and past participles, especially the latter, lingered on until the seventeenth century, and as archaisms in poetry much later. Examples of early NE. strong preterites are :— *borst (barst, brast), dolve, molt(e), swoll (swole)*, especially in the sixteenth century, and *holp* as an archaism down to the nineteenth century ; and of past participles :— *bursten, corven* beside the new formations *carven (kerven), dolven (dolve), molte(n), throshen* beside the new formation *threshen, yolden,* and *holpen* as an archaism down to the nineteenth century. The old past participles, *molten, swollen* are still used as adjectives

(§ 348).   Beside the pret. and pp. *burst* the form *bursted* was
formerly common.

§ 356. The principal parts of *fight* in ME. were:—

fiȝten   fauȝt (faȝt)   fǫuȝten (fuȝten)   fǫuȝten

The NE. present and past participle are regularly developed
from the corresponding ME. forms, see §§ 73, 7, 90. In
pronunciation the preterite is also regularly developed from
the ME. pret. sing. fauȝt (§ 84, 4), but the spelling *fought* is
either due to the analogy of preterites like *brought* (§ 90) or
to the influence of the past participle.

Class IV.

§ 357. This class includes the OE. verbs whose stems end
in a single liquid or a nasal, a few others which originally
belonged to classes V (§ 363) and VI (§ 374), and the
originally weak verb *wear*. The verbs *break, speak, tread,*
and *weave,* which in OE. belonged to class V, passed over
entirely into this class in early ME. through the stem-
vowels of the present and the preterite being alike in both
classes. The verbs *heave* (OE. hebban, ME. hęven) and
swear (OE. swerian, ME. swęren), which in OE. belonged
to class VI, passed over into this class through the ME.
present and the past participle being alike in both classes,
cp. *EME. Gr.* § 412.

§ 358. The principal parts of strong verbs belonging to
this class normally had:—

OE.	e	æ	ǣ (ē)	o
ME.	ę̄	a	ę̄ (ę̄)	ǭ

The NE. stem-vowels of the present and past participle are
regularly developed from ME. ę̄ (§§ 72, 122) and ǭ (§§ 76,
125), as in *speak, spoken* beside *tear, torn*; for the ea (= ei)
in *break* see § 72, note.

§ 359. Old preterites with short ă = ME. a, as *brack,*

spack, *stal* (*stall*, *stalle*) were often used in the sixteenth
century, and *brack*, *spack* are still very common in the
northern dialects down to the present day. The preterites
of this type began to be supplanted by new formations
already in late ME. In the fifteenth century the ă in the
preterite singular was generally lengthened to ā after the
analogy of the long vowels in the present, preterite plural,
and past participle, as bār, brāk, shār, spāk, stāl, tār, &c.,
and then later a final -e was added to indicate that the preceding vowel was long, as *bare*, *brake*, *spake*, &c. These and
similar preterites were the predominant type from the late
fifteenth down to the seventeenth century, and some of
them like *bare*, *brake*, *sware* occur as archaisms down to the
nineteenth century. They are still very common in some
of the modern dialects. Beside the preterites of this type
a new type of preterite began to be formed in the sixteenth
century with ǭ from the past participle, as *bore*, *broke*, *hove*
'heaved', *spoke*, *stole*, *swore*, *tore*, *wore*, *wove*. In the sixteenth
and early part of the seventeenth century there was a great
deal of fluctuation in the use of the types *brake*, *spake* and
broke, *spoke*, but during the seventeenth and early part of
the eighteenth century the former type was gradually supplanted by the latter. Down to the eighteenth and also in
the early part of the nineteenth century these new preterites
were often used for the past participle beside the old past
participles, as *bore*, *broke*, *shore*, *spoke* (*bespoke* is still common),
stole, *swore*, *tore*, *wore*, *wove*, beside *borne* (*born*) which became
differentiated in meaning in the eighteenth century, *broken*,
shorn (*shorne*), *spoken*, *stolen*, *sworn*, *torn*, *worn*, *woven*.

§ 360. Some of the verbs belonging to this class had weak
beside strong preterites and past participles in earlier NE.,
especially in the sixteenth and seventeenth centuries, as
heaved (also *heft* in the seventeenth century), *sheared*, *stealed*,
teared, *sweared*, *weaved*, beside *bore*, *borne* (*born*), &c. ; and we
still have *sheared* beside *shore*, *shorn*. The preterite and past

participle of *heave* have generally been *heaved* since the
sixteenth century.

§ 361. The stem-vowels in the principal parts of *tread*
underwent shortening in late ME. or early NE., see §§ 98,
100, whence *tread, trod, trodden*, but earlier NE. had forms
with long beside short stem-vowels as is evidenced by
numerous rhymes and sometimes by the spelling, as pret.
trode (troad) : *abode*, beside *trodde (trod)* ; pp. *troden (troaden)*,
troad beside *trod (trodden)*.

§ 362. In ME. the principal parts of *come* were:—**cumen**
(also written **comen**), pret. sing. **cam** (late ME. **cām**) beside
cǫm, pret. pl. **cāmen** beside **cǫmen**, pp. **cumen** (also written
comen).   NE. *come, came, come* regularly correspond to ME.
cumen (comen), cām, cumen (comen), see §§ 67, 69.   The
present and past participle was often written *cum (com)* down
to the seventeenth century.   The old preterite singular
forms *cam, come* (= **kūm** with **ū** from older **ǭ**, § 75) are
occasionally found in early NE.   In the sixteenth and
seventeenth centuries a weak beside a strong past participle
in -en was common, as *cumed (comed)* beside *cum(m)en,
com(m)en*.   And similarly the verbs *become* and *overcome*.

Class V.

§ 363. This class includes the OE. verbs whose stems end
in a single consonant other than a nasal or liquid.   In OE.
and ME. it only differed from class IV in the past participle.
In ME. class IV had **ǭ** and class V had **ę̄** in the past
participle.   Through the stem-vowels of the present and
preterite being alike in both classes the verbs *break, speak,
tread*, and *weave*, which originally belonged to class V, passed
over entirely into class IV in early ME. (§ 357).   The six
verbs *bequeath, fret, knead, mete, weigh*, and *wreak* have now
become weak, but some of them had remnants of old strong
beside the weak forms in earlier NE., see § 373.   The only
verbs which have remained strong are :—*bid (forbid), eat,*

get (*beget, forget*), *give* (*forgive*), *lie* 'lie down', *see*, and *sit*; and as some of these had a great variety of forms in ME. it will be most expedient to treat each verb separately.

§ 364. The principal parts of strong verbs belonging to this class normally had :—

OE.	e	æ	ǣ (ē)	e
ME.	ę̄	a	ę̄ (ē)	ę̄

The verbs which regularly had short **a** in the pret. singular in early ME. had **ā** beside **a** in late ME. and early NE. This **ā** was due to the analogy of the long vowel in the pret. plural and to the new long **ā** which arose in the pret. singular of verbs belonging to class IV (§ 359). The only verb of this type which has preserved the regularly developed form of the past participle is *eat*, pp. *eaten* (§ 72). Beside the early ME. past participles bę̄den, sę̄ten new past participles **biden** (bidden), **siten** (sitten) were formed direct from the present during the ME. period.

§ 365. The only NE. verb which has fairly well preserved the corresponding ME. principal parts is *eat*: present *eat* (ME. ę̄ten) and pp. *eaten* (ME. ę̄ten), but in the sixteenth century both the present and the past participle had forms with early shortening of the stem-vowel (cp. § 98) beside those with long vowel, as **ett(e)**, **etten** (still preserved in many dialects). In OE. and early ME., as in the other Germanic languages, this verb had a long vowel in the pret. singular, which was the same as that in the plural, OE. ǣt (ēt) = early ME. ę̄t (ę̄t) which would regularly have become *īt (written *eat, eet,* or *ete*) in the present standard language. This old preterite (written at various times *ete, eate, eat*) has been more or less common from the fourteenth down to the nineteenth century, and in earlier NE. it was often used for the past participle. Beside the form with long vowel early NE. had also one with short vowel (ĕt) which arose from shortening before ę̄ (ē) became ī (cp. § 98),

and this form, generally written *ate,* rarely *eat,* has remained
in the colloquial language down to the present day. A new
analogical pret. singular at arose in the thirteenth century,
which became obsolete in the sixteenth century. From at
was formed āt, later written ate, in the fifteenth century
(§ 359), which has been the predominant literary form since
the sixteenth century.

§ 366. The simple verb *get* (ON. geta, cp. *EME. Gr.*
§ 176) has had exclusively initial g· in all its parts from the
earliest date of its appearance in the language. The principal
parts in ME. were :—inf. gḙten, giten ; pret. sing. gat beside
gāt, later written gate (§ 359), pl. gēten ; pp. gḙten beside
gǫten with ǫ from class IV. In the sixteenth century the
present had ę beside ĕ, and also occasionally ĭ, but from then
onwards *get* has been the standard form ; *git* is still common
in the modern northern dialects. The pret. *gat* (*gatt*) became
obsolete in the standard language in the sixteenth century,
but it is still common in many of the modern dialects ; and
gate became obsolete in the seventeenth century. During
the sixteenth century a new preterite *got* arose with o from
the past participle gǫten, and this has been the standard
form since the seventeenth century. The past participle
had gǫten beside gḙten, git(t)en down to the sixteenth
century, and then these forms were gradually ousted by the
new preterite *got* used for the past participle, but *gotten,*
getten are still very common in the modern dialects, and
gotten is still the standard form in the compounds *begotten,*
forgotten. The compounds *beget* and *forget* had medial ·ȝ·
beside ·g· in ME., as inf. forȝḙten, forȝiten beside forgḙten ;
pret. sing. forȝat beside forgat (forgāt later written for-
gate) ; pp. forȝḙten beside forgḙten, see *EME. Gr.* §§ 176,
410. The forms with ·ȝ· became obsolete in the sixteenth
century, and from then onwards these compounds have had
the same forms as the simple verb, except that they have
preserved the old past participle in ·en.

§ 367. The principal parts of the OE. verbs **biddan** (ME.
bidden) 'pray, beg' and **bēodan** (ME. **bḝden**, cp. § 344)
'order, command' became mixed up in ME. both in form
and meaning; and similarly OE. **forbēodan** (ME. **forbḝden**)
'forbid' with those of the simple verb **bidden,** which during
the ME. period gave rise to the new inf. **forbidden** beside
forbḝden. The result was that *bid* and *forbid* had several
different forms in the present, preterite, and past participle
both in late ME. and early NE., especially in the sixteenth
century. In early NE. the present had **bidd(e), bid** beside
bḗde; pret. **bad, bāde, bọ̄d** (written *bode, bod*), and **bid**
formed from the pp. **bidden** and also used for the past
participle; a new pp. **bidden** beside the old form **bḗden**
was formed from the present during the ME. period, **bọ̄den**
with **ọ̄** from verbs of class IV (§ 358), **bid** (see above). From
the sixteenth century onwards the usual forms have been:
present *bid*, pret. *bade* (= **bæd, beid**), *bid*; pp. *bidden, bid*.
And similarly with the various forms of *forbid*, except that
the preterite is now always *forbade* (= **bæd**), and the pp.
forbidden.

§ 368. The verb *give* had in ME. a variety of forms with
initial ʒ· (often written **y·**) beside **g·** both in the present,
preterite, and past participle, as inf. ʒḗven, ʒiven beside
given; pret. sing. ʒaf, ʒafe, ʒāve, ʒọ̆ve beside gaf, gāve,
pl. ʒḗven, ʒḗven, ʒāven, ʒọ̆ven beside gḗven; pp. ʒḗven,
ʒọ̆ven, ʒiven, beside given, see *EME. Gr.* §§ 292, 410.
ʒ· beside **g·**forms existed side by side until the sixteenth
century, but during the sixteenth century the ʒ·forms were
gradually ousted by the **g·**forms, and from then onwards
give, pret. *gave,* pp. *given* have been the standard forms.
The preterite form **gaf (gaffe)** existed beside the new
formation **gāve** until well on into the sixteenth century,
and then became obsolete. Beside **gāve** there was also
a weak pret. **gived** from the sixteenth down to the eighteenth
century.

§ 369. The regular parts of *sit* were in ME. :—inf. **sitten**; pret. sing. **sat** beside **sāt,** later written **sate;** pp. **sẹ̄ten.** *sit,* often written *sitt(e)* in earlier NE., regularly corresponds to ME. **sitten.** The preterite from **sate,** often also used for the past participle, became obsolete in the sixteenth century ; **sat** was often written *satt(e)* down to the eighteenth century. Beside the old pp. **sẹ̄ten** a new pp. **sitten** with **i** from the present was formed in late ME., and then the former became obsolete in the sixteenth century. In the sixteenth century the pret. **sat** came to be used beside **sitten, sitt(e)** for the past participle, and since the end of the century it has been the predominant form, and is now the only form, but **sitten** is still very common in the dialects.

The old weak verb *spit* (OE. **spittan**) now forms its preterite and past participle after the analogy of *sit, sat, sat*; in the seventeenth and eighteenth centuries it also had a strong pp. *spitten.*

§ 370. The principal parts of *lie* 'lie down' were in ME. :—inf. **līen** ; pret. sing. **lai,** pl. **leien (lẹ̄ȝen)** ; pp. **leien (lein, lain).** NE. *lie, lay, lain* are regularly developed from the corresponding ME. forms **līen** (§ 73, 3), **lai** (§ 82, 1), **lain** (§ 82, 2). From the fourteenth down to the eighteenth century there was also a pp. **lien (line)** formed direct from the present, beside the regular form **lain.**

§ 371. In ME. the verb *see* had a large number of different forms in the preterite and past participle, as pret. **saȝ, sauȝ, saw** beside **seȝ, seiȝ, sei, sai, siȝ, sī;** pp. **sẹwen, sawen** beside **seien, sein, sain, sẹ̄n (sẹ̄ne = OE.** adj. **gesīene, gesēne** ' visible '), see *EME. Gr.* § 410. From the fourteenth century onwards the predominant forms were:—inf. **sẹ̄n, sẹ̄** ; pret. sing. **saw;** pp. **sẹ̄n (sẹ̄ne),** although some of the other forms were not uncommon down to the sixteenth century, but since then the standard forms have been *see, saw, seen,* beside a sporadic pret. and pp. *see'd.*

§ 372. The pret. *was* (ME. **was**), pl. *were* (ME. **wẹ̄ren,**

wēren) is the only preterite in NE. which has preserved the old distinction between the singular and plural. The present and past participle of *quethe* (OE. **cweþan,** ME. **quēþen)** became obsolete in the sixteenth century, but the old pret. singular *quoth* (OE. **cwæþ,** ME. **quaþ)** has been preserved as an archaism down to the present day (cp. § 132).

§ 373. The verbs *bequeath, fret* (§ 98), *knead, mete, weigh,* and *wreak* had become weak or had weak beside strong forms by the beginning of the NE. period, and some of them still had strong beside the weak past participle in the sixteenth or seventeenth century, as *fretten, knedden (knoden, knodden), meten (metten, moten), wroken* The forms with **ǒ** were due to the analogy of the verbs o class IV (§ 358).

Class VI.

§ 374. This class contained a fairly large number of verbs in OE. and ME., but only seven of them have remained strong in NE., the rest have all become weak except in the case of a few isolated past participles which are now used as adjectives, and the two verbs *heave* and *swear* which passed over into class IV (§ 357) ; *heave* is now also weak.

§ 375. The OE. and ME. normal vowels in the principal parts were:—

OE.	a	ō	ō	æ (a)
ME.	ā	ǭ	ǭ	ā

The following NE. verbs are regularly developed from the corresponding ME. forms, but with shortening of the vowel in the preterite (§ 99):—*forsake, forsook, forsaken ; shake, shook, shaken ; take,* (ON. **taka**), *took, taken* ; and pret. *stood.* From the sixteenth down to the nineteenth century the preterite was often used for the past participle, and this has been the standard past participle of *stand* since the sixteenth century. Beside the regular pp. **tāken** ME. also had **tān**

(cp. *EME. Gr.* §§ 250, 411), which was common in earlier
NE., especially in poetry, and generally written *tane, ta'en*.
Beside the strong forms, *shake* often had a weak preterite
and past participle *shaked* from the sixteenth down to the
nineteenth century. The old pp. *standen* beside a new weak
form *standed* was occasionally used in the sixteenth century,
and the weak form in the compounds *understanded, with-
standed* was very common in the sixteenth and early part of
the seventeenth century.

§ 376. The verb *(a)wake* has had a weak beside the strong
preterite and past participle from the fourteenth century down
to the present day. The usual preterite and past participle
now are *(a)woke* beside *(a)waked*, but it is remarkable that no
strong forms are found either in Shakespeare, Ben Jonson,
the 1611 edition of the Bible, or in Milton's poetry. The
pret. *(a)woke* has been in use for the past participle since the
seventeenth century, and from the seventeenth down to the
nineteenth century there has also been a strong pp. *(a)woken*
which is now obsolete or obsolescent. The stem-vowel in
(a)woke, (a)woken is difficult to explain satisfactorily. ǭ beside
ǭ existed already in late ME. and is generally explained as
being due to forms like **brǭke, spǭke; brǭken, spǭken**
(§ 359), but this is uncertain, because of the lack of a point
of contact between the two classes, cp. also § 342.

§ 377. NE. *draw* (ME. **drawen, draȝen**) and *drawn* (ME.
drawen, draȝen) are regularly developed from the corresponding ME. forms, see § 84, 2, but the pret. *drew* (ME.
drǫw, drǫuȝ, drǭȝ) is a late ME. new formation after the
analogy of preterites like *blew* (ME. **blęw**) : *blow* (ME.
blǫwen) of class VII (§ 384). Beside the strong forms
a weak preterite and pp. *drawed* was sometimes used in
earlier NE., and is still common in the Midland and
southern dialects.

§ 378. The pp. *slain* is regularly developed from ME. *slain*
(OE. **slægen**). The regular form of the present would be

*slea (ME. slę̄n, § 72), and this form existed down to the
seventeenth century. A new present *slay* beside the old
slę̄(n) was formed direct from the pp. *slain* so early as the
fifteenth century, and then gradually supplanted the old
form. The pret. *slew* (ME. slǫw, slǫuȝ, slǭȝ) is a new
formation which is found so early as the fifteenth century.

§ 379. The following verbs have become weak :—*ache,
bake, fare, flay, gnaw, grave (engrave), lade, laugh, shape, shave,
step, wade, wax.* The preterite of most of these verbs had
become entirely weak, or had weak beside strong forms,
before the end of the ME. period, so that only scanty
fragments were preserved in early NE., and even these
became obsolete in the eighteenth century, and some of
them earlier, as *fore, gnew, lough, shoope (shope), shove, wox.*
The old past participles *baken, flain, gnawn, waxen* became
obsolete in the seventeenth century, but a few of the old
past participles, used archaically as adjectives, have lingered
on to the present day, as *graven, engraven, laden, misshapen,
shaven, unwashen.*

Class VII.

§ 380. To this class belong those verbs which originally
had reduplicated preterites. In OE. they are divided into
two subdivisions according as the preterite had ē or ēo, but
as ēo regularly became ę̄ in ME. (cp. *EME. Gr.* § 65) all the
verbs of this class, which remained strong, had ę̄ in the
preterite in ME. The present and past participle had the
same stem-vowel both in OE. and ME. The verbs which
have remained strong or have strong beside weak forms in
NE. are here arranged according as the present had in
ME. :—a (= OE. ea), ǭ (= OE. ea before ld), ę̄ (= OE. ēa),
ǫw (= OE. āw), and ǫw (= OE. ōw), see *EME. Gr.*
§ 414.

§ 381. a : *fall, fell, fallen* regularly correspond to ME.
fallen, fel from older fę̄ll, fallen, cp. § 102, 1. Beside fel

ME. had also **fil** (see *EME. Gr.* § 99), which was common until towards the end of the sixteenth century.

§ 382. ǭ : *hold* (ME. hǭlden), *held, held* beside archaic *holden* (ME. hǭlden) regularly correspond to the ME. forms (§ 106). The pret. *held* is an early shortening of ME. hḗld (cp. § 97) ; *held* began to be used for the past participle in the sixteenth century, and in the seventeenth century gradually supplanted *holden* in the ordinary language.   Beside **held** late ME. had also a form **hild** which was not uncommon down to the end of the sixteenth century.   Beside the strong forms there was also a weak pret. and pp. *holded* in the sixteenth and seven-teenth centuries.   And similarly *behold* with isolated pp. *beholden* ' obliged ' used as an adjective.

§ 383. ȩ̄ : *beat* (ME. bȩten), *beat* (ME. bȩt), *beaten* (ME. bȩten).   The present *beat* and pp. *beaten* regularly correspond to the ME. forms (§ **72,** 3).   The pret. *beat*, also used for the past participle since the sixteenth century, has **ea** for **ee** (§ **71**) from *beat, beaten*.   Beside the present, preterite, and past participle with long vowel there were also forms with short vowel, as *bett, bett, betten* (*bett*) in the sixteenth and seventeenth centuries, and the pret. *bett*, pp. *betten* are still common in many dialects.

hew (ME. hȩwen), *hewed, hewn* (ME. hȩwen) beside *hewed*. *hew, hewn* regularly correspond to the ME. forms.   The weak pret. and pp. *hewed* began to appear so early as the fourteenth century, and by about 1500 had supplanted the old strong preterite **hȩw,** but in the past participle we still have *hewn* beside *hewed*.

§ 384. ǫw : *blow, blew, blown* are regularly developed from the corresponding ME. forms **blǫwen, blȩw, blǫwen ;** and similarly *know, throw*.   Beside the strong forms, *blow* also had a weak pret. and pp. *blowed* in the sixteenth and seven-teenth centuries.   *crow* has preserved the old pret. *crew* beside *crowed* which has been common since the sixteenth century ; the strong pp. *crown* beside *crowed* was common

down to the eighteenth century, and *crown* is still used as an
archaism.   *mow* and *sow* now have weak preterites, and past
participles *mowed, sowed* beside *mown, sown,* but the old
preterites *mew, sew* were common from the fifteenth down to
the eighteenth century, as they still are in many of the
northern and north Midland dialects.   After the analogy of
blew, blown : blow strong forms *snew, snown : snow* were
formed in the sixteenth century, and were common beside
the weak form *snowed* in the seventeenth century, and are
still so in most of the northern and north Midland dialects.
After the analogy of *blow : blown* strong past participles
shówn (shewn), strewn (strown), sewn were formed in early NE.
to the old weak verbs *show (shew), strew (strow), sew,* see
§§ 86 note, 87 note.

§ 385. ǫw: *grow, grew, grown* are regularly developed
from the corresponding ME. forms **grǫwen, gręw, grǫwen,**
see §§ 86, 1, 89, 4.

§ 386. **hung** is properly not the preterite and past
participle of *hang,* but of ME. **hingen** (= ON. wv. **hengja**),
which became a strong verb after the analogy of verbs like
swing, swung, swung (§ 351), and then *hing* became obsolete,
and *hung* became associated with *hang.*

§ 387. A few forms of the ME. verb **hǫten** (OE. **hātan**)
'to call' survived down to the seventeenth century, and a pp.
hight is still often used as an archaism in poetry.   The old
present **hǫte** had become obsolete before the end of the ME.
period, but the pp. **hoten** (ME. **hǫten**) is found as late as the
seventeenth century.   The old pret. **hęt** beside **heht, hiht,
hight** (= OE. **hēt** beside **hěht**) gave rise to various new
formations in ME. itself; from **hęt** a new present **hęten** was
formed, and this survived down to the latter half of the
sixteenth century; and in like manner from **hight** a new
present **hight** with pret. **highte,** pp. **hight** was formed; and
then later a weak pret. and pp. **highted** was formed.   With
the exception of the pp. *hight* all these new formations had

become obsolete by about the early part of the seventeenth century.

§ 388. The following verbs have become weak :—*dread, flow, fold, leap, let, read, row, sleep, sweep, walk, weep.* Some of them like *dread, read, sleep* had begun to have weak forms already in OE., see *EOE. Gr.* § 357, and nearly all the others had but scanty remnants of strong forms at the end of the ME. period. Down to the seventeenth century there was a strong beside a weak preterite and past participle of *leap*, viz. *lope* (*leep, leepe*), *lopen* with ǭ after the analogy of verbs of class IV (§ 358). Earlier NE. had also a few strong beside weak past participles, as *flown, folden, letten* still common in some dialects, *rown*, beside *flowed, folded, let, rowed.* The preterite and past participle of *dread* has been *dreaded* since the sixteenth century, but beside it there was also a pret. *dred(de), drad(de)*, and pp. *dred, drad* which had become obsolete by the end of the century.

B. WEAK VERBS

§ 389. Although many OE. and ME. strong verbs have become weak in NE., the number of weak verbs has always been infinitely larger than that of the strong in all periods of the language. For the history of the OE. weak verbs in ME. see *EME. Gr.* §§ 415–29.

§ 390. In early ME. the preterite singular of all weak verbs ended either in ·ede or ·de (·te), and the past participle in ·ed or ·d (·t). The final ·e disappeared in the preterite during the ME. period (*EME. Gr.* §§ 139–42), so that before the end of the period the preterite and the past participle had come to be alike in form. In early NE. the e in ed also disappeared in the preterite and past participle except when the present ended in d or t (§ 158), although the e has mostly continued to be written down to the present day, but in earlier NE., especially in the seventeenth and eighteenth

centuries, it was often omitted in writing and its omission
was indicated by ', as *amaz'd, seem'd*, &c.   After the e in ed
had disappeared or ceased to be pronounced the d regularly
remained after voiced sounds, but became t after voiceless
sounds, as *judged, laid, loved, paid, turned* beside *ceased,
hoped, thanked, wished*; in earlier NE. t was often written
where we now write ed, as *thankt (thank't), wisht (wish't)*, and
in many verbs we still have double spellings, as *blessed,
dressed, stepped, stripped, tossed, whipped* beside *blest, drest,
stept, stript, tost, whipt*.   From what has been stated above it
follows that the present general rule for the formation of the
preterite and past participle of weak verbs is :—Verbs ending
in a voiced sound have ·d, and those ending in a voiceless
sound have ·t, generally written ·ed in both cases, but those
ending in ·d or ·t add ·ed (= id), as *called, breathed, dined,
clothed, judged, lived, raised, seized, served, turned; ceased,
fixed, hissed, hoped, knocked, liked, pushed, thanked; divided,
dreaded, ended, nodded, waded; fainted, hated, lasted, permitted, stated, waited*.

§ 391. A considerable number of verbs deviate from the
general rule stated in the previous paragraph.   These
deviations are due partly to special sound changes which
took place in OE. and ME., and partly to analogical formations which arose in ME. or early NE.   Before beginning to
treat the history of the formation of the preterite and past
participle of these and the other verbs in NE , it will be
advisable to state here a few points which are chiefly of an
orthographical nature :—

1. ME. i, whether a simple vowel or the second element of
a diphthong, is generally written y when final in NE. (cp.
§ 170), whence the interchange between y and i in such
verbs as *carry : carried, lay : laid, pay : paid, pity : pitied,
study : studied, say : said* (§ 96) ; *defy : defied* ; but in some
verbs the preterite and the past participle are now formed
direct from the present without this interchange in spelling,

as *employ, employed ; obey, obeyed ; play, played ; pray, prayed ; stay, stayed.*

2. In late ME. it became fairly common to simplify double consonants finally, but medially to retain them, and to double single consonants after short vowels in order to indicate that the preceding vowel was short; and these double consonants have been preserved in the preterite and past participle of many verbs, as *begged : beg, dropped : drop, permitted : permit, stirred : stir, travelled : travel,* &c. See §§ **53–4**.

3. Verbs ending in **p, l, m, n** often have double written forms in the preterite and past participle, viz. **-t** beside **-ed,** but in a few verbs there is also a double pronunciation, as *dipt, dipped : dip, dropt, dropped : drop, smelt, smelled : smell, spilt, spilled : spill* ; but *burnt, burned : burn, dreamt* (= **dremt**), *dreamed* (= **drīmd**) *: dream, leant* (= **lent**), *leaned* (= **līnd**) *: lean.*

4. In NE. the past participle has regularly fallen together with the preterite, so that there is no longer any difference between them in form or meaning, but in a small number of verbs we have the old beside a new past participle, the one being used as the past participle proper, and the other as an adjective, as *loved : beloved* (= **bilavid**), *bent : bended* (on bended knee), *blessed* (*blest*) *: blessed* (= **blesid**), *passed : past.*

§ **392.** It has been stated above (§ **390**) that the preterite had the three different endings **-ede, -de, -te** in early ME., and that the final **-e** disappeared during the ME. period. In the following paragraphs we shall now deal with the history of these endings separately.

1. -ede

§ **393.** Those verbs which had the ending **-ede** in early ME. corresponded to : (*a*) The OE. first class of weak verbs which originally had a short stem-syllable, as **fremede : fremman** 'to perform' (*EOE. Gr.* § 368) ; (*b*) The OE.

second class of weak verbs, as **lōcode : lōcian** 'to look'
(*EOE. Gr.* § 380) ; (*c*) The verbs of French origin, as
blāmed(e) : blāmen, finisched(e) : finischen (cp. *EME. Gr.*
§ 432). After the final **-e** had disappeared during the ME.
period the preterite of all verbs of this type came to end in
-ed (*EME. Gr.* §§ 139–42). In early NE. the **e** in **-ed** also
disappeared except when the present ended in **d** or **t** (§ 158),
although the **e** has mostly continued to be written down to
the present day. The **d** then became **t** after voiceless
sounds, but remained after voiced sounds, as *asked, fetched,
finished, groped, hoped, liked, looked ; agreed, bathed, called,
earned, loved, offered, opened, pleased, prayed, spared, wondered ;
divided, ended, wounded ; hated, melted, tasted* ; for forms like
blest, drest, rapt, beside *blessed, dressed, rapped,* see § **390**.
By far the greater majority of all weak verbs now form their
preterite in the manner stated above.

2. -de

§ **394**. Those verbs which had the ending **-de** in early
ME. corresponded to : (*a*) The OE. first class of weak verbs
which originally had a long stem-syllable ending in a voiced
consonant, as **dēmde : dēman** 'to judge' (*EOE. Gr.* § 373) ;
(*b*) The OE. third class of weak verbs, as **lifde : libban** 'to
live' (*EOE. Gr.* § 380). The preterite of verbs of this type
underwent various changes in ME. besides the loss of the
final **-e** :—

1. Long vowels were shortened before double consonants
and consonant combinations, as **bledde,** pp. **ybled(d) :
blēden** 'to bleed'; **ledde,** pp. **yled(d) : lēden** 'to lead';
hidde, pp. **yhid(d) : hīden** 'to hide'; **cledde, cladde,** pp.
ycle(d), yclad(d) : clēþen 'to clothe' (*EME. Gr.* § 423);
hĕrde, pp. **yhĕrd : hēren** 'to hear'. After the loss of the
final **-e** in the preterite the **dd** was simplified to **d,** and this
simplification of the **dd** had generally taken place earlier in
the past participle, whence NE. *bleed, bled, bled ; hide, hid,*

hid (*hidden*, § 341); *clothe* (OE. clāþian): *clothed* beside *clad*; *lead, led, led; read* (§ 388), *read, read* with the spelling **ea** from the present; and similarly *breed, feed, speed; chide, chid, chid* (*chidden*, § 341). To this type of preterite and past participle now also belong *flee, fled* (ME. fledde, flēde), *fled; say, said* (ME. saide, OE. sægde), *said* (§ 96); *shoe, shod* (ME. shodde, shōde), *shod*. On the pret. and pp. *heard* (= hǝd) : *hear* (hiǝ), see § 120.

2. When the stem ended in **v, l, m, n**, or **nd, ld, rd** the preterite and past participle generally had **t** in ME. with shortening of a preceding long vowel (*EME. Gr.* §§ 270, 422), as lēven 'to leave', **lefte, yleft**; fēlen 'to feel', **felte, yfelt**; lēnen 'to lend', **lente, ylent**; **senden, sente, ysent**; bīlden 'to build', **bilte, ybilt**; **girden, girte, ygirt**. Some verbs have preserved and others now have this type of preterite and past participle in NE., as *bereave, bereft* (*bereaved*); *cleave, cleft; leave, left. deal, dealt; dwell, dwelt; feel, felt; kneel, knelt* (*kneeled*); *smell, smelt* (*smelled*); *spell, spelt* (*spelled*); *spill, spilt* (*spilled*); *spoil, spoilt* (*spoiled*). *dream, dreamt* (*dreamed*). *lean, leant* (*leaned*); *mean, meant; pen, pent* (*penned*). *bend, bent*, pp. *bent* beside *bended* now used as an adjective; *blend*, pret. and pp. *blended*, but in earlier NE. *blent; lend, lent; rend, rent; send, sent; spend, spent; wend*, pret. and pp. *wended*, the old pret. *went* is now used for the pret. of *go* (§ 411). *build, built*, but in earlier NE. the pret. *builded* was very common; *gild, gilt* (*gilded*). *gird, girt* (*girded*). *burn, burnt* (*burned*); *learn, learnt*, pp. *learnt* (*learned*), beside *learned* (lǝnid) now used as an adjective. To this type now also belongs *lose, lost*. The preterites *dem*(*p*)*t : deem, sem*(*p*)*t : seem* were in common use down to the seventeenth century, just as they still are in some of the dialects.

3. With one or two exceptions the preterite of all other verbs which ended in -**de** in early ME. was remodelled during the ME. period after the analogy of those verbs whose preterite ended in -**ede** (cp. *EME. Gr.* § 419), as *behaved :*

behave, felled : fell, and similarly *believe, fill, heal, live, rear, singe,* &c.   *rid* (OE. *hreddan,* § 136), *rid* (*ridded*) ; *spread* with early shortening (§ 98), *spread* (ME. **spredde**), *spread* ; and similarly *shed, shed* (ME. **schedde**), *shed* ; with these are now associated *shred, shred* ; *wed, wed* (*wedded*), which in OE. belonged to the second class of weak verbs (§ 393).

§ 395. NE. *lay, laid, laid* regularly correspond to ME. **leien, leide, yleid** (*EME. Gr.* § 107, i) ; *make, made, made* to ME. **māken, māde, ymād** (*EME. Gr.* § 428) ; and *have, had, had* to ME. **have(n), hād(d)e, (y)had** (*EME. Gr.* § 429).

3. -te

§ 396. Those verbs whose preterite ended in -te in early ME. corresponded to the OE. first class of weak verbs whose present ended in a voiceless consonant (*EOE. Gr.* §§ 368, 373). The e in -te disappeared during the ME. period, and the t, which thus became final, has remained in NE., although it is generally written -ed after the analogy of those verbs which had -ede in early ME. (§ 393), as *clip, clipt* (*clipped*) ; *dip, dipt* (*dipped*) ; *drench, drenched* ; and similarly *kissed, puffed, quenched, wished,* &c.

§ 397. Most of the verbs of this type underwent certain changes during the ME. period: (*a*) Long vowels were shortened before double consonants and consonant combinations, as pret. **mette,** pp. **ymet : mēten ;** pret. **kepte,** pp. **ykept : kēpen.** (*b*) When the stem ended in t the tt was simplified to t in the past participle, and also in the preterite after the loss of the final -e, as **ymet, mette** later **met : mēten ; yset, sette** later **set : setten.** (*c*) When the stem ended in st the tt was simplified to t already in OE. (*EOE. Gr.* § 373), as ME. pret. **caste,** pp. **ycast : casten.** See *EME. Gr.* §§ 424–5. NE. examples are : (*a*) *keep, kept* ; and similarly with the old strong verbs, *leap, leapt* (*leaped*) = **lept, līpt ;** *sleep, slept ; sweep, swept ; weep, wept.* See § 388.

(*b*) *meet, met; shoot, shot*; after the analogy of *bite, bit, bit* (*bitten*, § 339) we now have *light, lit* beside *lighted*; to this type also belonged in early NE. the verbs *greet, heat*, which now form their preterite and past participle in -ed (= -id); and in *sweat* (§ 98), *wet* (§ 98) we still have pret. and pp. *sweat, wet* beside the new formations *sweated, wetted. set, set*; and similarly *cut, hit, hurt, let* (§ 388), *put, slit, spilt; whet*, pret. and pp. *whet* beside the new formation *whetted. knit* and *lift* now have the pret. and pp. *knitted, lifted*, but in earlier NE. the common forms were *knit, lift*, and the old pp. *knit* is still preserved as an adjective, as *well knit*. (*c*) *cast, cast;* and similarly *burst* (§ 355), *cost, thrust*. The other verbs of this type now form their preterite and past participle in -ed (= -id), as *fasted, lasted, rested, thirsted*, &c., and *casted* was also common in earlier NE.

§ 398. OE. had twenty verbs belonging to class I of weak verbs which (except **bringan**) had umlaut in the present, but not in the preterite and past participle, see *EOE. Gr.* § 379. Some of these verbs became obsolete in ME., and the preterite and past participle of others were remodelled in ME. and early NE. after the analogy of the present stem-form, as *dwell, dwelt* (ME. **dwelte**, OE. **dwealde**), *dwelt* (ME. **ydwelt**, OE. **gedweald**, § 394, 2); *quell, quelled* (OE. **cwealde**), *quelled* (OE. **gecweald**); *reach, reached* (ME. **rauȝte**), *reached* (**yrauȝt**), but the pret. and pp. *raught* was common down to the seventeenth century; *stretch, stretched* (OE. **streahte**), *stretched* (OE. **gestreaht**); *work, worked* (ME. **wrǫuȝte**), *worked* (**ywrǫuȝt**), but the pret. and pp. *wrought* (§ 90) was common down to the eighteenth century, and the old past participle *wrought* is still used as an adjective. Only a few NE. verbs have preserved the regular old formation of the preterite and past participle. Those verbs which had in ME. pret. -ǫuȝte, pp. -ǫuȝt now regularly have -*ought* (= ǭt, § 90), as *beseech, besought; bring, brought; buy, bought; seek, sought; think, thought*. The pret. and pp. *sold*

(ME. sọlde, ysọld): *sell* is regularly developed from the corresponding ME. forms (§ 106); and similarly *told : tell*. The pret. and pp. *taught : teach* regularly corresponds to ME. tauȝte, ytauȝt (§ 84, 5); the pret. and pp. *caught : catch* was a ME. new formation (*EME. Gr.* § 426), the pret. and pp. *catched* was also common in earlier NE. The pret. *methought* (ME. me þŭȝte) is due to the influence of *thought* (ME. þọuȝte).

C. MINOR GROUPS

1. PRETERITE-PRESENTS.

§ 399. Only a small number of the OE. and ME. preterite-presents have been preserved in the standard language of the present day, viz. *can : could, dare : durst, may : might, shall : should,* and the forms of the old preterites *must, ought,* which are now also used as presents. With the exception of *dare* all these verbs are now used with widely extended meanings and functions from what they were in OE. and ME. In dealing with the preterite-presents we shall follow the same order as that in the *EME. Gr.* §§ 434–9, and shall generally include the form of the second pers. singular which is now obsolete except in liturgical language and poetry.

§ 400. Early NE. preserved some of the forms of the ME. verb witen, pres. sing. wọt, pl. witen; pret. wiste, present participle witing(ē); pp. wist. We still have *to wit* with the meaning 'namely'; the old present sing. in the phrase 'God wot' with early shortening (cp. § 100), but in early NE. the forms *wots, wotteth* were common with -s, -eth from the present of other verbs; the pret. and pp. *wist* was common in the sixteenth and seventeenth centuries; and the old present participle has been preserved in *unwitting; wotting* formed direct from *wot* was also sometimes used in the sixteenth and seventeenth centuries.

§ 401. *can* (ME. can) beside the unaccented forms kən,

kn with vocalic **n** (§ 175), *canst* (ME. **canst**); pret. *could* (ME. **coude, couþe**) with l after the analogy of *should* and *would;* *could* (**kud**) is the old unaccented form from which has been made a new unaccented form **kəd**, the old accented form would now be **kaud written *could*. We have preserved the present participle *cunning*, and the old pp. *couth* (ME. **couþ**) in *uncouth*, see § 77, 1. The contracted form *can't* (= **kānt**) with lengthening of **a** to **ā** arose in the sixteenth century before ME. **a** became **æ** in NE. (§ 62).

§ 402. *dare* from late ME. **dār** beside **dar** (cp. § 359), the latter form is still common in the modern dialects; the second pers. sing. *darst* (ME. **darst**), often written *dar'st*, was common down to the seventeenth century. From the sixteenth century onwards the third person singular has had *dares* beside *dare* (ME. **dār**). The preterite has had *dared* beside *durst* (ME. **durste**) since the sixteenth century. The old pp. *durst* (ME. **durst**) had become supplanted by the new formation *dared* by about 1600 in the standard language, but it is still used in some of the modern dialects.

§ 403. Late ME. had the accented form **schaul** beside unaccented **schal** (§ 102, 1). **schaul, shaul** became **shǫl** about the end of the sixteenth century (§ 84). **shǫl** and **shal** (= **shæl**) existed side by side down to the eighteenth century, and then the former became obsolete, and **shæl** written *shall* came to be used for both the accented and unaccented form, and from it has been formed the new unaccented forms **shəl, shl** with vocalic l, see § 102, 1. Second person sing. *shalt* (ME. **schalt**) from which was later formed the unaccented form **shəlt**. For *shan't* (= **shānt**) 'shall not' see § 187. In the preterite ME. had the accented form **schǫlde** beside unaccented **schŏlde**; the latter has not survived in NE. **schǫlde** regularly became **shūld** in early NE., and this pronunciation was common until the end of the eighteenth century (§ 105); from early NE. **shūld** was formed the unaccented form **shu(l)d** which has now become the accented form, and from it has been formed a new unaccented form shəd, see § 105.

§ 404. The present first and third pers. sing. *may* regularly corresponds to ME. mai (§ 82, 1). The early ME. form of the second pers. singular was miȝt (OE. meaht, later miht) which became obsolete in late ME. Beside miȝt there arose in the fourteenth century maist, maiest formed from mai, to which the NE. forms *mayest, mayst* regularly correspond. In the preterite ME. had miȝte beside mouȝte; the former has regularly become NE. *might*, and *mought* (= ME. mouȝte) was very common down to the end of the seventeenth century, and is still common in some of the modern dialects.

§ 405. The ME. present first and third pers. sing. mǭt, which regularly became mūt written *mote* and sometimes also *mought* in early NE. (§ 75), became obsolete during the sixteenth century, and its place was taken by *must* which is properly the old preterite form (ME. muste, moste, OE. mōste) now used for both tenses.

§ 406. *owe* (ME. ǫwen, ǭȝen, OE. āgan) has had weak beside strong forms since the late ME. period, and apart from isolated forms it is now always weak with pret. and pp. *owed*. The change of meaning from *habēre* to *dēbēre* began to take place so early as the OE. period, see *N. E. D.* s. v. The old pret. *ought* (= ME. ǫuȝte, OE. āhte) was often used as the preterite beside the new formation *owed* until about the end of the seventeenth century, but *ought* is now isolated from *owed*, and is used both with present and preterite meaning. The old pp. *owen, oune* (ME. ǫwen, OE. āgen) continued to be used as such down to the seventeenth century, and in the form *own* it is still in general use as an adjective.

§ 407. After the analogy of the preterite-presents, the old weak verb *need* has had the third pers. sing. *need* beside *needs* since the sixteenth century, but the former is now only used in such combinations as *it need not, why need it?*

2. Anomalous Verbs.

§ 408. *be* (= bǐ): The ordinary ME. forms of the present
indicative were: sing. **am, art, is,** pl. **ắre(n)** beside **bḗn,
bḗþ.** Beside the accented form *am* (= æm) we now have
the unaccented forms **əm, m**; and similarly *is* (= iz) beside
z, but **s** after voiceless consonants (§ 175); *art* (= āt) regularly corresponds to ME. **art.** The ME. accented form
āre(n), which would now be *ę̄ə (§ 119, note), became
obsolete in earlier NE.; the old unaccented form *are* now
pronounced **ā** (§ 108) then came to be used for the accented
form, and from it a new unaccented form **ə** has been formed
(§ 175). The full forms **bḗn, bḗþ** had become obsolete by
the end of the ME. or beginning of the NE. period, but the
form *be* (= bǐ) was in common use down to the seventeenth
century, and then became obsolete except in formal and
stilted language. The pret. *was* (ME. **was**), pl. *were* (ME.
wḗren, wę̄ren) is the only NE. preterite which has preserved
the old distinction between the singular and plural, but *was*
for *were,* especially *you was* used in addressing a single
person, was very common in the earlier NE. colloquial
language, and is still so in many of the modern dialects.
In the standard pronunciation we now have accented *was*
(= **woz,** § 132) beside unaccented **wəz**; and accented **wę̄ə**
(§ 120) beside unaccented **wə̆** (§ 175). In the sixteenth
century the old second pers. sing. *were* (= ME. **wḗre, wę̄re**)
was supplanted by the new formations *wast, wert* with **t**
from *art,* and these forms were very common in the seventeenth and eighteenth centuries; in the 1611 edition of the
Bible the former is used for the indicative and the latter
for the subjunctive. Subjunctive present accented **bī,** unaccented **bi,** written *be* in both cases; pret. accented **wę̄ə**
beside unaccented **wə̆,** written *were* in both cases; from the
sixteenth century onwards the common form of the second

pers. singular has been *wert* (= **wə̄t**), but in the sixteenth
and seventeenth centuries there were also the forms *werest,*
werst with ·st from the preterite of ordinary verbs. Inf.
accented **bī** beside unaccented **bi** (ME. **bę̄n**). Present
participle **bī-ing;** pp. accented **bīn** beside unaccented **bin**
written *been.*

§ 409. *have :* The v in *have* disappeared in the second and
third persons singular of the present and in the preterite
and past participle during the ME. period ; early NE. also
had the unaccented forms *ha'*, *a* 'have' corresponding to
ME. **ha** (*EME. Gr.* § 429), whence NE. *hast, has (hath),* pret.
and pp. *had,* see § 69, note 1, and for the various unaccented
forms of this verb see § 175.

§ 410. *do :* The present of *do* (ME. **dǭ, dǭn**) now has
accented beside unaccented forms, viz. **dū** (§ 75) beside **du,**
də ; dast beside **dəst ; daz, daþ** beside **dəz, dəþ ;** early NE.
also had the accented forms **dŭ·ist, dŭ·iþ** written *doest, doeth.*
For the unaccented forms with **u, a, ə,** see §§ 99, 175. *did*
(ME. **dide) ;** pp. *done* (ME. **dǭn**) with early shortening of **ū**
to **u** later **a** (§ 67) after ME. **ǭ** had become **ū** in early NE.
The pronunciation of the contracted form *don't* (= **dount**) is
due to the influence of the spelling (§ 75, note 2). The ·th
of the third pers. singular remained longer in *doth* and *hath*
than in other verbs ; both these forms were common in the
eighteenth century.

§ 411. *go* (= ME. **gǭn**), pp. *gone* (ME. **gǭn**) with early NE.
shortening of **ǭ** to **o** (§ 100). In the preterite ME. had
wente (= NE. *went*) beside ȝę̄de, ȝǭde, the former being
properly the preterite of **wenden** (§ 394, 2); the latter became
obsolete in the ordinary language in late ME., but it was
often used as an archaism in poetry during the sixteenth
century with both present and preterite meaning ; and some
writers like Spenser ignorantly used *yede* as the present and
yode as the preterite.

§ 412. *will* (ME. **wille, wile, wil**), *wilt* (ME. **wilt) ;** beside

wille, &c. ME. also had **wolle, wole,** and **wulle, wule,**
which were common in the forms **wol, wul** in early NE.
The contracted form *won't* (= **wount**) is from **wol + not,**
see § 103, 3, note 1. In the preterite ME. had the accented
form **wǭlde** beside unaccented **wŏlde**; the latter has not
survived in NE. **wǭlde** regularly became **wūld** in early NE.,
and this pronunciation was common until the end of the
eighteenth century (§ 105); from early NE. **wūld** was formed
the unaccented form **wu(l)d** which has now become the
accented form, and from which a new unaccented form **wǝd**
has been formed, both written *would*. For the various
unaccented forms of this verb, see § 175.

INDEX

The numbers after a word refer to the paragraphs in the Grammar.

198 *Index*

furrow 44. 1, 67. 1, 107. 1
further (*v.*) 114. 3
further (*adj.*) 239
furthermost 313
furze 114. 3, 255
future 185

gage 140
gaiety 82. 6
gain 82. 6
gait 69 n. 2
gall 102. 1
gallop 156
gallows 62, 297
gambol 156
game 69
gang 63
gaol 11 n.
gap 62
gape 69
garden 13. 2, 108, 159. 2
garland 110
garlic 97, 173. 1
garment 108
garner 110
garrison 253
gasp 93. 1
gate 69 n. 2, 267
gather 62, 230
gauge 140
gauntlet 85
gay 82. 6, 267
gaze 255
geese 17, 71. 2
gem 52, 279
gender 64
general 13. 8, 153, 156, 279
generosity 253
generous 153
genial 151
genius 29, 71. 10, 151
gentle 64, 279
gentry 297
genuine 46, 159. 2
geography 22
georgics 22
get 58, 98, 135. 2, 363, 366
ghastly 50, 267
gherkin 50, 267

ghost 50, 76. 1, 267
giant 30. 1, 57
gibe 11 n.
giddy 65. 2
gift 65. 1, 215, 222, 267
gigantic 146
gild 73. 6, 394. 2
gipsy 243. 2
gird 114. 3, 394. 2
girdle 114. 3, 247, 297
give 17, 219, 267, 363, 368
glad 13. 1, 62, 186, 267, 308
gladly 170. 2
glare 119
glass 13. 2, 93. 1, 267, 288. 3
glaze 13. 6, 69, 240, 255
glazier 29
glede 'kite' 71. 8
glee 20
glide 73. 1, 340
gloom 75. 1
glorious 151
glory 125. 3, 170. 4, 186
gloss 93. 2
glove 34. 2, 99, 289. 1
glow 89. 4
glue 45
gnarl 268
gnash 48. 1, 268
gnat 48. 1, 268
gnaw 48. 1, 84. 2, 195, 268, 379
go 34. 8, 76. 1, 267, 411
goad 36
goat 17, 36, 57, 76. 1, 267, 296
gobbet 53
goblin 154
God 66. 1
gold 34. 8, 57, 103. 2, 105
golden 186
gone 17, 100
good 37. 3, 57, 99, 229, 311
goodness 54, 157. 3

goose 37. 1, 75. 1, 245, 267, 296
gooseberry 244
gorgeous 22. 3, 57
gosling 66. 3, 244
gospel 93. 2, 157. 1, 243. 1
gossip 213, 243. 1
govern 34. 2, 67. 1, 165
gown 40. 1, 77. 1
grace 69
graceful 156
gracious 185
grain 82. 6
grammar 62, 165, 267
grammarian 146
grandeur 151
grandfather 232
grandmother 232
grant 85
grape 69
grasp 243. 1
grass 54, 93. 1, 190, 245, 267
grave 13. 6, 69, 379
gray 14. 1, 82
graze 69, 255
grease 72. 6
great 19. 6, 57, 72 n. 1, 309, 310
greedy 71. 6
green 17, 20, 71. 2, 190, 198, 267
Greenwich 20, 48. 9, 52, 97, 182, 276
greet 71. 2, 397
grew 23. 6, 86. 1
grey 21. 1, 82
greyhound 82. 5
gridiron 136
grief 31. 1, 71. 10
grieve 31. 1, 71. 10
grin 136
grind 353
grindstone 65. 4, 232
gripe 340
grisly 65. 5, 244
gristle 48. 8
grit 97
groan 36, 76. 1
groat 76 n. 2
groin 88. 2, 232

pupil 159. 1
purchase 117. 2, 160, 275
pure 44. 9, 129, 191
purity 79
purpose 156, 255
purse 213
pursue 79, 185
pursuit 46, 57, 79, 243. 2
push 44. 2, 133, 390
puss 133
put 44. 2, 57, 58, 133, 397
pygmy 26

quack 132
quaint 179
quality 13. 4, 42, 132, 179
qualm 102. 4
quantity 132
quarrel 132, 157. 1
quarry 132
quart 109
quarter 13. 4, 109, 179, 261
quay 14. 4, 57. 83, 261
queen 71. 2, 179, 198, 261
quell 398
quench 227, 277, 396
quern 112
quest 42
question 179, 261
quick 54, 65. 1, 179, 261
quiet 57, 73. 8, 179
quince 297
quinsy 253
quire 121
quoit 42, 179, 261
quote 261
quoth 372

race 69
radical 28. 1, 151, 156
radish 259
rafter 93. 1
raid 76 n. 2
rail 82. 6
rain 82. 2]

raise 14. 1, 82. 5, 255, 390
raisin 82. 6, 159. 2
ramp 85
ran 63
random 201
range 140
ransom 85, 201
rare 13. 7, 119
rase (v.) 11 n.
raspberry 48. 10, 207, 244
rather 94
raven 69
ravine 73. 8
raw 84. 1
ray 82. 6
raze (v.) 11 n.
reach 72. 1, 398
read 70, 72. 2, 190, 388, 394. 1
read (pret.) 64
ready 19. 2, 64
real 19. 8
reality 19. 9
realize 73. 8
realm 55. 5, 87. 3, 188
reap 72. 5
rear 19. 8, 122, 394. 3
reason 19. 1, 57, 72. 6, 161, 190, 250. 1
reasonable 34. 4, 153
receipt 55. 1, 208
receive 21. 4, 72. 6
recent 52, 71. 10
recognize 269
record 155
recruit 46
red 58, 98, 190
redeem 71. 10
reed 20, 71. 3
refuse (sb.) 162
refuse (v.) 255
regret 64
regular 44. 8, 152
regulate 152
reign 48. 4, 82. 6, 198, 269
rein 21. 1
rejoice 88. 1, 245
relative 13. 8, 150
relief 71. 10

religion 279
remain 82. 6
remark 108
remedy 64, 150
remnant 156
remorse 115
rend 394. 2
renown 77. 5
repent 206
reprieve 31. 1, 71. 9
request 64
require 121, 179
requisite 159. 3
rescue 45
research 243. 5
resemble 250
resent 250
reserve 146
resign 250. 2
resolution 80
resort 116
resource 243. 5
result 67. 5, 250. 2
resume 250. 2
revenge 64
revolve 103 n. 2
reward 13. 4, 109
rhyme 26
rhythm 26
rib 65. 1, 54, 210
ribbon 143
rice 73. 8
rich 65. 6, 190
riches 297
rick 97
rid 136, 394. 3
ridden 65. 1
riddle 17, 97, 157. 1, 186, 229, 247, 297
ride 28. 4, 73. 1, 336, 337, 338, 339
rider 230
ridge 279
right 11 n., 50, 73. 7, 271
ring 28. 1, 65. 1, 350, 351
rise 17, 255, 336, 339
risen 65. 1, 250
rite 11 n.
rive 340
river 219